Building Serverless Web Applications

Build scalable web apps using Serverless Framework on AWS

Diego Zanon

BIRMINGHAM - MUMBAI

Building Serverless Web Applications

Copyright © 2017 Packt Publishing

First published: July 2017

Production reference: 2040817

Published by Packt Publishing Ltd.
Livery Place
35 Livery Street
Birmingham
B3 2PB, UK.

ISBN 978-1-78712-647-3

www.packtpub.com

Credits

Author
Diego Zanon

Reviewer
Chintan Mehta

Commissioning Editor
Aaron Lazar

Acquisition Editor
Nitin Dasan

Content Development Editor
Rohit Kumar Singh

Technical Editor
Vibhuti Gawde

Copy Editor
Pranjali Chury

Project Coordinator
Vaidehi Sawant

Proofreader
Safis Editing

Indexer
Aishwarya Gangawane

Graphics
Jason Monteiro

Production Coordinator
Arvindkumar Gupta

About the Author

Diego Zanon is a full-stack developer for both JavaScript and .NET applications. He is passionate about understanding and trying new technologies and frameworks, especially those designed to solve scalability problems. In his free time, he likes to contribute to Stack Overflow and write in his blog.

Diego is a computer engineer with experience on a wide range of projects, from industrial systems to e-commerce websites, for customers around the world, including the USA, Brazil, Netherlands, and Kazakhstan.

This book is dedicated to my sweet wife, Carol, for standing by my side and making my life better.

About the Reviewer

Chintan Mehta is a cofounder af KNOWARTH Technologies (`https://www.knowarth.com`) and heads Cloud/RIMS/DevOps. He has a diploma in computer hardware and network certification and has rich progressive experience in systems and server administration of Linux, AWS Cloud, Devops, RIMS, and Server Administration on open source technologies. He is also an AWS Certified Solutions Architect-Associate.

Chintan's roles during his career in infrastructure and operations include requirement analysis, architecture design, security design, high availability and disaster recovery planning, automated monitoring, automated deployment, building processes to help customers, performance tuning, infrastructure setup and deployment, and application setup and deployment along with setting up various offices at different locations with a fantastic sole ownership to achieve operation readiness for the organizations he has been associated with.

He headed the Managed Cloud Services practice at his previous job and received multiple awards for his valuable contribution to the business of the group. He was involved in creating solutions and consulting to build SAAS, IAAS, and PAAS services on Cloud. He also led the ISO 27001:2005 implementation team as a joint management representative. Chintan has authored *Hadoop Backup and Recovery Solutions* and reviewed *Liferay Portal Performance Best Practices*.

> *First, I would like to congratulate the author, who has done a wonderful job along with the tremendous team at Packt, for this effort. I would like to especially thank my wonderful wife, Mittal, and my sweet son, Devam, for putting up with the long days, nights, and weekends where I was camped out in front of my laptop.*

www.PacktPub.com

For support files and downloads related to your book, please visit www.PacktPub.com.

Did you know that Packt offers eBook versions of every book published, with PDF and ePub files available? You can upgrade to the eBook version at www.PacktPub.com and as a print book customer, you are entitled to a discount on the eBook copy. Get in touch with us at service@packtpub.com for more details.

At www.PacktPub.com, you can also read a collection of free technical articles, sign up for a range of free newsletters and receive exclusive discounts and offers on Packt books and eBooks.

https://www.packtpub.com/mapt

Get the most in-demand software skills with Mapt. Mapt gives you full access to all Packt books and video courses, as well as industry-leading tools to help you plan your personal development and advance your career.

Why subscribe?

- Fully searchable across every book published by Packt
- Copy and paste, print, and bookmark content
- On demand and accessible via a web browser

Customer Feedback

Thanks for purchasing this Packt book. At Packt, quality is at the heart of our editorial process. To help us improve, please leave us an honest review on this book's Amazon page at https://www.amazon.com/dp/1787126471.

If you'd like to join our team of regular reviewers, you can e-mail us at customerreviews@packtpub.com. We award our regular reviewers with free eBooks and videos in exchange for their valuable feedback. Help us be relentless in improving our products!

Table of Contents

Preface

Serverless is a buzzword created to identify cloud services that are totally managed by the provider and have a different billing model where you pay only for the time that you use them, measured in a granularity of tenths of a second and not hours. Serverless Computing allows a wide range of applications to benefit from reduced costs, faster development, and much less trouble with availability and scalability. Those are enough reasons for you to start learning how to build serverless applications.

Besides teaching you what is and how to use serverless, this book offers a broader view on the subject. Serverless is frequently associated with FaaS and people don't realize that you can do much more with serverless than just running functions on demand. Serverless offers many services for databases, security, notifications, and others. I will teach you how to use them.

This book can be divided into the following three parts:

- **Introduction**: This is where you will be introduced to the serverless concepts and tools that will be used in this book. You will learn about AWS services and the Serverless Framework. This introduction ranges from Chapter 1, *Understanding the Serverless Model*, to Chapter 3, *Using the Serverless Model*.
- **Building a serverless application**: From Chapter 4, *Hosting the Website*, to Chapter 7, *Managing a Serverless Database*, you will follow how to develop and host a serverless application and build the frontend, backend, and data access layer.
- **Advanced features**: This book ends with Chapter 8, *Securing the Serverless Application*, to Chapter 10, *Testing, Deploying, and Monitoring*, giving you the knowledge of how to use serverless to implement security and real-time notifications in addition to how to test, deploy, and monitor your application.

What this book covers

Chapter 1, *Understanding the Serverless Model*, introduces the concept and its pros and cons along with some use cases.

Chapter 2, *Getting Started with AWS*, gives an introduction to new AWS users and describes which tools will be used throughout the book.

Chapter 3, *Using the Serverless Framework*, teaches you how to configure and use the Serverless Framework, which is a must-have tool to build serverless applications.

Chapter 4, *Hosting the Website*, helps you to configure your domain and host your website with HTTPS support.

Chapter 5, *Building the Frontend*, uses the approach of Single-Page Applications to design a React frontend.

Chapter 6, *Developing the Backend*, covers how to design a RESTful interface and build the backend code using Node.js.

Chapter 7, *Managing a Serverless Database*, shows how to use SimpleDB and DynamoDB to store data for a serverless project.

Chapter 8, *Securing the Serverless Application*, covers the standard security practices and how to implement authentication and authorization in a serverless application.

Chapter 9, *Handling Serverless Notifications*, demonstrates how to build serverless notifications using the publisher-subscriber pattern.

Chapter 10, *Testing, Deploying, and Monitoring*, shows how to test a serverless solution, what are the standard practices to deploy your application in production, and what you need to monitor.

What you need for this book

This book assumes previous knowledge of web development using JavaScript and Node.js. While you have many options of programming languages to develop a serverless application, all code examples of this book uses Node, so some basic knowledge of Node.js is necessary at least to understand how npm and the JavaScript ES6 syntax are used.

There are many cloud providers that offer serverless services, but this book focuses on AWS. You don't need to have prior knowledge of AWS because we will cover the basics too, but you will need to create an account to develop and test the code examples. If it is a brand new account, AWS offers a free tier of 12 months for you to learn and develop without any cost.

Who this book is for

This book was designed for web developers who want to use cloud services to be more productive, reducing the time wasted on configuration and maintenance of the infrastructure or for developers who want to build solutions using existing services to solve common problems with very little effort.

Also, as I work as a full-stack developer, my job requires me to understand a little bit of everything such as frontend, backend, databases, security, and DevOps. So I tried to give in this book a broad view of web development using the serverless concept. If you have a similar role or, at least, want to learn more about the different layers of web development, this book will suit you well.

Conventions

In this book, you will find a number of text styles that distinguish between different kinds of information. Here are some examples of these styles and an explanation of their meaning.

Code words in text, database table names, folder names, filenames, file extensions, pathnames, dummy URLs, user input, and Twitter handles are shown as follows: "This example defines a `<HelloReact/>` HTML element and the rendered output will use the value of the `name` property".

A block of code is set as follows:

```
class HelloReact extends React.Component {
  render() {
    return <div>Hello, {this.props.name}!</div>;
  }
}

ReactDOM.render(
  <HelloReact name="World"/>,
  document.getElementById('root')
);
```

When we wish to draw your attention to a particular part of a code block, the relevant lines or items are set in bold:

```
[default]
exten => s,1,Dial(Zap/1|30)
exten => s,2,Voicemail(u100)
exten => s,102,Voicemail(b100)
exten => i,1,Voicemail(s0)
```

Any command-line input or output is written as follows:

```
aws s3 sync ./path/to/folder s3://my-bucket-name --acl public-read
```

New terms and **important** words are shown in bold. Words that you see on the screen, for example, in menus or dialog boxes, appear in the text like this: "Clicking the **Next** button moves you to the next screen."

 Warnings or important notes appear in a box like this.

 Tips and tricks appear like this.

Reader feedback

Feedback from our readers is always welcome. Let us know what you think about this book—what you liked or disliked. Reader feedback is important for us as it helps us develop titles that you will really get the most out of.

To send us general feedback, simply e-mail feedback@packtpub.com, and mention the book's title in the subject of your message.

If there is a topic that you have expertise in and you are interested in either writing or contributing to a book, see our author guide at www.packtpub.com/authors.

Customer support

Now that you are the proud owner of a Packt book, we have a number of things to help you to get the most from your purchase.

Downloading the example code

You can download the example code files for this book from your account at http://www.packtpub.com. If you purchased this book elsewhere, you can visit http://www.packtpub.com/support and register to have the files e-mailed directly to you.

You can download the code files by following these steps:

1. Log in or register to our website using your e-mail address and password.
2. Hover the mouse pointer on the SUPPORT tab at the top.
3. Click on Code Downloads & Errata.
4. Enter the name of the book in the Search box.
5. Select the book for which you're looking to download the code files.
6. Choose from the drop-down menu where you purchased this book from.
7. Click on Code Download.

Once the file is downloaded, please make sure that you unzip or extract the folder using the latest version of:

- WinRAR / 7-Zip for Windows
- Zipeg / iZip / UnRarX for Mac
- 7-Zip / PeaZip for Linux

The code bundle for the book is also hosted on GitHub at `https://github.com/PacktPubl ishing/Building-Serverless-Web-Applications`. We also have other code bundles from our rich catalog of books and videos available at `https://github.com/PacktPublishing/`. Check them out!

Downloading the color images of this book

We also provide you with a PDF file that has color images of the screenshots/diagrams used in this book. The color images will help you better understand the changes in the output. You can download this file from `https://www.packtpub.com/sites/default/files/down loads/BuildingServerlessWebApplications_ColorImages.pdf`.

Errata

Although we have taken every care to ensure the accuracy of our content, mistakes do happen. If you find a mistake in one of our books—maybe a mistake in the text or the code—we would be grateful if you could report this to us. By doing so, you can save other readers from frustration and help us improve subsequent versions of this book. If you find any errata, please report them by visiting `http://www.packtpub.com/submit-errata`, selecting your book, clicking on the Errata Submission Form link, and entering the details of your errata. Once your errata are verified, your submission will be accepted and the errata will be uploaded to our website or added to any list of existing errata under the Errata section of that title.

To view the previously submitted errata, go to `https://www.packtpub.com/books/content/support`and enter the name of the book in the search field. The required information will appear under the Errata section.

Piracy

Piracy of copyrighted material on the Internet is an ongoing problem across all media. At Packt, we take the protection of our copyright and licenses very seriously. If you come across any illegal copies of our works in any form on the Internet, please provide us with the location address or website name immediately so that we can pursue a remedy.

Please contact us at `copyright@packtpub.com` with a link to the suspected pirated material.

We appreciate your help in protecting our authors and our ability to bring you valuable content.

Questions

If you have a problem with any aspect of this book, you can contact us at `questions@packtpub.com`, and we will do our best to address the problem.

1
Understanding the Serverless Model

Serverless is a model where the developer doesn't need to worry about servers: configuring, maintaining, or updating is none of their business. Although it is not an entirely new concept, the services that are offered nowadays are much more powerful and enable a wider range of applications. If you want to build cost-effective and scalable solutions, you should dive deeper into this subject and understand how it works.

In this chapter, we will cover the following topics:

- What is serverless?
- The main goals of serverless
- Pros and cons
- Use cases

After this chapter, you will be ready to start our hands-on approach, building an online store demo application, one piece per chapter.

Introducing serverless

Serverless can be a model, a type of architecture, a pattern, or anything else you prefer to call it. For me, serverless is an adjective, a word that qualifies a *way of thinking*. It's a way to abstract how the code that you write will be executed. *Thinking* serverless is to not think in servers. You code, you test, you deploy, and that's (almost) enough.

Serverless is a buzzword. You still need servers to run your applications, but you should not worry about them *that much*. Maintaining a server is none of your business. The focus is on development and writing code, and not in the operation.

DevOps is still necessary, although with a smaller role. You need to automate the deployment and have at least a minimal monitoring of how your application is operating and how much it costs, but you don't need to start or stop machines to match the usage and neither do you need to replace failed instances or apply security patches to the operating system.

Thinking serverless

A serverless solution is entirely *event-driven*. Every time that a user requests some information, a trigger will notify your cloud vendor to pick your code and execute it to retrieve the answer. In contrast, a traditional solution also works to answer requests, but the code is always up and running, consuming machine resources that were reserved specifically for you, even when no one is using your system.

In a serverless architecture, it's not necessary to load the entire codebase into a running machine to process a single request. For a faster loading step, only the code that is necessary to answer the request is selected to run. This small piece of the solution is referenced as a **function**. So we only run functions on demand.

Although we call it simply as a function, it's usually a zipped package that contains a piece of code that runs as an entry point along with its dependencies.

In the following diagram, the serverless model is illustrated in a sequence of steps. It's an example of how a cloud provider could implement the concept, though it doesn't have to implement it in this way:

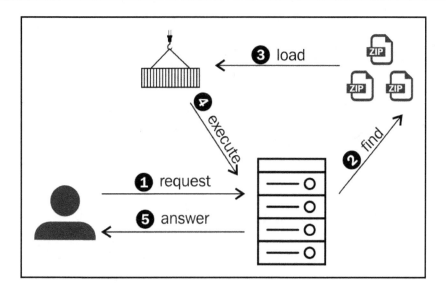

Let's understand the following steps shown in the preceding diagram:

1. The user sends a request to an address handled by the cloud provider.
2. Based on the message, the cloud service tries to locate which package must be used to answer the request.
3. The package (or function) is selected and loaded into a Docker container.
4. The container is executed and outputs an answer.
5. The answer is sent to the original user.

What makes the serverless model so interesting is that you are only billed for the time that was needed to execute your function, usually measured in fractions of seconds, not hours of use. If no one is using your service, you pay nothing.

Also, if you have a sudden peak of users accessing your application, the cloud service will load different instances to handle all simultaneous requests. If one of those cloud machines fails, another one will be made available automatically, without needing to configure anything.

Serverless and PaaS

Serverless is often confused with **Platform as a Service (PaaS)**. PaaS is a kind of cloud computing model that allows developers to launch applications without worrying about the infrastructure. According to this definition, they have the same objective! And they do. Serverless is like a rebranding of PaaS, or you can call it the next generation of PaaS.

The main difference between PaaS and serverless is that in PaaS you don't manage machines, but you are billed by provisioning them, even if there is no user actively browsing your website. In PaaS, your code is always running and waiting for new requests. In serverless, there is a service that is listening for requests and will trigger your code to run only when necessary. This is reflected in your bill. You will pay only for the fractions of seconds that your code was executed and the number of requests that were made to this listener. Also, serverless has an immutable state between invocations, so it's always a fresh environment for every invocation. Even if the container is reused in a subsequent call, the filesystem is renewed.

IaaS and On-Premises

Besides PaaS, serverless is frequently compared with **Infrastructure as a Service** (**IaaS**) and On-Premises solutions to expose its differences. IaaS is another strategy to deploy cloud solutions where you hire virtual machines and is allowed to connect to them to configure everything that you need in the guest operating system. It gives you greater flexibility, but it comes with more responsibilities. You need to apply security patches, handle occasional failures, and set up new servers to handle usage peaks. Also, you pay the same per hour whether you are using 5% or 100% of the machine s CPU.

On-Premises is the traditional kind of solution where you buy the physical computers and run them inside your company. You get total flexibility and control with this approach. Hosting your own solution can be cheaper, but it happens only when your traffic usage is extremely stable. Over or under provisioning computers is so frequent that it's hard to have real gains using this approach, even more when you add the risks and costs to hire a team to manage those machines. Cloud providers may look expensive, but several detailed use cases prove that the **return of investment** (**ROI**) is larger running on the cloud than On-Premises. When using the cloud, you benefit from the economy of scale of many gigantic data centers. Running on your own exposes your business to a wide range of risks and costs that you'll never be able to anticipate.

The main goals of serverless

To define a service as serverless, it must have at least the following features:

- **Scale as you need**: There is no under or over-provisioning
- **Highly available**: It is fault tolerant and always online
- **Cost-efficient**: You will never pay for idle servers

Scalability

With IaaS, you can achieve infinite scalability with any cloud service. You just need to hire new machines as your usage grows. You can also automate the process of starting and stopping servers as your demand changes. But this is not a fast way to scale. When you start a new machine, you usually need to wait for around 5 minutes before it can be usable to process new requests. Also, as starting and stopping machines is costly, you only do this after you are certain that you need. So, your automated process will wait some minutes to confirm that your demand has changed before taking any action.

> **Infinite scalability** is used as a way to highlight that you can usually grow without worrying if the cloud provider has enough capacity to offer. That's not always true. Each cloud provider has limitations that you must consider if you are thinking in large applications. For example, AWS limits the number of running virtual machines (IaaS) of a specific type to 20 and the number of concurrent Lambda functions (serverless) to 1,000.

IaaS is able to handle well-behaved usage changes, but it can't handle unexpected high peaks that happen after announcements or marketing campaigns. With serverless, your scalability is measured in milliseconds and not minutes. Besides being scalable, it's very fast to scale. Also, it scales per invocation without needing to provision capacity.

When you consider a high usage frequency in a scale of minutes, IaaS suffers to satisfy the needed capacity while serverless meets even higher usages in less time.

In the following graph, the left-hand side graph shows how scalability occurs with IaaS. The right-hand side graph shows how well the demand can be satisfied using a serverless solution:

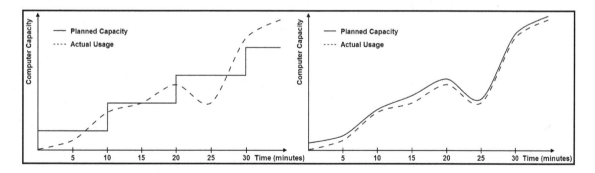

With an On-Premises approach, this is a bigger problem. As the usage grows, new machines must be bought and prepared, but increasing the infrastructure requires purchase orders to be created and approved, you need to wait the new servers to arrive and you need to give time to your team to configure and test them. It can take weeks to grow, or even months if the company is very big and requests many steps and procedures to be filled in.

Availability

A highly available solution is the one that is fault tolerant to hardware failures. If one machine goes out, you must keep running the application with a satisfactory performance. If you lose an entire data center due to a power outage, you must have machines in another data center to keep the service online. Having high availability generally means to duplicate your entire infrastructure, placing each half in a different data center.

Highly available solutions are usually very expensive in IaaS and On-Premises. If you have multiple machines to handle your workload, placing them in different physical places and running a load balancing service can be enough. If one data center goes out, you keep the traffic in the remaining machines and scale to compensate. However, there are cases where you will pay extra without using those machines.

For example, if you have a huge relational database that is scaled vertically, you will end up paying for another expensive machine as a slave just to keep the availability. Even for NoSQL databases, if you set a MongoDB replica set in a consistent model, you will pay for instances that will act only as secondaries, without serving to alleviate read requests.

Instead of running idle machines, you can set them in a cold start state, meaning that the machine is prepared, but is off to reduce costs. However, if you run a website that sells products or services, you can lose customers even in small downtimes. A cold start for web servers can take a few minutes to recover, but needs several more minutes for databases.

Considering these scenarios, in serverless, you get high availability for *free*. The cost is already considered in what you pay to use.

Another aspect of availability is how to handle **Distributed Denial of Service (DDoS)** attacks. When you receive a huge load of requests in a very short time, how do you handle it? There are some tools and techniques that help mitigate the problem, for example, blacklisting IPs that go over a specific request rate, but before those tools start to work, you need to scale the solution, and it needs to scale really fast to prevent the availability from being compromised. In this, again, serverless has the best scaling speed.

Cost efficiency

It's impossible to match the traffic usage with what you have provisioned. With IaaS or On-Premises, as a rule of thumb, CPU and RAM usage must always be lower than 90% for the machine to be considered healthy, and ideally CPU should be using less than 20% of the capacity with normal traffic. In this case, you are paying for 80% of waste when the capacity is in an idle state. Paying for computer resources that you don't use is not efficient.

Many cloud vendors advertise that you just pay for what you use, but they usually offer significant discounts when you provision for 24 hours of uptime in a long term (one year or more). It means that you pay for machines that you will keep running even in very low traffic hours. Also, even if you want to shut down machines to reduce costs, you need to keep at least a minimum infrastructure 24/7 to keep your web server and databases always online. Regarding high availability, you need extra machines to add redundancy. Again, it's a waste of resources.

Another efficiency problem is related with the databases, especially relational ones. Scaling vertically is a very troublesome task, so relational databases are always provisioned considering max peaks. It means that you pay for an expensive machine when most of the time you don't need one.

In serverless, you shouldn't worry about provisioning or idle times. You should pay exactly the CPU and RAM time that is used, measured in fractions of seconds and not hours. If it's a serverless database, you need to store data permanently, so this represents a cost even if no one is using your system. However, storage is very cheap compared to CPU time. The higher cost, which is the CPU needed to run the database engine that runs queries, will be billed only by the amount of time used without considering idle times.

Running a serverless system continuously for one hour has a much higher cost than one hour in a traditional infra. However, the difference is that serverless is designed for applications with variable usage, where you will never keep one machine at 100% for one hour straight. The cost efficiency of serverless is not perceived in websites with flat traffic.

The pros and cons of serverless

In this section, we will go through the various pros and cons associated with serverless computing.

Pros

We can list the following strengths:

- Fast scalability
- High availability
- Efficient usage of resources
- Reduced operational costs
- Focus on business, not on infrastructure
- System security is outsourced
- Continuous delivery
- Microservices friendly
- Cost model is startup friendly

Let's skip the first three benefits, since they were already covered in the previous pages, and let's take a look at the others.

Reduced operational costs

As the infrastructure is fully managed by the cloud vendor, it reduces the operational costs since you don't need to worry about hardware failures, applying security patches to the operating system, or fixing network issues. It effectively means that you need to spend less sysadmin hours to keep your application running.

Also, it helps to reduce risks. If you make an investment to deploy a new service and that ends up as a failure, you don't need to worry about selling machines or disposing the data center that you have built.

Focus on business

Lean software development states that you must spend time in what aggregates value to the final product. In a serverless project, the focus is on business. Infrastructure is a second-class citizen.

Configuring a large infrastructure is a costly and time-consuming task. If you want to validate an idea through a **Minimum Viable Product** (**MVP**) without losing time to market, consider using serverless to save time. There are tools that automate the deployment, which we will use throughout this book and see how they help the developer to launch a prototype with minimum effort. If the idea fails, infrastructure costs are minimized since there are no payments made in advance.

System security

The cloud vendor is responsible for managing the security of the operating system, runtime, physical access, networking, and all related technologies that enable the platform to operate. The developer still needs to handle authentication, authorization, and code vulnerabilities, but the rest is outsourced to the cloud provider. It's a positive feature if you consider that a large team of specialists are focused on implementing the best security practices, and patching new bug fixes as soon as possible to serve their hundreds of customers. That's the definition of economy of scale.

Continuous delivery

Serverless is based on breaking a big project into dozens of packages, each one represented by a top-level function that handles requests. Deploying a new version of a function means uploading a ZIP file to replace the previous one and updating the event configuration that specifies how this function can be triggered.

Executing this task manually, for dozens of functions, is an exhausting task. Automation is a must-have feature when working in a serverless project. In this book, we'll use the Serverless Framework that helps developers manage and organize solutions, making a deployment task as simple as executing a one-line command. With automation, continuous delivery is a feature that brings many benefits, such as the ability to deploy at any time, short development cycles, and easier rollbacks.

Another related benefit when the deployment is automated is the creation of different environments. You can create a new test environment, which is an exact duplicate of the development environment, using simple commands. The ability to replicate the environment is very important for building acceptance tests and to progress from deployment to production.

Microservices friendly

Microservices is a topic that will be better discussed later in this book. In short, a Microservices architecture is encouraged in a serverless project. As your functions are single units of deployment, you can have different teams working concurrently on different use cases. You can also use different programming languages in the same project and take advantage of emerging technologies or team skills.

Cost model

Suppose that you have built an online store with serverless. The average user will make some requests to see a few products and a few more requests to decide whether they will buy something or not. In serverless, a single unit of code has a predictable time to execute for a given input. After collecting some data, you can predict how much a single user costs on average, and this unit cost will remain almost constant as your application grows in usage.

Knowing how much a single user costs and keeping this number fixed is very important for a startup. It helps to decide how much you need to charge for a service or earn through ads or sales to have a profit.

In a traditional infrastructure, you need to make payments in advance, and scaling your application means increasing your capacity in steps. So, calculating the unit cost of a user is a more difficult task and it's a variable number.

In the following diagram, the left-hand side shows traditional infrastructures with stepped costs and the right-hand side depicts serverless infrastructures with linear costs:

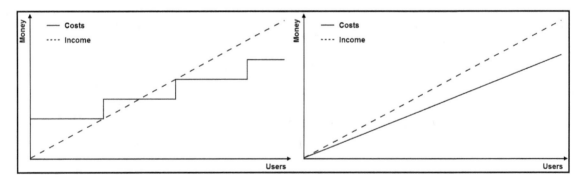

Cons

Serverless is great, but no technology is a silver bullet. You should be aware of the following issues:

- Higher latency
- Constraints
- Hidden inefficiencies
- Vendor dependency
- Debugging difficulties
- Atomic deploys
- Uncertainties

We will address these drawbacks in detail now.

Higher latency

Serverless is event-driven and so your code is not running all the time. When a request is made, it triggers a service that finds your function, unzips the package, loads it into a container, and makes it available to be executed. The problem is that those steps take time: up to a few hundreds of milliseconds. This issue is called a cold start delay and is a trade-off that exists between the serverless cost-effective model and the lower latency of traditional hosting.

There are some solutions available to minimize this performance problem. For example, you can configure your function to reserve more RAM memory. It gives a faster start and overall performance. The programming language is also important. Java has a higher cold start time than JavaScript (Node.js).

Another solution is to benefit from the fact that the cloud provider may cache the loaded code, which means that the first execution will have a delay but further requests will benefit from a smaller latency. You can optimize a serverless function by aggregating a large number of functionalities into a single function. The benefit is that this package will be executed with a higher frequency and will frequently skip the cold start issue. The problem is that a big package will take more time to load and provoke a higher first start time.

As a last resort, you could schedule another service to ping your functions periodically, such as once every 5 minutes, to prevent putting them to sleep. It will add costs, but it removes the cold start problem.

There is also a concept of serverless databases that references services where the database is fully managed by the vendor, and it costs only the storage and the time to execute the database engine. Those solutions are wonderful, but they add a second layer of delay for your requests.

Constraints

If you go serverless, you need to know what the vendor constraints are. For example, on AWS, you can't run a Lambda function for more than 5 minutes. It makes sense because if you spend long time running code, you are using it the wrong way. Serverless was designed to be cost efficient in short bursts. For constant and predictable processing, it will be expensive.

Another constraint on AWS Lambda is the number of concurrent executions across all functions within a given region. Amazon limits this to 1,000. Suppose that your functions need 100 milliseconds on average to execute. In this scenario, you can handle up to 10,000 users per second. The reasoning behind this restriction is to avoid excessive costs due to programming errors that may create potential runways or recursive iterations.

AWS Lambda has a default limit of 1,000 concurrent executions. However, you can file a case into AWS Support Center to raise this limit. If you say that your application is ready for production and that you understand the risks, they will probably increase this value.

When monitoring your Lambda functions using Amazon CloudWatch (more in `Chapter 10`, *Testing, Deploying, and Monitoring*), there is an option called *throttles*. Each invocation that exceeds the safety limit of concurrent calls is counted as one throttle. You can configure a CloudWatch alert to receive an e-mail if this scenario occurs.

Hidden inefficiencies

Some people see serverless as a NoOps solution. That's not true. DevOps is still necessary. You don't need to worry much about servers because they are second-class citizens and the focus is on your business. However, adding metrics and monitoring your applications will always be a good practice. It's so easy to scale that a specific function may be deployed with a poor performance that takes much more time than necessary and remains unnoticed forever because no one is monitoring the operation.

Also, over or under provisioning is also possible (in a smaller sense) since you need to configure your function, setting the amount of RAM memory that it will reserve and the threshold to timeout the execution. It's a very different scale of provisioning, but you need to keep it in mind to avoid mistakes.

Vendor dependency

When you build a serverless solution, you trust your business to a third-party vendor. You should be aware that companies fail and you can suffer downtimes, security breaches, and performance issues. Also, the vendor may change the billing model, increase costs, introduce bugs into their services, have poor documentation, modify an API forcing you to upgrade, and terminate services. A whole bunch of bad things may happen.

What you need to weigh is whether it's worth trusting in another company or making a big investment to build everything by yourself. You can mitigate these problems by doing a market search before selecting a vendor. However, you still need to count on luck. For example, Parse was a vendor that offered managed services with really nice features. It was bought by Facebook in 2013, which gave more reliability due to the fact that it was backed by a big company. Unfortunately, Facebook decided to shut down all servers in 2016, giving one year of notice for customers to migrate to other vendors.

Vendor lock-in is another big issue. When you use cloud services, it's very likely that one specific service has a completely different implementation than another vendor, making those two different APIs. You need to rewrite code in case you decide to migrate. It's already a common problem. If you use a managed service to send e-mails, you need to rewrite part of your code before migrating to another vendor. What raises a red flag here is that a serverless solution is entirely based in one vendor, and migrating the entire codebase can be much more troublesome.

To mitigate this problem, some tools such as the Serverless Framework support multiple vendors, making it easier to switch between them. Multivendor support represents safety for your business and gives power to competitiveness.

Debugging difficulties

Unit testing a serverless solution is fairly simple because any code that your functions rely on can be separated into modules and unit tested. Integration tests are a little bit more complicated because you need to be online to test using external services.

When it comes to debugging to test a feature or fix an error, it's a whole different problem. You can't hook into an external service to see how your code behaves step-by-step. Also, those Serverless APIs are not open sourced, so you can't run them in-house for testing. All you have is the ability to log steps, which is a slow debugging approach, or extract the code and adapt it to host into your own servers and make local calls.

Atomic deploys

Deploying a new version of a serverless function is easy. You update the code and the next time that a trigger requests this function, your newly deployed code will be selected to run. This means that, for a brief moment, two instances of the same function can be executed concurrently with different implementations. Usually, that's not a problem, but when you deal with persistent storage and databases, you should be aware that a new piece of code can insert data into a format that an old version can't understand.

Also, if you want to deploy a function that relies on a new implementation of another function, you need to be careful in the order that you deploy those functions. Ordering is often not secured by the tools that automate the deployment process.

The problem here is that current serverless implementations consider that deployment is an atomic process for each function. You can't batch deploy a group of functions atomically. You can mitigate this issue by disabling the event source while you deploy a specific group, but that means introducing downtime into the deployment process. Another option would be to use a Monolith approach instead of a Microservices architecture for serverless applications.

Uncertainties

Serverless is still a pretty new concept. Early adopters are braving this field, testing what works, and which kind of patterns and technologies can be used. Emerging tools are defining the development process. Vendors are releasing and improving new services. There are high expectations for the future, but the future isn't here yet. Some uncertainties still worry developers when it comes to building large applications. Being a pioneer can be rewarding, but risky.

Technical debt is a concept that compares software development with finances. The easiest solution in the short run is not always the best overall solution. When you take a bad decision in the beginning, you pay later with extra hours to fix it. Software is not perfect. Every single architecture has pros and cons that append technical debt in the long run. The question is: how much technical debt does serverless aggregate to the software development process? Is it more, less, or equivalent to the kind of architecture that you are using today?

Use cases

In this section, we'll cover which use cases fit better for the serverless context and which you should avoid. As the concept is still evolving, there are still unmapped applications, and you should not be restricted. So feel free to exercise your creativity to think and try new ones.

Static websites

Let's see the following few examples of static websites:

- Company website
- Portfolio
- Blog
- Online documentation

Static hosting is the simplest and oldest kind of serverless hosting. A static website, by definition, doesn't require server-side logic. You just need to map your site URLs to HTML files. In this book, we are going to use Amazon S3 to distribute HTML, CSS, JavaScript, and image files. Using Amazon Route 53, you give AWS the rights to route all domain requests to an S3 bucket that acts like a simple and cheap filesystem.

Hosting static files on a storage system is by far the best solution. It's cheap, fast, scalable, and highly available. There is no drawback. There is no function with cold start, no debugging, no uncertainties, and changing vendors is an easy task.

If you are thinking of using WordPress to build a static site, please reconsider. You would need to spin up a server to launch a web server and a database that stores data. You start paying a few dollars per month to host a basic site and that cost greatly increases with your audience. For availability, you would add another machine and a load balance, and the billing would cost at least dozens of dollars per month. Also, as WordPress is so largely used, it's a big target for hackers and you will end up worrying about periodic security patches for WordPress and its plugins.

So, how should you build a static site with a serverless approach? Nowadays, there are dozens of tools. I personally recommend **Jekyll**. You can host on GitHub pages for free, use **Disqus** to handle blog comments, and easily find many other plugins and templates. For my personal blog, I prefer to use Amazon because of its reliability and I pay just a few cents per month. If you want, you can also add CloudFront, which is a **Content Delivery Network** (**CDN**), to reduce latency by approximating users to your site files.

Lean websites

Once you learn how to build a serverless website, it's extremely fast to transform an idea into a running service, removing the burden of preparing an infrastructure. Following the lean philosophy, your prototype reaches the market to validate a concept with minimum waste and maximum speed.

Small e-commerce websites

In this section, I've used the qualifier *small*. This is because there are many studies that correlate the time to load a page with the probability for the customer to buy something. A few tens of milliseconds later may result in loss of sales. As already discussed, serverless brings reduced costs, but the cold start delay may increase the time to render a page. User-facing applications must consider whether this additional delay is worth it.

If the e-commerce sells to a small niche of customers in a single country, it's very likely that the traffic is concentrated during the day and reduces to almost nothing at late night. This use case is a perfect fit for serverless. Infrequent access is where most of the savings happens.

A real story to back this use case was described on Reddit. Betabrand, a retail clothing company, made a partnership with Valve to sell some products to promote one game. Valve created a blog post to advertise the deal and after a few minutes, the website broke because it couldn't handle the instant peak of a massive number of users. Valve pulled out the post and Betabrand had the mission to improve their infrastructure in one weekend.

Betabrand solved the problem building a small website using serverless. Valve advertised them again and they were able to handle 500,000 users in 24 hours, with peaks of 5,000 concurrent users. The post starts saying that it had an initial cost of only US$ 0.07, but it was corrected in comments to US$ 4.00 for backend and US$ 80.00 to transfer large (non-optimized) images, which is still an impressive low cost for such a high traffic (source: `http s://www.reddit.com/r/webdev/3oiilb`).

Temporary websites

Consider, in this section, websites that are built just for short events, like conferences, that receive a big number of visitors. They need to promote the event, display the schedule and maybe collect e-mails, comments, photos, and other kinds of data. Serverless helps handling the scale and provides a fast development.

Another related use case is for ticketing websites. Suppose that a huge, popular concert will start selling tickets at midnight. You can expect a massive number of fans trying to buy tickets at the same time.

Triggered processing

A common example is a mobile application that sends an image to a RESTful service. This image is stored and it triggers a function that will process it to optimize and reduce its size, creating different versions for desktop, tablet, and phones.

Chatbots

Most chatbots are very simple and designed for specific use cases. We don't build chatbots to pass the Turing test. We don't want them to be so complex and clever as to deceive a human that it's another human talking. What we want is to provide a new user interface to make it easier to interact with a system under certain conditions.

Instead of ordering a pizza through an application using menus and options, you can type a message like "I want a small pepperoni pizza" and be quickly done with your order. If the user types "Will it rain today?", it is perfectly fine for the pizza chatbox to answer "I couldn't understand. Which kind of pizza do you want for today? We have X, Y, and Z." Those broad questions are reserved for multipurpose AI bots such as Siri, Cortana, or Alexa.

Considering this restricted scenario, a serverless backend can be pretty useful. In fact, there is a growing number of demos and real-world applications that are using serverless to build chatbots.

IoT backends

Internet of Things (**IoT**) is a trending topic and many cloud services are providing tools to easily connect a huge number of devices. Those devices usually need to communicate through a set of simple messages, and they require a backend to process them. Thinking of this use case, Amazon offers AWS IoT as a serverless service to handle the broadcast of messages and AWS Lambda for serverless processing. Configuring and managing those services is so easy that they are becoming a common choice for IoT systems.

Scheduled events

You can set up your code to be executed on a regular, scheduled basis. Instead of running a dedicated machine to execute a code, one per hour, which creates some database reads or small file processing, you can use serverless and save costs.

Actually, that's a great way to introduce new features using serverless into a running solution since scheduled events are usually composed of simple tasks in separated modules.

Big Data

There is a growing number of applications that are substituting traditional big data tools such as Hadoop and Spark for serverless counterparts. Instead of managing clusters of machines, you can create a big data pipeline, converting your input to data streams and loading chunks of data into concurrent serverless functions.

The benefit of this approach is the reduced management and ease of use. However, as you have a constant processing of data, you can expect higher costs. Also, on AWS, a Lambda function can't run for more than 5 minutes, and this limit may force changes to reduce chunks of data to smaller sizes before processing.

What you should avoid

Avoid applications that have the following features:

- CPU-intensive with long running tasks
- Constant and with predictable traffic
- Real-time processing
- Multiplayer-intensive games

Regarding multiplayer games, you can build a serverless backend that handles the communication between players with very low latency through serverless notifications. It enables turn-based and card games, but may not fit so well for first person shooters, for example, which require constant and frequent server-side processing.

Summary

In this chapter, you learned about the serverless model and how it is different from other traditional approaches. You already know what the main benefits are and the advantages that it may offer for your next application. Also, you are aware that no technology is a silver bullet. You know what kind of problems you may have with serverless and how to mitigate some of them.

Now that you've understood the serverless model, we are ready to dive into the tools and services that you can use to build a serverless application. In the next chapter, you will learn which services AWS offers that can be considered as serverless, followed by a brief explanation on how they work and a set of code examples.

2
Getting Started with AWS

All major public cloud vendors currently provide serverless products. In this book, the focus will be on AWS, which is often considered the best option with regards to features, costs, and reliability. As we need to use a large number of AWS services throughout the book, this chapter introduces them to help you to get familiar with the building blocks of our sample application.

The main topics covered in this chapter are as follows:

- Handling user accounts
- Using the AWS, CLI, and the SDK services
- Deploying your first Lambda function
- Other AWS serverless products
- The architecture of our sample application
- Estimating costs

After this chapter, you will be able to start playing with AWS.

Amazon Web Services

AWS is the largest cloud vendor in terms of revenues. Often considered the best with regards to features, it offers great serverless products. This is why we have chosen AWS. If you prefer to use another cloud vendor, the following providers are other great options for serverless:

- **Google Cloud Engine**: This is where you can use Google Cloud Functions for serverless code execution with Node.js, and Google Cloud Datastore as a serverless database. Also, Google has integrated the Firebase platform, which offers many tools and serverless services for mobile and web applications like storage, authentication, and messaging.
- **Microsoft Azure**: This offers Azure Functions for serverless code execution, supporting C#, Node.js, Python, and PHP.
- **IBM Cloud**: This offers IBM Bluemix OpenWhisk for serverless code execution, supporting C#, Node.js, Java, and Swift.

All code examples in this book were designed for AWS using Node.js. They can be ported to other clouds, but this won't be an easy task. As previously stated in `Chapter 1`, *Understanding the Serverless Model*, one of the disadvantages of serverless is the vendor lock-in. However, you can use this book to learn the concepts and maybe mix services from different vendors. For example, you could use Azure Functions with Amazon SimpleDB.

If you are just starting with AWS and don't have any previous experience, that's not a problem since we'll start right from the basics. You can start by creating a new account at `https://aws.amazon.com`. For 12 months, you benefit from a free tier (`https://aws.amazon.com/free`) that is designed to enable you to learn and get hands-on experience for free while building demo applications. There are also some services that offer a permanent free tier that goes beyond the 12 months period.

The next sections will cover a selection of services that will be used in this book. Note that AWS has an official categorization of products (`https://aws.amazon.com/products`) that is different from this book's categories. This is because, instead of grouping services in their main field of application, we are grouping them based on how they will be used in our use case. For example, the IoT service will be used for notifications and not to connect devices. Also, Cognito is commonly used in mobile applications, but we will use its security features for a website:

- Security services
    - AWS IAM
    - Amazon Cognito

- Management
    - AWS SDKs
    - AWS CLI
    - AWS CloudFormation
    - Amazon CloudWatch
- Frontend services
    - Amazon S3
    - Amazon Route 53
    - Amazon CloudFront
    - AWS Certificate Manager
- Messaging and notifications
    - Amazon SNS
    - AWS IoT
- Backend services
    - AWS Lambda
    - Amazon API Gateway
- Database services
    - Amazon SimpleDB
    - Amazon DynamoDB

Handling user accounts and security

We will start covering security topics because you need to know how to properly configure user access and how to give permissions to the tools that we'll use to automate our infrastructure.

AWS IAM

When you create your AWS account, you receive a root user with full access. It can create/delete and start/stop any service. That's great for learning, but you shouldn't use it when developing a real project. In information security, the principle of least privilege requires that a user or program must be able to access only the information or resources that are necessary for its legitimate purpose. In case your access keys are compromised, the damage will be reduced if the access scope is restricted.

Traceability is another important aspect. You shouldn't share your user with others. It's really important that each person has their own user. AWS offers CloudTrail as a tool to track user activity and API usage.

So, you need to learn how to create user accounts and application keys with restricted access using **Identity and Access Management** (**IAM**). As we don't have applications keys yet, we will configure security using the IAM Management Console.

Creating users and groups

Take a look at the following steps to learn how to create a user and associate a group to restrict the user access:

1. Browse to the IAM website at `https://console.aws.amazon.com/iam`:

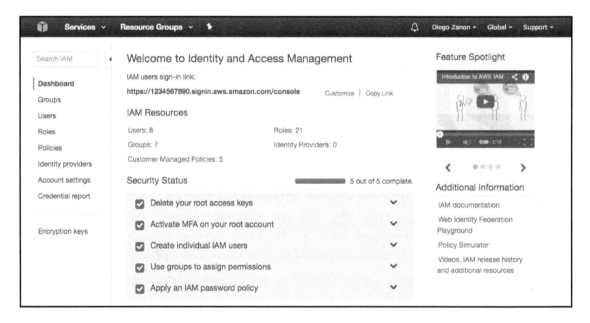

2. Click on **Users** in the left-hand side menu.

3. Choose **Add user** as shown in the following screenshot:

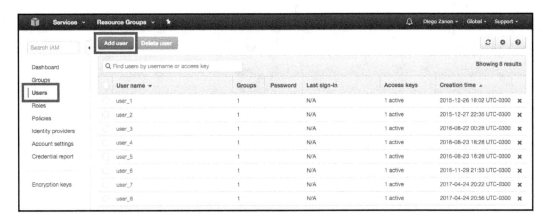

4. Type a username. Here, you can add multiple users at once by clicking on the **Add another user** option.
5. Check the **Programmatic access** box to enable API access using the CLI and the SDK.
6. Click on **Next: Permissions**, as shown in the following screenshot:

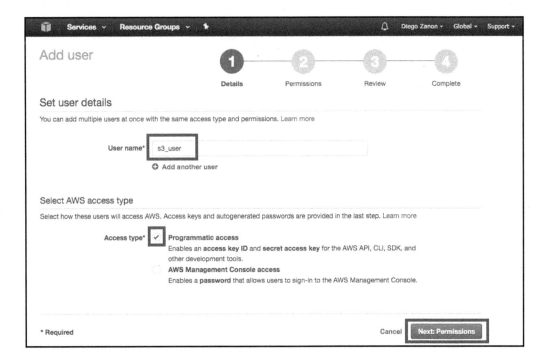

7. Now we need to create a group for this user. If you don't have one already, click on **Create group**:

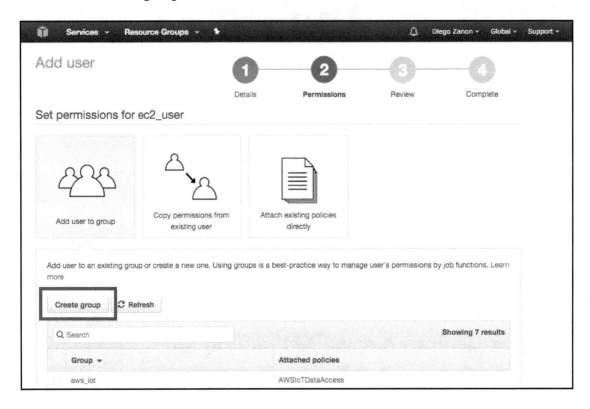

8. Choose a group name and select a policy. In this example, we will use a **Simple Storage Service (S3)** policy with full access. Click on **Create group** to continue and then click on **Next: Review**:

9. Review the selected data and click on **Create user**:

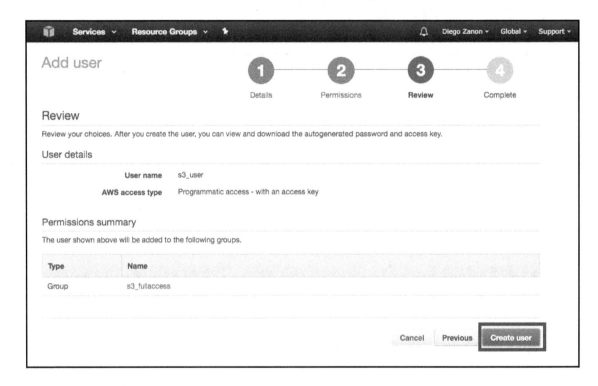

10. Write down the access key ID and secret access key displayed in the **Access key ID** and **Secret access key** boxes. They will be needed later to configure the CLI and the SDK:

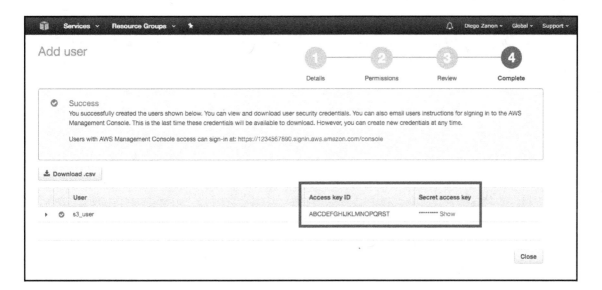

In this chapter, we will run examples for S3, SNS, Lambda, and API Gateway. You can take the opportunity and give proper access to each of these services. The **AdministratorAccess** policy type gives full access to all AWS resources and should be avoided if you are using this account to deploy applications to production.

Sign in with a non-root user account

The previous user was created with programmatic access only. You can edit the user or create another one to allow access to the Management Console by performing the following steps:

1. On the **Add user** screen, you need to check the **AWS Management Console access** option:

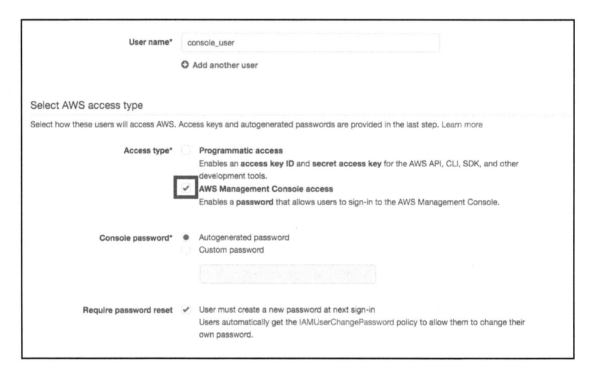

2. You can keep the **Autogenerated password** and **Require password reset** options checked. After selecting a group and confirming, you will receive a password and a link to access the AWS account with this non-root user:

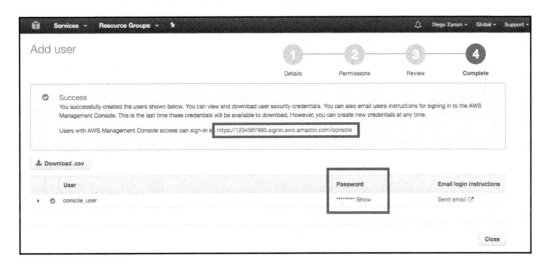

3. The access link has the format as
   `https://your_aws_account_id.signin.aws.amazon.com/console`. You just need to follow the link and type your new credentials.

4. If you don't want to disclose the AWS Account ID or if you prefer to use a friendly name, like your company name, you can create an account alias. On the IAM Console Management, select **Dashboard** and click on **Customize**:

5. Now, the user can sign in using a link that follows this format:
   `https://your_alias.signin.aws.amazon.com/console`

Amazon Cognito

Handling authentication in a secure way is a complex problem, but this use case is so common that many frameworks and services were built dedicated to solve it. Nowadays, you just need to copy a few lines of code and you are good to go.

Cognito is Amazon's solution for this problem. More than solving how you authenticate accounts, it provides an easy way to sync data between different devices. When you log in using a Cognito account, you receive a temporary AWS token that is used to store and retrieve data specific to the user, like preferences, user profile, or saved game data.

We'll explore more about this service through code examples in `Chapter 8`, *Securing the Serverless Application*.

Managing AWS resources

All services offered by Amazon are configured through RESTful interfaces named AWS API. You can access them using the following services:

- AWS Management Console
- AWS SDKs
- AWS CLI

Take look at the following diagram, which depicts the services offered by Amazon:

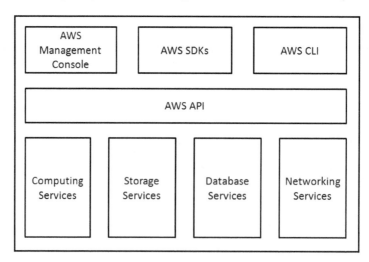

Rough schematic of the AWS architecture

AWS Management Console

The console is the graphical user interface provided by Amazon and is accessed through the official website at `https://console.aws.amazon.com`. It's the easiest interface for beginners and useful to learn new services, but it's not complete. There are some features that can't be accessed or configured using the console, such as managing your SimpleDB data. Also, in some cases, it requires a lot of manual work. If you have a repetitive task, it's better to automate it using the SDK or the CLI.

AWS SDKs

The SDK is the best way to manage your AWS resources through reusable code. Using the SDK, you can automate your infrastructure and handle errors using very simple commands. There are SDKs for many different programming languages like Java, Python, Ruby, and others. In this book, we will use exclusively the SDK for Node.js. The official documentation is available at `http://docs.aws.amazon.com/AWSJavaScriptSDK/latest /index.html`.

 All code examples in this book use Node.js, which is a cross-platform JavaScript runtime with an event-driven model. Basic knowledge of Node.js is expected from the reader since we will not cover the basics. Also, we will use Node's default package manager, `npm`, to install dependencies.

Let's learn about using the SDK for Node.js by performing the following steps:

1. Start a new Node project using `npm init` and run the npm command to install the AWS SDK:

    ```
    npm install aws-sdk --save
    ```

2. After installing, you need to set the access keys that will be used by the SDK to connect to AWS. These keys were generated in the previous section, when we created a new user.
3. The following are a few options to set the credentials:
    *   Setting the credentials with hardcoded keys
    *   Loading a JSON file on disk
    *   Setting a credentials file
    *   Setting environment variables

You should always avoid hardcoding AWS keys, especially in open source projects on GitHub. You don't want to risk accidentally committing your private keys.

4. I prefer to configure them through environment variables. If you are running on macOS or Linux, add the following lines to the ~/.bash_profile file. Replace YOUR-KEY and YOUR-REGION by the real values:

```
export AWS_ACCESS_KEY_ID=YOUR-KEY
export AWS_SECRET_ACCESS_KEY=YOUR-KEY
export AWS_REGION=YOUR-REGION
```

5. If you are running on Windows, execute the following commands on command prompt as the admin, replacing the values of the keys and region:

```
setx AWS_ACCESS_KEY_ID YOUR-KEY
setx AWS_SECRET_ACCESS_KEY YOUR-KEY
setx AWS_REGION YOUR-REGION
```

6. If you don't have a preferred region, you can use us-east-1 (Northern Virginia, US East). When you use the AWS Management Console, you can set the region where you are going to manage the resources through the upper-right drop-down menu.

Both the configurations are persistent, but they will work only for the next time that you open the command line.

7. You can test your setup creating a new file named index.js and running the following code to list your S3 buckets. As a simplified definition, you can consider a **bucket** as a repository of files. Now, if you have proper access, this example will return your bucket list or an empty array, if there is none. If you don't have access or had a problem setting the credentials, it will return an error:

```
const AWS = require('aws-sdk');
const s3 = new AWS.S3();

s3.listBuckets((err, data) => {
  if (err) console.log(err, err.stack); // an error occurred
  else console.log(data.Buckets); // successful response
});
```

AWS CLI

The CLI is the command-line interface. For experienced users, it's a great tool to access information and manage resources. If you already have Python installed, you just need to run `pip`, which is the default package manager for Python, to install the CLI:

```
pip install awscli
```

The configuration of the CLI is very similar to the one used by the SDK. The only difference is that you need to add another environment variable: AWS_DEFAULT_REGION. You need this because the SDK uses AWS_REGION instead of the AWS_DEFAULT_REGION variable.

To test if your setup is correct, you can execute the `ls` (list) command to list S3 buckets:

```
aws s3 ls
```

Considering an AWS account with one bucket, the preceding command line derives the following output:

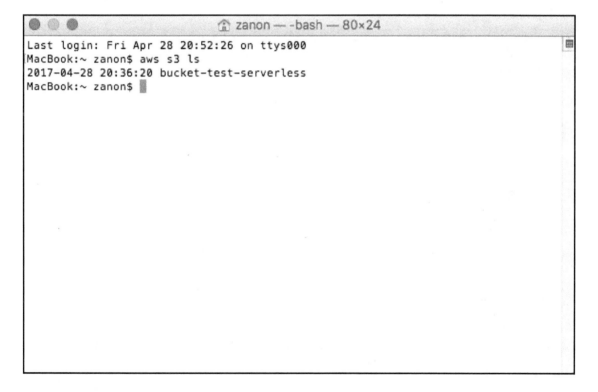

AWS CloudFormation

CloudFormation gives to developers the possibility to script the entire infrastructure using templates. This approach is called as *Infrastructure as a Code*. It's a powerful feature because it makes it easy to reproduce the configuration of servers and resources into another region or in a different account. Furthermore, you can version control your scripts to help you with the development of your infrastructure. As a quick start, AWS offers many sample templates (`https://aws.amazon.com/cloudformation/aws-cloudformation-templates`) for common use cases.

In this book, we will not use CloudFormation directly, but in the next chapter, we'll start using the Serverless Framework that extensively uses CloudFormation under the hood to manage resources. That's how you can easily duplicate your solution to different environments, making a production deployment an exact copy of the development or staging environment.

Amazon CloudWatch

CloudWatch is a monitoring service for your AWS resources. It is often used to monitor virtual machines, but it is not restricted to it and plays an important role even when your operation is based only on serverless functions. With CloudWatch, you can monitor errors, throttles, number of invocations, duration, and costs. You can also expand monitoring further with custom plugins.

This subject will be covered in `Chapter 10`, *Testing, Deploying, and Monitoring*.

Frontend services

This section describes the main services related to frontend development. While an introduction is made here, you will find detailed examples in `Chapter 4`, *Hosting the Website*, when we will host our application frontend using a serverless approach.

Amazon S3

Amazon Simple Storage Service (**S3**) is a service where you can save any type of file such as images, log files, and backups. Starting here with a bit of nomenclature, Amazon calls each file as an **object** and, to store files, you need a root folder that is called as a **bucket**. In your account, you can have multiple buckets to better organize your data. You can also have folders inside a bucket, but can't have buckets within buckets.

An interesting feature is that each file receives a unique URL in the following format:

```
https://s3.amazonaws.com/bucketname/filename
```

With this format, the bucket name must be unique through all accounts to guarantee unique URLs. It means that you can't create a bucket with a common name like "my-photos" because it will already be taken. Be creative and count on luck when choosing a name.

You can restrict the file access if it's a backup or another kind of private data, but what we will explore here is to let the files be publicly available to store our frontend data. This is a powerful feature. For example, you can use it to stream videos. You just need to add a `<video>` HTML5 tag that references the URL of an mp4 file. For a nice looking player, you could use something like `http://videojs.com`, which is open source.

We will take advantage of S3 as it is a very cheap storage service and it has the flexibility to share files to build our low cost and serverless frontend. In our bucket, we'll add all static files of our frontend, including HTML, CSS, JavaScript, images, and so on. With proper configuration, which will be detailed in `Chapter 4`, *Hosting the Website*, it will be ready to serve our content with high availability, scalability, and low costs.

Using S3 with the CLI

The Management Console is very useful to upload and download files from S3, but so is the CLI. Let's play with the CLI in this section to gain more familiarity. We will create a bucket and store a file by performing the following steps. Those will be useful later for the AWS Lambda demo:

1. First, choose a bucket name and use the make-bucket command:

   ```
   aws s3 mb s3://my-bucket-name
   ```

2. Now, create a file named `test.txt` and write something to it.
3. Copy the file to your new bucket setting the **Access Control List** (**ACL**) as public content:

   ```
   aws s3 cp test.txt s3://my-bucket-name/ --acl public-read
   ```

4. List the bucket contents using the following command line:

```
aws s3 ls s3://my-bucket-name
```

5. Download the file as test2.txt by using the following command line:

```
aws s3 cp s3://my-bucket-name/test.txt test2.txt
```

 For more commands, refer to the official guide at http://docs.aws.amazo n.com/cli/latest/userguide/using-s3-commands.html.

Amazon Route 53

Route 53 provides a DNS service where you can buy and host your site's domain. You may prefer to buy your domain from another seller, like GoDaddy or Namecheap, but if you want to serve your serverless frontend using AWS services, you need to use Route 53 to host it.

When you configure a subdomain (like in mysubdomain.mydomain.com), you can set an A record (IP address) or CNAME (alias to another address), but the root domain (mydomain.com) requires an A record. If you host your frontend using S3, you receive an endpoint to set a CNAME record, but you don't get a fixed IP to set an A record. Since Route 53 is an AWS service, it accepts an S3 endpoint in the A record option and solves this issue.

Configuring your domain requires a simple setup, but it often confuses web developers who are not used to DNS management. This service will receive more attention later, specifically in Chapter 4, *Hosting the Website*.

Amazon CloudFront

CloudFront is a **Content Delivery Network (CDN)**. It is a special service with the objective of improving your website speed and availability. It achieves this by reducing the distance between users and files using Amazon's infrastructure around the world, which contains more than 60 edge locations, where each one of them can be used to host copies of your files.

A signal traveling at light speed from Sydney (Australia) to New York (USA) takes 53 milliseconds. A ping message needs a roundtrip, covering twice the distance and taking double the time. Also, there are other factors that increase this time: light travels 33% slower on fiber optics (glass), there is no straight line connecting both cities, and equipment like repeaters and switches will slow down transfer speeds. The result is a measured latency between 200 milliseconds and 300 milliseconds. By comparison, providing the content in the same city may reduce the latency to 15 milliseconds.

This difference is usually not significant for most applications. In a serverless website, the cold start delay has a bigger impact. If your use case is very sensitive to high latencies, you should avoid serverless or you can use CloudFront to minimize the impact, at least in the frontend.

To reduce costs, CloudFront won't replicate your content automatically throughout the world. It will replicate only where a demand for it exists. For example, when a request is made from a British city, the DNS will route the request to the nearest edge location and if it does not have yet a local copy of the file, it will be copied temporarily (cached). When another user in a nearby city requests the same file, it will benefit from a lower latency and fast response.

AWS Certificate Manager

Certificate Manager is a service where you can request free SSL/TLS certificates to make your website support HTTPS. A certificate used to be an expensive purchase for small sites, ranging from US$ 100 to US$ 500 per year. To help make certificates (and HTTPS) accessible to everyone, Let's Encrypt (`https://letsencrypt.org`) was created as a nonprofit certificate authority company, which operates based on donations and sponsorship. You can get free certificates and they will be accepted by all major browsers.

Following Let's Encrypt, Amazon launched its own service named AWS Certificate Manager. It's restricted to AWS customers, but it's also free and easier to use. Once you issue a new certificate and associate it with a CloudFront distribution, Amazon will also be responsible by automatically renewing the certificate when necessary. We will cover this service in `Chapter 4`, *Hosting the Website*.

Messaging and notifications

This section covers which services you can use on AWS to send notifications to your users.

Amazon SNS

Amazon **Simple Notification Service** (**SNS**) implements the publish-subscribe messaging pattern. When you create an SNS topic, it becomes available for other services to subscribe to it. If someone publishes a message in this topic, all subscribed services will be alerted.

It's a very simple and powerful service. You can use it to dynamically attach different services that are able to handle a specific kind of notification. For example, an application can send a notification to an SNS topic to alert that you have received a new file to process. You can subscribe to this topic using an HTTP endpoint and SNS will send a message to your web service with the file location that needs processing. Later, you can add another endpoint, using a Lambda function programmed to do another kind of processing.

Let's perform the following steps to create a simple demo using the CLI as an example:

1. Create an SNS topic using the following command line:

    ```
    aws sns create-topic --name email-alerts
    ```

2. The result is an **Amazon Resource Name** (**ARN**) that you need to save. The ARN will be created with a format of this example: `arn:aws:sns:us-east-1:1234567890:email-alerts`

3. Subscribe to a topic using the e-mail protocol, so you will receive an e-mail every time that an application publishes to this topic:

    ```
    aws sns subscribe --topic-arn the_previous_arn --protocol email \
       --notification-endpoint myemail@example.com
    ```

4. Open your e-mail account and confirm that you want to subscribe to events.
5. Publish a test message and see it working by using the following command line:

    ```
    aws sns publish --topic-arn the_previous_arn --message "test"
    ```

For more commands, refer to the official guide at `http://docs.aws.amazo` `n.com/cli/latest/userguide/cli-sqs-queue-sns-topic.html`.

AWS IoT

AWS IoT (Internet of Things) will be used in our solution to handle serverless notifications. Although the name indicates the usage of IoT devices, we will use this service exclusively for users connected through browsers. This is becasuse hooking a web page into a notification service to receive updates, through a subscription mechanism and not data polling, requires the usage of WebSockets, which are supported by IoT and not supported by Amazon SNS. So, although the IoT name may sound as a strange choice, we will use it because it is the only AWS service capable of handling our use case.

AWS IoT implements the publish-subscribe pattern using the **Message Queuing Telemetry Transport** (**MQTT**) protocol. We will see code examples in `Chapter 9`, *Handling Serverless Notifications*, while implementing live comments for product review pages of our sample website.

Backend services

In this section, we will go through the services that are needed to build the backend with some practical examples.

AWS Lambda

Lambda is the flagship product of the serverless concept. The ability to run functions on demand with zero administration and its particular pricing model is the main drive that aroused interest in the developer community. We can say that we have serverless databases, serverless notifications, and serverless frontends, but those are merely extensions of the main feature, that is, serverless code executions.

Lambda currently only supports Node.js (JavaScript), Python, Java, and C# languages, but there is a third-party framework named Apex (`https://github.com/apex/apex`) that adds support for Go, Rust, and Clojure by injecting Node.js shims in the deployment build.

Creating a Lambda function

In this book, we will use the Serverless Framework extensively to make the deployment of Lambda functions easier; however, to see how useful the framework is, in this chapter, we will use the AWS Management Console for comparison.

We will now create a Lambda function to process log files. This function will be triggered when a new log file is added to an S3 bucket and the result of the Lambda function is to create an SNS notification if there is an error in the file.

Let's take a look at the following steps, which are necessary to execute:

1. Browse the following link: `https://console.aws.amazon.com/lambda`. Select **Get Started Now** to start creating a new function:

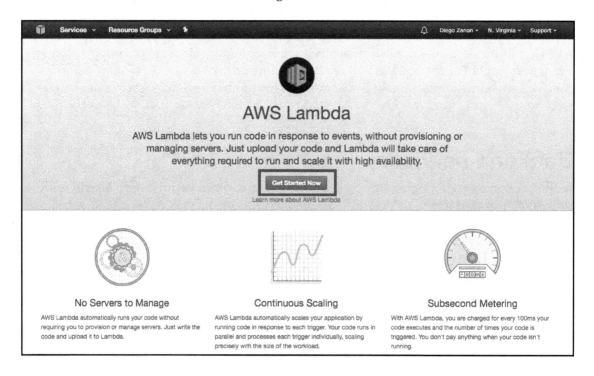

2. AWS offers many templates with sample configuration and code. For example, you could use a template of a Lambda function that processes bounced e-mails. This option is interesting for marketing campaigns to remove e-mail addresses that don't exist. However, in this example, we will select a **Blank Function** template:

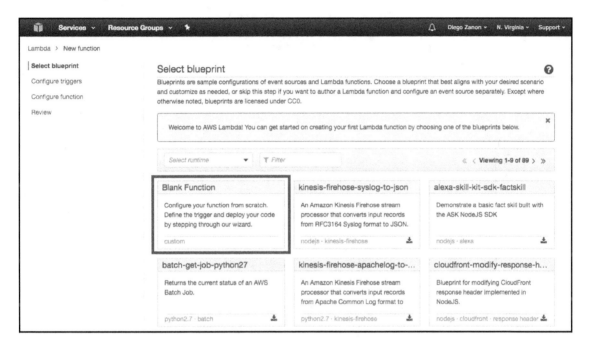

3. A Lambda function can be triggered by many different sources. In the next screen, you will see a list of all available options. Select **S3**:

- On a side note, take a look at some use cases of the available triggers:
  - **Amazon S3**: You can select a bucket name with **Event type** as **Object Created (All)** and **Prefix** images/. In this setting, when you upload an image to this bucket within the images folder, you will trigger a Lambda function for post-processing and image optimization.
  - **SNS**: You can use this service to handle notifications. For example, you could create an SNS topic named Process Order that would be activated by your application when a new order is received. SNS could be configured to send an e-mail for a specific list of employees and trigger a Lambda function to execute some logic.
  - **CloudWatch Logs**: This service helps you to monitor your AWS resources and take automated actions. You could trigger Lambda functions to handle alert messages and execute specific actions according to its content.

4. After selecting **S3**, you will be presented with some configuration options. Select the bucket that we have created previously with the CLI. For the **Event type**, select **Object Created (All)** to trigger the function whenever a new file is created. For **Prefix**, type `logs/` to consider only files in the logs folder and in the **Suffix**, type `txt` to consider only text files. Finally, check the **Enable trigger** option and click on **Next**:

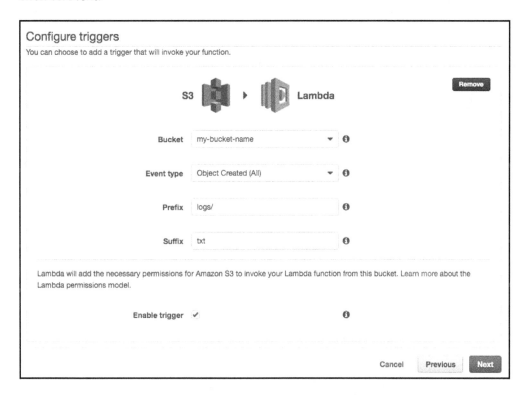

5. Type a name for your Lambda function, for example, `processLog`, and select the **Node.js 6.10** option for **Runtime**:

6. Now we need to implement the code that will be executed by the Lambda function using the **Edit code inline** option. In this example, we are using S3.getObject to retrieve the file created and SNS.publish to create a notification if there is the error word in this file. For the SNS topic ARN, you can use the same that was previously created with the CLI:

```javascript
const AWS = require('aws-sdk');
const s3 = new AWS.S3();
const sns = new AWS.SNS();

exports.handler = (event, context, callback) => {
  const bucketName = event.Records[0].s3.bucket.name;
  const objectKey = event.Records[0].s3.object.key;
  const s3Params = {
    Bucket: bucketName,
    Key: objectKey
  };

  s3.getObject(s3Params, (err, data) => {
    if (err) throw err;

    // check if file have errors to report
    const fileContent = data.Body.toString();
    if (fileContent.indexOf('error') !== -1) {
      const msg = `file ${objectKey} has errors`;
      const snsParams = {
        Message: msg,
        TopicArn: 'my-topic-arn'
      };
      sns.publish(snsParams, callback);
    }
  });
};
```

The aws-sdk module is available for all Lambda functions. If you want to add another dependency that is not the aws-sdk module or a core module of Node, you need to upload a ZIP file to AWS containing your function and the module.

7. As we have used the inline option to write the code instead of uploading a ZIP file, the code will be placed inside an `index.js` file. Also, the module that we have created exports a function named `handler`. In this case, we need to configure the Lambda handler with the `index.handler` name. For the **Role** box, we need to create a new one because a Lambda function can't execute without proper access. Even if you create a Lambda using an administrator account, you must give explicit permissions for which kind of services and resources the Lambda will be able to access:

8. Type a role name for this role and click on **Edit** to modify the default policy document. Add the following JSON object and finish by clicking on **Allow**:

  You will need to replace the S3 and SNS ARNs to your respective ARNs.

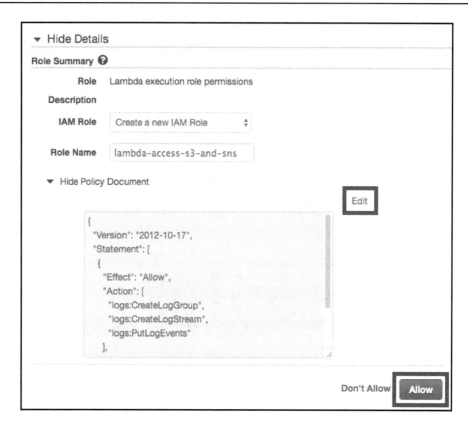

Use the following JSON object:

```
{
  "Version": "2012-10-17",
  "Statement": [
    {
      "Effect": "Allow",
      "Action": ["s3:GetObject"],
      "Resource": "arn:aws:s3:::my-bucket-name/*"
    },
    {
      "Effect": "Allow",
      "Action": ["sns:Publish"],
      "Resource": "arn:aws:sns:us-east-1:1234567890:email-alerts"
    }
  ]
}
```

9. The last step is to configure the **Advanced settings**. Set the amount of RAM memory that should be allocated for this function and the timeout value that AWS must wait for this function to finish its execution. You may need to increase the timeout value depending on the size of the log files that you are going to use for testing:

10. Click on **Next** and you will be redirected to a **Review** page where you need to confirm the function creation.

11. To test this function, we can use the Management Console, which lets us create custom input events, but, in this case, we can use the CLI to upload a new file and trigger the Lambda function. If the file has the word "error", you should receive an e-mail message with the file name.

    Take a look at the following CLI command to trigger this Lambda function:

    ```
    aws s3 cp log1.txt s3://my-bucket-name/logs/
    ```

12. If you have any issues, you can try using the Management Console to see the error message that appears. In this case, use the following JSON object as the event trigger, replacing the bucket name:

```
{
  "Records": [
    {
      "s3": {
        "bucket": {
          "name": "my-bucket-name"
        },
        "object": {
          "key": "logs/log1.txt"
        }
      }
    }
  ]
}
```

Amazon API Gateway

API Gateway is a service that helps you to build RESTful APIs. You need to configure your resources, set the supported HTTP verbs and specify what will handle the requests. You can use it to redirect requests to EC2 instances (virtual machines) or external web servers, but what we'll explore here is to use it to trigger Lambda functions.

Besides, API Gateway has other interesting features. For example, after creating your API endpoints, you can use API Gateway to automatically generate a client SDK for many different platforms, where you can easily test and distribute it to be used by third-party developers. Also, you can create third-party API keys to access your content with fine-grained access permissions, request quota limits, and throttling.

In our architecture, API Gateway will act as a thin layer that exists only to expose our Lambda functions to the world. Additionally, you can set security controls to allow only authenticated users to trigger your code. We are going to use this service in the next chapter, where we'll talk about how to configure our endpoints using the Serverless Framework, we will see more in Chapter 6, *Developing the Backend*, while building our backend code, and lastly, in Chapter 8, *Securing the Serverless Application*, when our security measures will be explained.

Expose your Lambda function using API Gateway

Let's use the API Gateway to expose our previous Lambda function to be accessible using a URL by performing the following steps:

1. First, go to the API Gateway Management Console by visiting this link `https://c onsole.aws.amazon.com/apigateway`and click on **Create API**.

2. Under the **Create new API** header, select the **New API** option and type the API name. For example: `log-processor`:

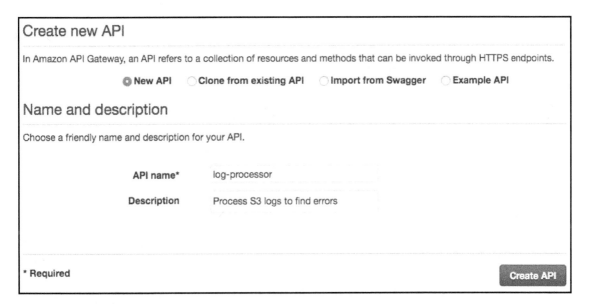

3. Under **Resources**, click on the **Actions** dropdown and choose **Create Method**:

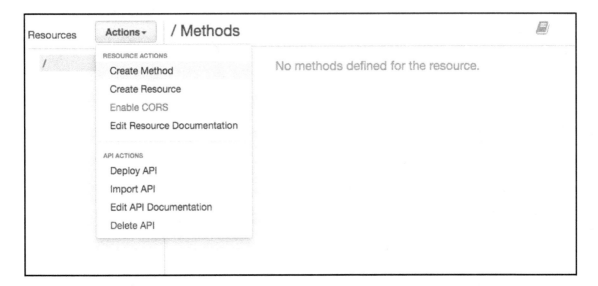

4. In the new dropdown, select the **POST** HTTP verb.

5. Under **- POST - Setup**, select **Lambda Function** as our **Integration type**. Select the region in which you have deployed our previous Lambda function and its corresponding name and click on **Save** button:

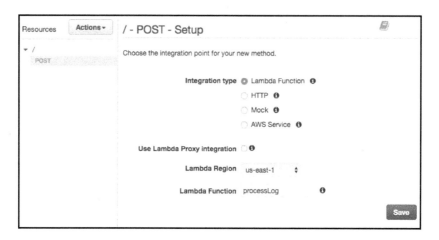

6. A popup will request that you allow this method to access the Lambda function. Accept it.

7. Under **Resources**, click again in the **Actions** drop-down and choose **Deploy API**.

8. A popup will request a stage to be selected. You can select **[New Stage]** and name it as `dev`:

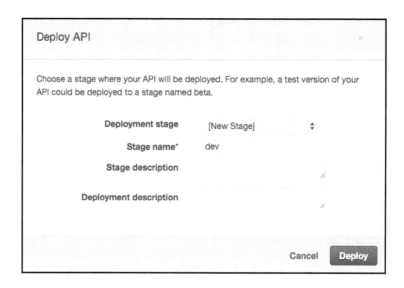

9. Click on **Deploy**. The next screen will show where the API Gateway was deployed. The URL will follow this format, such as `https://[identifier].execute-api.[region].amazonaws.com/dev`.

10. If you try this URL in your browser, the result will be an authentication error that happens because the browser will try a `GET` request that was not defined. As we have defined only a `POST` resource, we need another way to test. You can use the API Gateway test feature that is accessible under the **Resources** feature in the left menu, followed by selecting the `POST` verb and clicking on **Test**.

11. You need to provide a **Request Body**. In our case, it will be a JSON object with a format similar to a new S3 object event:

```
{
  "Records": [
    {
      "s3": {
        "bucket": {
          "name": "my-bucket-name"
        },
        "object": {
          "key": "logs/log1.txt"
        }
      }
    }
  ]
}
```

12. You just need to change the bucket name for the name that you used previously, and the API Gateway will trigger the Lambda function to process the `log1.txt` file that we have uploaded before.

Another way to test this integration with the API Gateway is using **Postman**, which is a very popular tool to test any kind of RESTful APIs. Postman can be installed as a Chrome extension or as a macOS application.

Database services

In this section, we will see a brief explanation about the SimpleDB and DynamoDB products. Both of them will be covered in details in `Chapter 7`, *Managing a Serverless Database*.

Amazon SimpleDB

SimpleDB is a NoSQL database that can be defined as a serverless database because it scales automatically, it is highly available without needing to pay for provisions, and you are only billed by the seconds that the database engine needs to execute your queries.

You can use SimpleDB to make queries using a SQL-like syntax, but SimpleDB is very limited in terms of functionalities. It's so limited that it only stores string fields! If you store a datetime data type, you need to save it as a string ISO representation to avoid localization issues and to be able to make the `where` clauses. If you want to store numbers, use zero-padding. And how can we make `where` clauses with negative numbers? It is done by adding a large offset to all numbers to avoid storing negatives! As you can see, building a system on top of SimpleDB can be hard. There are many considerations and you can have performance problems when running with large datasets. Hence, SimpleDB is usually useful only for small projects.

 You can see more tips on how to handle data types by following this link: `https://aws.amazon.com/articles/Amazon-SimpleDB/1232`

SimpleDB is the only serverless database offered by AWS. If you want a better serverless solution, you would need to try other cloud providers. You currently have the following options: Google Firebase storage, Google Cloud Datastore, or FaunaDB.

SimpleDB is one of the oldest AWS services, announced in late 2007. However, it continues to be one of very few services that don't have a Management Console. If you want a GUI to easily query and manage your SimpleDB data, you can install a third-party solution. In this case, I suggest the **SdbNavigator Chrome Extension** as a good option. You only need to add an access key and a secret key to connect to your database. As a security measure, create a new user account using IAM with restricted privileges to SimpleDB.

Amazon DynamoDB

DynamoDB is a fully managed NoSQL database designed to be highly scalable having a fast and consistent performance. Unlike SimpleDB, DynamoDB has all the common features that you expect in a NoSQL database and can be extensively used in large projects. However, DynamoDB has a flaw for our use case: it is *not* a serverless database. It requires provisioning of resources, so you *can't* say that DynamoDB is truly serverless. If you pay for provisioned capacity, you need to worry about the *servers* because you may end up provisioning more or less than necessary and paying for availability even when no one is using your database.

Fortunately, AWS has a permanent free tier that is very generous. You can serve more than 100 million read/write requests per month for free and this offer is not restricted to new AWS users. Considering this advantage, the low price to grow your user base, the possibility to automate the throughput provisioning, DynamoDB is a good choice for most serverless applications and this is proven by the numerous examples of projects and demos created by the serverless community using DynamoDB. It is very hard to see SimpleDB being used even for small projects, since DynamoDB is free for low usage.

So, even if you have a large project and end up having to pay for provisioned resources that you would not use, DynamoDB requires much less management and can be a cheaper option than running a traditional database solution. For all these reasons, we are going to cover SimpleDB usage in this book, but our sample application will run on DynamoDB.

The serverless architecture of our online store

In this book, we will build a real-world use case of a serverless solution. This sample application is an online store with the following requirements:

- List of available products
- Product details with user rating
- Add products to a shopping cart
- Create account and login pages

We will describe and implement each feature in the next chapters. For a better understanding of the architecture, the following diagram gives a general view of how the different services that we covered in this chapter are organized and how they interact:

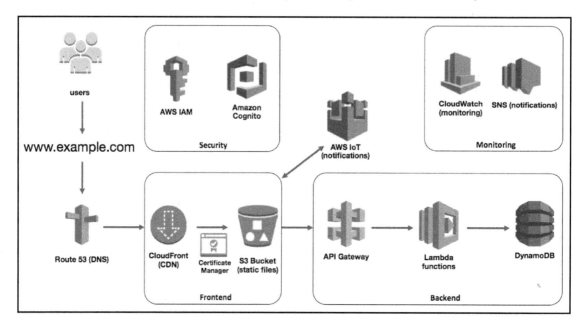

Estimating costs

In this section, we will estimate the costs of our sample application demo based on some usage assumptions and Amazon's pricing model. All pricing values used here are from mid 2017 and considers the cheapest region, US East (Northern Virginia).

This section covers an example to illustrate how costs are calculated. Since the billing model and prices can change over time, always refer to the official sources to get updated prices before making your own estimations. You can use Amazon's calculator, which is accessible at this link: `http://c alculator.s3.amazonaws.com/index.html`. If you still have any doubts after reading the instructions, you can always contact Amazon's support for free to get commercial guidance.

Assumptions

For our pricing example, we can assume that our online store will receive the following traffic *per month*:

- 100,000 page views
- 1,000 registered user accounts
- 200 GB of data transferred considering an average page size of 2 MB
- 5,000,000 code executions (Lambda functions) with an average of 200 milliseconds per request

Route 53 pricing

We need a hosted zone for our domain name and it costs US$ 0.50 per month. Also, we need to pay US$ 0.40 per million DNS queries to our domain. As this is a prorated cost, 100,000 page views will cost only US$ 0.04.

Total: US$ 0.54

S3 pricing

Amazon S3 charges you US$ 0.023 per GB/month stored, US$ 0.004 per 10,000 requests to your files, and US$ 0.09 per GB transferred. However, as we are considering the CloudFront usage, transfer costs will be charged by CloudFront prices and will not be considered in S3 billing.

If our website occupies less than 1 GB of static files and has an average per page of 2 MB and 20 files, we can serve 100,000 page views for less than US$ 20. Considering CloudFront, S3 costs will go down to US$ 0.82 while you need to pay for CloudFront usage in another section. Real costs would be even lower because CloudFront caches files and it would not need to make 2,000,000 file requests to S3, but let's skip this detail to reduce the complexity of this estimation.

On a side note, the cost would be much higher if you had to provision machines to handle this number of page views to a static website with the same availability and scalability.

Total: US$ 0.82

CloudFront pricing

CloudFront is slightly more complicated to price since you need to guess how much traffic comes from each region, as they are priced differently. The following table shows an example of estimation:

Region	Estimated traffic	Cost per GB transferred	Cost per 10,000 HTTPS requests
North America	70%	US$ 0.085	US$ 0.010
Europe	15%	US$ 0.085	US$ 0.012
Asia	10%	US$ 0.140	US$ 0.012
South America	5%	US$ 0.250	US$ 0.022

As we have estimated 200 GB of files transferred with 2,000,000 requests, the total will be US$ 21.97.

Total: US$ 21.97

Certificate Manager pricing

Certificate Manager provides SSL/TLS certificates for free. You only need to pay for the AWS resources you create to run your application.

IAM pricing

There is no charge specifically for IAM usage. You will be charged only by what AWS resources your users are consuming.

Cognito pricing

Each user has an associated profile that costs US$ 0.0055 per month. However, there is a permanent free tier that allows 50,000 monthly active users without charges, which is more than enough for our use case.

Besides that, we are charged for Cognito Syncs of our user profiles. It costs US$ 0.15 for each 10,000 sync operations and US$ 0.15 per GB/month stored. If we estimate 1,000 active and registered users with less than 1 MB per profile, with less than 10 visits per month in average, we can estimate a charge of US$ 0.30.

Total: US$ 0.30

IoT pricing

IoT charges starts at US$ 5 per million messages exchanged. As each page view will make at least 2 requests, one to connect and another to subscribe to a topic, we can estimate a minimum of 200,000 messages per month. We need to add 1,000 messages if we suppose that 1% of the users will rate the products and we can ignore other requests like disconnect and unsubscribed because they are excluded from billing. In this setting, the total cost would be of US$ 1.01.

Total: US$ 1.01

SNS pricing

We will use SNS only for internal notifications, when CloudWatch triggers a warning about issues in our infrastructure. SNS charges US$ 2.00 per 100,000 e-mail messages, but it offers a permanent free tier of 1,000 e-mails. So, it will be free for us.

CloudWatch pricing

CloudWatch charges US$ 0.30 per metric/month and US$ 0.10 per alarm and offers a permanent free tier of 50 metrics and 10 alarms per month. If we create 20 metrics and expect 20 alarms in a month, we can estimate a cost of US$ 1.00.

Total: US$ 1.00

API Gateway pricing

API Gateway starts charging US$ 3.50 per million of API calls received and US$ 0.09 per GB transferred out to the Internet. If we assume 5 million requests per month with each response with an average of 1 KB, the total cost of this service will be US$ 17.93.

Total: US$ 17.93

Lambda pricing

When you create a Lambda function, you need to configure the amount of RAM memory that will be available for use. It ranges from 128 MB to 1.5 GB. Allocating more memory means additional costs. It breaks the philosophy of avoiding provision, but at least it's the only thing you need to worry about. The good practice here is to estimate how much memory each function needs and make some tests before deploying to production. A bad provision may result in errors or higher costs.

Lambda has the following billing model:

- US$ 0.20 per 1 million requests
- US$ 0.00001667 GB-second

 Running time is counted in fractions of seconds, rounding up to the nearest multiple of 100 milliseconds.

Furthermore, there is a permanent free tier that gives you 1 million requests and 400,000 GB-seconds per month without charges.

In our use case scenario, we have assumed 5 million requests per month with an average of 200 milliseconds per execution. We can also assume that the allocated RAM memory is 512 MB per function:

- **Request charges**: Since 1 million requests are free, you pay for 4 million that will cost US$ 0.80.
- **Compute charges**: Here, 5 million executions of 200 milliseconds each gives us 1 million seconds. As we are running with a 512 MB capacity, it results in 500,000 GB-seconds, where 400,000 GB-seconds of these are free, resulting in a charge of 100,000 GB-seconds that costs US$ 1.67.
- **Total**: US$ 2.47

SimpleDB pricing

Take a look at the following SimpleDB billing where the free tier is valid for new and existing users:

- US$ 0.14 per machine-hour (25 hours free)
- US$ 0.09 per GB transferred out to the internet (1 GB is free)
- US$ 0.25 per GB stored (1 GB is free)

Take a look at the following charges:

- **Compute charges**: Considering 5 million requests with an average of 200 milliseconds of execution time, where 50% of this time is waiting for the database engine to execute, we estimate 139 machine hours per month. Discounting 25 free hours, we have an execution cost of US$ 15.96.
- **Transfer costs**: Since we'll transfer data between SimpleDB and AWS Lambda, there is no transfer cost.
- **Storage charges**: If we assume a 5 GB database, it results in US$ 1.00, since 1 GB is free.
- **Total**: US$ 16.96, but this will not be added in the final estimation since we will run our application using DynamoDB.

DynamoDB

DynamoDB requires you to provision the throughput capacity that you expect your tables to offer. Instead of provisioning hardware, memory, CPU, and other factors, you need to say how many read and write operations you expect and AWS will handle the necessary machine resources to meet your throughput needs with consistent and low-latency performance.

One read capacity unit represents one strongly consistent read per second or two eventually consistent reads per second, where objects have a size up to 4 KB. Regarding the writing capacity, one unit means that you can write one object of size 1 KB per second. Considering these definitions, AWS offers in the permanent free tier 25 read units and 25 write units of throughput capacity, in addition to 25 GB of free storage. It charges as follows:

- US$ 0.47 per month for every **Write Capacity Unit (WCU)**
- US$ 0.09 per month for every **Read Capacity Unit (RCU)**
- US$ 0.25 per GB/month stored
- US$ 0.09 GB per GB transferred out to the Internet

Since our estimated database will have only 5 GB, we are on the free tier and we will not pay for transferred data because there is no transfer cost to AWS Lambda.

Regarding read/write capacities, we have estimated 5 million requests per month. If we evenly distribute them, we will get two requests per second. In this case, we will consider that it's one read and one write operation per second.

We need to estimate now how many objects are affected by a read and a write operation. For a write operation, we can estimate that we will manipulate 10 items on average and a read operation will scan 100 objects. In this scenario, we would need to reserve 10 WCU and 100 RCU. As we have 25 WCU and 25 RCU for free, we only need to pay for 75 RCU per month, which costs US$ 6.75.

Total: US$ 6.75

Total pricing

Let's summarize the cost of each service in the following table:

Service	Monthly Costs
Route 53	US$ 0.54
S3	US$ 0.82
CloudFront	US$ 21.97
Cognito	US$ 0.30
IoT	US$ 1.01
CloudWatch	US$ 1.00
API Gateway	US$ 17.93
Lambda	US$ 2.47
DynamoDB	US$ 6.75
Total	**US$ 52.79**

It results in a total cost of ~ US$ 50 per month in infrastructure to serve 100,000 page views. If you have a conversion rate of 1%, you can get 1,000 sales per month, which means that you pay US$ 0.05 in infrastructure for each product that you sell.

Summary

In this chapter, you were introduced to the services that will be used throughout this book. You already know how to create new AWS users with restricted privileges, how to use the AWS CLI and the Node SDK, and what the frontend, backend, and notification services are. This chapter finished showing how each service fits in our sample application architecture and you learned how to estimate its costs.

In the next chapter, you'll be introduced to the Serverless Framework that plays an important role in our development workflow, automating tasks and organizing the code. You'll learn how to configure, deploy Lambda functions, and structure the beginning of our sample application.

3
Using the Serverless Framework

When developing a serverless project, you can group multiple features into a single big Lambda function or break each feature into its own small function. If you follow the second option, you will end up managing the deployment of dozens of different functions, each one of them with its own configuration and dependencies. Automating this process could be a real challenge, but it becomes an easy task when you use the Serverless Framework in your workflow. Besides handling the release process, the framework helps you architect the solution and manage different environments, and it provides a clean and succinct syntax for versioning the infrastructure.

In this chapter, you will learn how to configure and use the Serverless Framework. We will cover the following topics:

- How to set up and start using the framework
- Deploying a hello-world application
- Creating endpoints and enabling CORS
- Configuring events to trigger functions
- Accessing other AWS resources

After this chapter, you'll have learned the basics of how to build the backend of a serverless project.

Serverless Framework

There are many tools that have been developed to help manage serverless projects. The Serverless Framework is currently the most popular and will be used extensively in this book. This section will help you configure, use, and understand how it will fit in your workflow.

Understanding the Serverless Framework

The Serverless Framework is a powerful Node.js *command-line tool*, not a cloud service. Its objective is to help developers be more productive by simplifying how they can use and manage cloud resources. It provides a set of commands that will help you quickly start a new project, add functions, endpoints, triggers, configure permissions, and more. In summary, the framework will manage your project, automate the deployment of your code, and integrate with many different services:

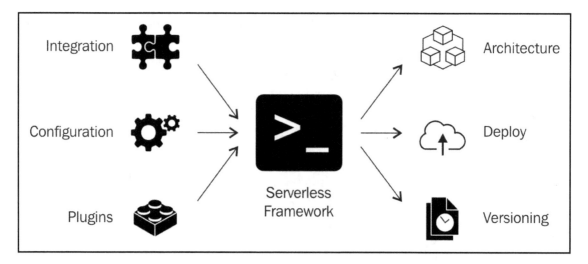

We have the following as input:

- **Integration**: Describes what and how different cloud services will trigger our Lambda functions
- **Configuration**: Sets permissions for Lambda functions, and defines the limits (timeout and RAM memory) under which they will run
- **Plugins**: Extends the framework functionalities with custom code

Here is what the framework provides:

- **Architecture**: Helps to define an architecture that will keep our project consistent.
- **Deploy**: Automates code deployment. You can deploy anytime with a single command.
- **Versioning**: Helps versioning the code configuration, which means versioning the infrastructure. Duplicating the same infrastructure into another region or environment is a trivial task.

Currently, it supports the following cloud providers: AWS, Microsoft Azure, Google Cloud Platform, and IBM OpenWhisk. Migrating from one cloud to another is possible, but it is not simple. The framework uses the same commands for management tasks and tries to use similar settings, but each one of them requires different configurations and setups.

Another important characteristic is that the Serverless Framework is open source and MIT licensed, so it can be used for free, even in commercial products.

Other frameworks

Serverless is a concept that promotes the development of applications without worrying about the servers that will operate them. It's a concept and doesn't specify the tools that will be used, nor the cloud vendors that host the applications. However, taking advantage of the word's hype, the creators of **JAWS** renamed their project to **Serverless Framework** at the end of 2015 and bought the `serverless.com` domain. To further improve their open source project, they started a venture-backed company named *Serverless, Inc.*

The Serverless Framework is currently the best tool to build a general-purpose serverless project, but **do not** confuse a product with the concept. The framework promotes serverless applications, but offers **only a subset** of what you can do with serverless. There are many other services and frameworks out there with different features and objectives.

For example, Apex is another framework to manage AWS Lambda functions with an interesting feature that provides support for Go, Rust, and Clojure, even without native support by Lambda. There are also dozens of other tools. For more options, you can take a look at this curated list: `https://github.com/anaibol/awesome-serverless`.

Installing the framework

As the Serverless Framework uses Node.js, you can use npm to install it:

```
npm install serverless@1.x --global
```

The `@1.x` suffix asks npm to download a package compatible with the 1.x version. This restriction is suggested because this book was written following the 1.18 specification of the framework and the examples may not be compatible with a future 2.x version.

 The Serverless Framework requires Node.js v6.5 or higher. Make sure that you have an updated version. You can check this by running `node --version`. If you need to update your Node version, consider using v6.10 because this is the latest version that AWS uses to run Lambda functions.

To confirm that the framework was installed successfully, you can check its version by running the following command:

```
serverless --version
```

 Instead of using the `serverless` command, you can use the abbreviation `sls` for all commands. For example, `sls --version`.

Also, for each option that starts with two dashes, such as in `--version`, there will always exist a shorter alternative using just one letter, such as `-v` in this case.

Configuring the framework

The Serverless Framework uses the AWS SDK to manage your account resources, so the configuration that is needed is to set your credentials where the SDK can access them. As described in `Chapter 2`, *Getting Started with AWS*, we have already created a user and set its **Access key** and **Secret access key** into environment variables.

What is missing here is properly restricting this user access. For learning purposes, it's perfectly fine to use an administrator account with full access. However, if you are building a real product, follow the principle of least privilege and set access only for what is expected to be used by the framework. In the previous chapter, you learned how to configure it using the IAM console (`https://console.aws.amazon.com/iam`).

The minimum access requirements are **Lambda**, **CloudFormation**, **IAM**, and **CloudWatch**. While setting permissions, you can anticipate and give access that will be needed later in our sample project. The framework will also need access to **API Gateway**, **IoT**, **SimpleDB**, and **DynamoDB**.

Managing permissions in a team

When working in a team, it's mandatory that everyone must have their own user for a fine-grained set of permissions. Also, it allows audit and traceability which are very important. Audit discourages wrongdoings by team members and traceability is useful for unfortunate cases, for example, if your site is compromised, you can discover the source of the invasion. If you want those features, you must configure **AWS CloudTrail** to store into S3 the log files of the AWS API usage.

If each team member has a unique account, you can restrict access to the production environment for a reduced group of people. Access to production is a great responsibility that should only be entrusted to experienced people to avoid failures due to distraction or lack of knowledge.

Creating a new project

Let's start by creating a new folder to store our project data. Name it `hello-serverless` and set the command prompt directory to this folder. Now, run the following command:

```
serverless create --template aws-nodejs --name hello-serverless
```

Take a look at the following screenshot:

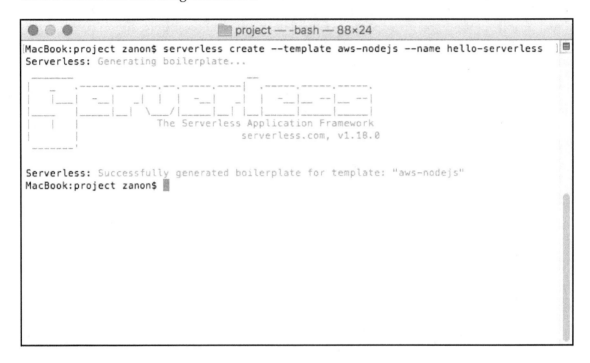

This command creates one *service* that is used to group related functions. You can compare a service as a bounded context as defined in **Domain-Driven Design** (**DDD**). For example, in this book, the sample application is an online store. We can say that features that will be implemented to exhibit products and handle sales are part of one context. The features that handle user accounts and profile data are part of another context. We will discuss serverless architectures in Chapter 6, *Developing the Backend*.

After executing the command, the following two files are created:

- The handler.js file
- The serverless.yml file

Let's see the context of each one and understand their role.

The handler.js file

This file contains the main function that will be executed by AWS Lambda. For a simple example, consider the following code:

```
module.exports.hello = (event, context, callback) =>
{

    const response =
    {
        statusCode: 200,
        body: JSON.stringify({
            message: `Hello, ${event.name}!`
        })
    };

    callback(null, response);
};
```

 Our `response` object has the properties `statusCode` and `body`. This schema is mandatory when you want to trigger Lambda functions using the API Gateway and when the Lambda is configured as a proxy, which is the default option selected in the Serverless Framework. Instead of configuring headers, status codes, and other parameters in the API Gateway, the Lambda proxy setting allows this configuration to be part of the code. This is the recommended practice for most use cases.

The function named `hello` will be configured as our main entry. It receives three arguments such as `event`, `context`, and `callback`. The `event` variable is our input data, and `callback` is the function that must be executed after the Lambda execution finishes and it receives an error object as the first parameter and a `response` object as the second one, and the `context` is an object that provides data related to our function execution. An example of the `context` content is displayed in the following JSON:

```
{
  "callbackWaitsForEmptyEventLoop": true,
  "logGroupName": "/aws/lambda/hello-serverless-dev-hello",
  "logStreamName":
    "2017/07/15/[$LATEST]01a23456bcd7890ef12gh34i56jk7890",
  "functionName": "hello-serverless-dev-hello",
  "memoryLimitInMB": "1024",
  "functionVersion": "$LATEST",
  "invokeid": "1234a567-8901-23b4-5cde-fg67h8901i23",
  "awsRequestId": "1234a567-8901-23b4-5cde-fg67h8901i23",
  "invokedFunctionArn": "arn:aws:lambda:us-east-1:1234567890:
```

```
        function:hello-serverless-dev-hello"
   }
```

In this example, we return `status code 200 (OK)`, and the response `body` will return a message that uses the event as an input variable.

The serverless.yml file

This is a configuration file that uses the YAML standard, which has the aim of being more readable by humans. The name YAML is a recursive acronym meaning *YAML Ain't Markup Language*.

When we created the service, we used the argument `aws-nodejs`. It creates a file with the following content:

```
service: hello-serverless

provider:
  name: aws
  runtime: nodejs6.10

functions:
  hello:
    handler: handler.hello
```

Let's take a look at the following settings depicted in the preceding code example:

- `service`: This is just the service name that we have specified while creating the service.
- `provider`: This sets the cloud provider and the runtime. We have selected AWS and the latest Node.js version available.
- `functions`: This is where we define the Lambda functions.

There are more options available, but we will cover them as we need them.

Configuring the Lambda limits

While setting the `serverless.yml` file, you can configure your function limits. The RAM memory size has the default value of 1,024 MB. The possible values range from 128 MB to 1,536 MB in chunks of 64 MB.

Another possible setting is the `timeout` property. If your function exceeds the expected time, it will be aborted. The default value is 6 seconds and the possible values range from 1 second to 300 seconds (5 minutes):

```
functions:
  hello:
    handler: handler.hello
    memorySize: 128 # measured in megabytes
    timeout: 10 # measured in seconds
```

 In YAML syntax, a comment begins with the hash sign (#) and continues until the end of the line.

You can also change the default values by modifying the provider settings. These values will be used when your function doesn't specify them:

```
provider:
  name: aws
  runtime: nodejs6.10
  memorySize: 512
  timeout: 30
```

Deploying a service

Deploying a service is a simple task. We just need to run the following command:

```
serverless deploy
```

You can see the results in the following screenshot:

```
● ● ●                    📁 project — -bash — 80×24
MacBook:project zanon$ serverless deploy
Serverless: Packaging service...
Serverless: Creating Stack...
Serverless: Checking Stack create progress...
.....
Serverless: Stack create finished...
Serverless: Uploading CloudFormation file to S3...
Serverless: Uploading artifacts...
Serverless: Uploading service .zip file to S3 (411 B)...
Serverless: Updating Stack...
Serverless: Checking Stack update progress...
..............
Serverless: Stack update finished...
Service Information
service: hello-serverless
stage: dev
region: us-east-1
api keys:
  None
endpoints:
  None
functions:
  hello: hello-serverless-dev-hello
MacBook:project zanon$ ▊
```

By default, it will deploy your functions in a `stage` named `dev` and in the `region` named `us-east-1`. The `stage` is used to simulate different environments. For example, you can create one for development and another for `production`, or you can use one for `v1` and another for `v2` if you want to create versioned APIs. Regarding the region, it's used to identify which AWS `region` will be used to host your Lambda functions.

Here are two options to change the default values:

- The first one is to modify the `serverless.yml` file, as shown in the following code example:

```
provider:
  name: aws
  runtime: nodejs6.10
  stage: production
  region: eu-west-1
```

- The second option is to use the arguments of the deploy command:

```
serverless deploy --stage production --region eu-west-1
```

 Under `provider`, you can set the configuration file to the `dev` stage, only when you want to deploy to `production`, you can do so using the stage argument with the command line. Using two different approaches for two different environments is a good way to avoid mistakes.

When we use the `deploy` command, it can take a couple of minutes to execute, even for small projects. The performance issue is related with CloudFormation, which needs to update the stack across AWS machines. After deploying the function for the first time, we can use the `deploy function` command for code updates because this command will simply swap the ZIP package of the function. As it doesn't need to execute any CloudFormation code, this is a much faster way of deploying changes. The following example shows how to use this command:

```
serverless deploy function --function hello
```

 Always remember to update the function's code using the `deploy function` command for fast deployment. If you need to update any kind of configuration, such as permissions or Lambda limits, you need to run the `deploy` command (without the `function` part).

Invoking a function

We just created and deployed a Lambda function. Now, let's see how this function can be invoked by performing the following steps:

1. Inside your project folder, create an `event.json` file with the following content. This file will serve as our input data:

```
{
    "name": "Serverless"
}
```

2. The next step is to invoke the function and confirm that it is working as expected. You can do so by executing the `invoke` command:

```
serverless invoke --function hello --path event.json
```

Passing the event.json file as input is not mandatory. We are using it because our example uses the input data to create the response object.

The following screenshot shows the invoke result:

3. If you have functions deployed to multiple stages/regions, you can invoke them by specifying the stage/region explicitly. For example, take a look at the following command:

```
serverless invoke --function hello --stage test --region eu-west-1
```

4. The last observation is that you can invoke functions locally. This invoke will execute the function using your machine instead of running the function hosted on AWS. For this, just use the invoke local command:

```
serverless invoke local --function hello --path event.json
```

We will see later that we can give or restrict permissions to Lambda functions. However, if you execute the code locally, it won't use the configured roles. The Lambda will execute under your local SDK credentials, so testing Lambda locally can be useful, but you need to know that you won't be testing it with the same permissions that will be used when the function is hosted on AWS.

Retrieving logs

When a Lambda function fails due to an unhandled exception, the result will be a generic message:

```
{
   "errorMessage": "Process exited before completing request"
}
```

To troubleshoot errors, we need to retrieve the execution logs. You can do so by appending the `--log` option to the `invoke` command:

```
serverless invoke --function hello --log
```

It will result in an error message similar to this one:

```
START RequestId: 1ab23cde-4567-89f0-1234-56g7hijk8901
Version: $LATEST2017-05-15 15:27:03.471 (-03:00)
    1ab23cde-4567-89f0-1234-56g7hijk8901
ReferenceError: x is not defined
    at module.exports.hello (/var/task/handler.js:9:3)
END RequestId: 1ab23cde-4567-89f0-1234-56g7hijk8901
REPORT RequestId: 1ab23cde-4567-89f0-1234-
56g7hijk8901
Duration: 60.26 ms
Billed Duration: 100 ms
Memory Size: 128 MB
Max Memory Used: 17 MB

Process exited before completing request
```

Besides using the `--log` command when invoking a function, you can retrieve logs from the Lambda functions that are deployed without invoking new executions. The command for this is as follows:

```
serverless logs --function hello
```

The following is a screenshot with an example of log messages:

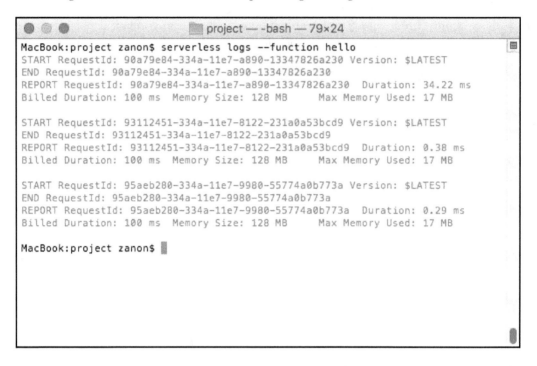

```
MacBook:project zanon$ serverless logs --function hello
START RequestId: 90a79e84-334a-11e7-a890-13347826a230 Version: $LATEST
END RequestId: 90a79e84-334a-11e7-a890-13347826a230
REPORT RequestId: 90a79e84-334a-11e7-a890-13347826a230  Duration: 34.22 ms
Billed Duration: 100 ms  Memory Size: 128 MB    Max Memory Used: 17 MB

START RequestId: 93112451-334a-11e7-8122-231a0a53bcd9 Version: $LATEST
END RequestId: 93112451-334a-11e7-8122-231a0a53bcd9
REPORT RequestId: 93112451-334a-11e7-8122-231a0a53bcd9  Duration: 0.38 ms
Billed Duration: 100 ms  Memory Size: 128 MB    Max Memory Used: 17 MB

START RequestId: 95aeb280-334a-11e7-9980-55774a0b773a Version: $LATEST
END RequestId: 95aeb280-334a-11e7-9980-55774a0b773a
REPORT RequestId: 95aeb280-334a-11e7-9980-55774a0b773a  Duration: 0.29 ms
Billed Duration: 100 ms  Memory Size: 128 MB    Max Memory Used: 17 MB

MacBook:project zanon$
```

One problem with this feature is that you *must* specify the function name. You can't have a generic view of how all functions are executing, which would be desirable in a project with dozens of functions.

When running in production, using the command line to watch for logs can be troublesome. You can reduce the amount of results using the `--filter string` command to show only messages that contain a specific string. This is useful in finding error messages, for example, using `--filter Error`.

The `--filter string` option is case sensitive. If you want to find error messages, use `--filter Error` because most exception messages will start the error word with an uppercase letter, for example: `ReferenceError`

Another option is to filter by time. You can use `--startTime time` to filter only the recent messages. For example, you could replace "time" with `30m` to see only messages that happened 30 minutes ago.

Take a look at the following example:

serverless logs --function hello --filter error --startTime 30m

Also, you can add a listener that will output all new log messages received. In this case, you need to add the `--tail` command.

Here's an example:

serverless logs --function hello --tail

Adding endpoints

Endpoints are the addresses that are exposed to the Internet through the API Gateway.

Take a look at the following steps to create an endpoint for our Lambda example:

1. Endpoints are added by setting HTTP events in the `serverless.yml` file. In the following example, we specify that a GET HTTP verb used in the `my-service/resource` path will trigger this Lambda function:

```
functions:
  hello:
    handler: handler.hello
    events:
      - http: GET my-service/resource
```

2. After editing the configuration file, deploy the service again using the following command:

serverless deploy

Take a look at the following screenshot:

```
● ● ●                        🗀 project — -bash — 86×24
[MacBook:project zanon$ serverless deploy                                          ]🖻
Serverless: Packaging service...
Serverless: Uploading CloudFormation file to S3...
Serverless: Uploading artifacts...
Serverless: Uploading service .zip file to S3 (444 B)...
Serverless: Updating Stack...
Serverless: Checking Stack update progress...
..............
Serverless: Stack update finished...
Service Information
service: hello-serverless
stage: dev
region: us-east-1
api keys:
  None
endpoints:
  GET - https://dxch4zvl5j.execute-api.us-east-1.amazonaws.com/dev/my-service/resource
functions:
  hello: hello-serverless-dev-hello
MacBook:project zanon$ ▌
```

This time, in addition to the Lambda function update, the `deploy` command will create an API Gateway resource configured with the preceding path and method. In the previous chapter, we deployed an API Gateway resource that triggered a Lambda function, and it required a lot of steps. Do you see now how powerful the Serverless Framework is? If you have dozens of functions and endpoints, a single command is enough to deploy all of them. This automation and ease of use is what makes the framework so interesting.

3. In the preceding screenshot, we can see that the framework lists the endpoint address that was created. It uses the following format:

```
https://[key].execute-api.[region].amazonaws.com/[stage]/[path]
```

4. If you use your browser to open this URL, you will see a `response` object containing our hello-world message. When using the API Gateway, the `event` variable will include much more data, adding information about headers and the request context. Most of this is not useful for us, but we need to use the `event` object to find the input data. As this is a `GET` request, we can add a query string to the end of the URL to pass variables values and retrieve them, looking for the `queryStringParameters` property inside the `event` object. Look at the following URL example:

```
https://[key].execute-api.us-east-1.amazonaws.com/dev/my-service/resource?name=Serverless&foo=bar
```

The `?name=Serverless&foo=bar` file is the query string that will be mapped to a JSON object inside the `queryStringParameters` property of our `event` variable, as shown here:

```
{
    "name": "Serverless",
    "foo": "bar"
}
```

5. As we are now using the API Gateway instead of invoking the Lambda function directly, the `event` object received will be set with different properties. In this case, we need to adapt our Lambda function to handle it properly. The following example uses `event.queryStringParameters.name` instead of `event.name`:

```
module.exports.hello = (event, context, callback) => {

    const response = {
        statusCode: 200,
        body: JSON.stringify({
            message: `Hello, ${event.queryStringParameters.name}!`
        })
    };

    callback(null, response);
};
```

6. To test, deploy the function again, and browse the endpoint address with the query string.

We will cover other HTTP verbs in `Chapter 6`, *Developing the Backend*.

Cross-Origin Resource Sharing

If you try to call this API address inside a website through an Ajax call, it will throw an exception. This is because **Cross-Origin Resource Sharing (CORS)** is not enabled by default in API Gateway. CORS is a mechanism that allows a resource to be requested from a web page hosted in another domain. By default, it is disabled to force administrators to give permissions for cross-domain requests only when it makes sense and for specific domains.

We are building a website that will be hosted inside AWS, but the web page will be accessed through our own domain, such as www.example.com, and not from www.amazonaws.com. As a result, we need to enable CORS to allow our frontend code to consume our services. If you have a Lambda function that should be accessed only by another Lambda or internal AWS service, CORS is not necessary.

To enable CORS, we need to modify our `handler.js` function to include the `"Access-Control-Allow-Origin"` header:

```
module.exports.hello = (event, context, callback) => {
  const response = {
    statusCode: 200,
    headers: {
      "Access-Control-Allow-Origin": "https://www.example.com"
    },
    body: JSON.stringify({
      message: "Hello, ${event.queryStringParameters.name}!"
    })
  };

  callback(null, response);
};
```

You can add only *one* origin per function. This is a problem when we need to support multiple origins, and this requirement is very common. For example, the following addresses are considered different origins because they have different protocols (HTTP versus HTTPS) or different subdomains (none versus www):

- http://example.com
- https://example.com
- http://www.example.com
- https://www.example.com

To support multiple origins, you need to use the following command:

```
"Access-Control-Allow-Origin": "*"
```

Another solution, which is very common in traditional web servers, is to dynamically write the *response* headers based on the *request* headers that you can find inside the event object. If its origin is contained in a predefined whitelist, you can build the response object using the corresponding origin.

Removing a service

After finishing this example, we can delete our test function and API. The remove command will delete all AWS resources that were created, but it will leave the project files intact. The syntax is pretty straightforward:

```
serverless remove
```

If you have deployed services to stages or regions that are not configured in the current version of your serverless.yml file, you can use the --stage and --region options to selectively remove them:

```
serverless remove --stage production --region eu-west-1
```

When you make a new deployment to the API Gateway, you receive an API key that is used to compose your API address, for example, `https://[key].execute-api.[region].amazonaws.com`. This key is important and will be saved into our frontend code. If you remove your services and recreate them again, a new key will be generated and the frontend key will need to be updated.

Going beyond the basics

In this section, we will explore what more we can do using the Serverless Framework.

Using npm packages

When you use the Serverless Framework to deploy your Lambda function, it creates a ZIP file with everything that is inside your project folder. If you need to use a module that is not a Node.js core module or the AWS SDK, you just need to use Node's default workflow to add dependencies.

Take a look at the following steps:

1. Create a `package.json` file to store your project dependencies and use `npm install <your-module> --save` to download your required module.
2. With the `node_modules` folder inside your project directory, the ZIP file will be deployed to AWS with the necessary dependencies.
3. In the following example, the Lambda function of the file `handle.js` uses an npm module called `cat-names`:

```
module.exports.catNames = (event, context, callback) => {

  const catNames = require('cat-names');

  const response = {
    statusCode: 200,
    body: JSON.stringify({
      message: catNames.random()
    })
  };

  callback(null, response);
};
```

4. The framework will zip everything that it finds inside the project folder, except what you configure in the `serverless.yml` file to be ignored. The following example uses the `package` configuration to remove some files that are commonly present in a project folder, but that should never be included in the ZIP file:

```
service: cat-names
provider:
   name: aws
   runtime: nodejs6.10
functions:
   catNames:
      handler: handler.catNames
package:
   exclude:
      - package.json
      - event.json
      - tests/**
      - LICENSE
      - README.md
```

 Hidden files and folders are not included in the ZIP package by default, for example, the `.gitignore` file and the `.serverless` folder, which are part of serverless projects, don't need to be explicitly excluded.

5. To test, just deploy and invoke the `catNames` function by using the following command:

```
serverless deploy
serverless invoke --function catNames
```

Accessing other AWS resources

By default, Lambda functions execute without any permissions. If you want to access S3 buckets, DynamoDB tables, or any kind of Amazon resource, your user must have access to them and you must give explicit permissions to your service.

This configuration is done in the `serverless.yml` file under the `provider` tag. The following example shows you how to give permissions to an S3 bucket:

```
provider:
  name: aws
  runtime: nodejs6.10
  iamRoleStatements:
    - Effect: "Allow"
      Action:
        - 's3:PutObject'
        - 's3:GetObject'
      Resource: "arn:aws:s3:::my-bucket-name/*"
```

To test this statement, we can modify our `handle.js` file to write and read files using the following code:

```
module.exports.testPermissions = (event, context, callback) => {
  const AWS = require('aws-sdk');
  const s3 = new AWS.S3();
  const bucket = 'my-bucket-name';
  const key = 'my-file-name';
  const write = {
    Bucket: bucket,
    Key: key,
    Body: 'Test'
  };

  s3.putObject(write, (err, data) => {
    if (err) return callback(err);

    const read = { Bucket: bucket, Key: key };
    s3.getObject(read, (err, data) => {
      if (err) return callback(err);

      const response = {
        statusCode: 200,
        body: data.Body.toString()
      };

      callback(null, response);
    });
  });
};
```

In this example, we are writing a file that contains the `Test` string to a bucket and, after finishing the writing, we read the same file and return its contents in our response.

Events

The Serverless Framework currently supports the following events:

- **Amazon API Gateway**: This creates RESTful interfaces by triggering Lambda functions through HTTP messages
- **Amazon S3**: This triggers functions for post-processing when a new file is added or to take an action when a file is removed
- **Amazon SNS**: This handles SNS notifications with Lambda functions
- **Schedule**: This triggers functions based on scheduled tasks
- **Amazon DynamoDB**: This triggers a function when a new entry is added to a table
- **Amazon Kinesis**: This uses Lambda functions to process Kinesis streams
- **Amazon Alexa**: This triggers functions with Alexa Skills
- **AWS IoT**: This handles messages sent to IoT topics
- **Amazon CloudWatch**: This handles CloudWatch events and log messages using Lambda functions

In this list, there are only two services that we haven't seen yet. The first one is Amazon Kinesis, which is a service created to process and analyze streaming data generated by different sources, and the other one is Amazon Alexa, which is Amazon's intelligent personal assistant. Both of them are beyond the scope of this book.

We will not cover all event types because the list is extensive, and each one of them requires different configurations. You can see how to use them in the official documentation at `http s://serverless.com/framework/docs/providers/aws/events`. In this chapter, we have already exemplified the API Gateway by creating an endpoint for our Lambda function. Now, we will take a look at two more examples: one for Amazon S3, to see how easy it is to create S3 events in comparison to the example from the previous chapter, and the other example is to **Schedule** triggers, which are very useful in running scheduled tasks.

The S3 event

In the previous chapter, we configured S3 to trigger a Lambda function when a new file is added to a bucket and its name matches certain rules. The same configuration can be applied here using the following configuration in our `serverless.yml` file:

```
functions:
  processLog:
    handler: handler.processLog
    events:
      - s3:
          bucket: my-bucket-name
          event: s3:ObjectCreated:*
          rules:
            - prefix: logs/
            - suffix: .txt
```

 The bucket name needs to be a new one. Due to limitations, you can't add events to an existing bucket.

Schedule events

Scheduling Lambda executions is a very important feature for many use cases. This setup is easily done by the framework by modifying the `serverless.yml` file using the `schedule` event. In the next example, the `processTask` function will be executed every 15 minutes:

```
functions:
  processTask:
    handler: handler.processTask
    events:
      - schedule: rate(15 minutes)
```

This setting accepts either the `rate` or `cron` expression.

The `cron` syntax is compounded by six required fields in the following order: `Minutes | Hours | Day-of-month | Month | Day-of-week | Year`. In the next example, the `cron` expression is used to schedule a function to run from Monday to Friday at 9:00 am (UTC):

```
- schedule: cron(0 9 ? * MON-FRI *)
```

Take a look at the following link for more details about this setting:

`http://docs.aws.amazon.com/AmazonCloudWatch/latest/events/ScheduledEvents.html`

Serving HTML pages with Lambda

A very common misunderstanding is that Lambda was designed to serve only JSON data. That's not true. As we have control over the response result, we can properly set the headers to serve HTML content. This is exemplified in the following code:

```javascript
module.exports.hello = (event, context, callback) => {

  const html = `
    <!DOCTYPE html>
    <html>
      <head>
        <title>Page Title</title>
      </head>
      <body>
        <h1>Hello</h1>
      </body>
    </html>`;

  const response = {
    statusCode: 200,
    headers: {
      'Access-Control-Allow-Origin': '*',
      'Content-Type': 'text/html'
    },
    body: html
  };

  callback(null, response);
};
```

This approach can be useful for server-side rendering. In Chapter 5, *Building the Frontend*, we will discuss Single-Page Applications, which use client-side rendering, and traditional web applications, which use server-side rendering. Serverless supports both models and it is up to the developer to choose the option that best suits their use case.

Using configuration variables

The Serverless Framework allows the usage of variables in our `serverless.yml` configuration file. This flexibility is useful in centralizing configurations that can be referenced at multiple places.

There are many options for using variables. Let's try them out by editing our configuration file:

- **Reference environment variables**:

  Take a look at the environment variable used in the following code snippet:

  ```
  provider:
    name: aws
    runtime: nodejs6.10
    stage: ${env:DEPLOYMENT_STAGE}
  ```

- **Load variables from CLI options**:

  Take a look at the local variable used in the following code snippet:

  ```
  iamRoleStatements:
    - Effect: "Allow"
      Action:
        - 's3:PutObject'
        - 's3:GetObject'
      Resource: "arn:aws:s3:::{opt:bucket-name}/*"
  ```

- **Store variables in another configuration file**:

  Take a look at the usage of a variable defined in another file in the following code snippet:

  ```
  functions:
    hello:
      handler: handler.hello
      events:
        - schedule: ${file(my-vars.yml):schedule}
  ```

Plugins

An interesting feature offered by the Serverless Framework is that it is extendable through plugins. You can use plugins for new CLI commands or functionalities that will be executed by hooking into existing commands.

To show how useful they can be, we will test a serverless plugin that supports Lambda development with TypeScript. When we execute the `deploy` command, the plugin will compile the code and create a JavaScript version that will be zipped and used by Lambda with the Node.js runtime.

To add this plugin to our project, we need to proceed with the following steps:

1. Install the plugin using npm:

   ```
   npm install serverless-plugin-typescript --save-dev
   ```

2. Add the plugin reference to the end of our `serverless.yml` file:

   ```
   plugins:
     - serverless-plugin-typescript
   ```

3. Write a TypeScript file and save it with the name `handler.ts`, as shown in the following code:

   ```
   export async function hello(event, context, callback) {

     const response = {
       statusCode: 200,
       body: JSON.stringify({
         message: 'Hello, TypeScript!'
       })
     };

     callback(null, response);
   }
   ```

4. Deploy and test using the following command:

   ```
   serverless deploy
   serverless invoke --function hello
   ```

Showing deployment information

If you want to know what functions were deployed and their related endpoints, you can use the `info` command:

```
serverless info
```

The following screenshot shows this command output:

```
MacBook:project zanon$ serverless info
Service Information
service: hello-serverless
stage: dev
region: us-east-1
api keys:
  None
endpoints:
  GET - https://dxch4zvl5j.execute-api.us-east-1.amazonaws.com/dev/my-service/resource
functions:
  hello: hello-serverless-dev-hello
MacBook:project zanon$
```

Scaffolding

Scaffolding is a technique that helps developers by providing a sample solution for a common problem. With a *boilerplate*, you can build a new project, taking advantage of the fact that some features are already configured, developed, and well tested. You start modifying the solution to meet your own requirements following the practices recommended by someone who has more experience than you with this technology and using a code that was used, tested, and improved by a lot of different people. This is the benefit of using open source projects. Also, it's a useful way to learn a new technology through *imitation*. You learn by seeing how someone else has solved the problem that you want to solve.

Let's perform the following steps to scaffold a project:

1. To scaffold a project, run the following command:

```
serverless install --url <github-project-url>
```

2. For example, you can run the following command to scaffold a serverless service to send e-mails:

```
serverless install \
  --url https://github.com/eahefnawy/serverless-mailer
```

 The Serverless Framework team maintains an extensive list of useful examples. Check it out by visiting `https://github.com/serverless/exa mples`.

3. The objective of this book is to build a sample serverless store. You can find all code that was developed with this objective on GitHub at `https://github.com/z anon-io/serverless-store`. This project can also be scaffolded using the same command:

```
serverless install \
  --url https://github.com/zanon-io/serverless-store
```

 The \ (backslash) character in this command was added because the command doesn't fit in one line. It is optional and works for Linux and macOS. On Windows, the ^ (caret) is the corresponding symbol.

Summary

In this chapter, you learned what the Serverless Framework is and how it will help us to build serverless applications. After configuring the framework, you have created a hello-world service, added endpoints, enabled CORS, and deployed it to be accessed through a public URL. You also learned how to add npm packages and access AWS resources.

In the next chapter, we will host the frontend following the serverless concept. This will be done using Amazon S3, and we will configure a CloudFront distribution to add a free TLS certificate to support HTTPS connections.

4
Hosting the Website

The frontend is the easiest layer to go serverless. You just need a service to host your website's static files, and the user's browser will download the files, render the pages and execute the client-side JavaScript code. On AWS, the service we will use to host the frontend pages is Amazon S3. In this chapter, you'll also learn how to configure and optimize your website by adding a CDN and the supporting HTTPS connections.

In summary, we are going to cover the following topics:

- Using Amazon S3 to host static files
- Configuring Route 53 to associate your domain name with S3
- Using CloudFront to serve files through a CDN
- Requesting a free SSL/TLS certificate to support HTTPS connections

After this chapter, you'll have learned how to host a frontend in a serverless infrastructure.

Serving static files with Amazon S3

Amazon S3 is extremely useful because it is a cheap service that provides high availability and scalability, requiring zero management effort. The infrastructure is fully managed by AWS. In this section, we are going to use S3 to host our website static files such as HTML, CSS, JavaScript, and images. You will see that this is done by uploading the files to a bucket and configuring S3 to enable website hosting.

Besides hosting static websites, you can also host complex applications. You just need to have a clear separation of concerns: the *frontend* files (HTML/CSS/JavaScript) will be hosted on S3 and will be used by the browser to render the web page and request additional data to the *backend* code, which will be hosted and executed by Lambda functions. As we are going to discuss in `Chapter 5`, *Building the Frontend*, you can build your frontend as an SPA. This requires the browser to render the pages. Alternatively, you can use Lambda to serve server-side rendered pages.

Creating a bucket

In `Chapter 2`, *Getting Started with AWS*, we created a bucket using the CLI. In this section, we are going to use the Management Console to create another bucket so you can see the configuration options that S3 offers.

Let's perform the following steps to create a bucket:

1. The first step is to browse the S3 console at `https://console.aws.amazon.com/s3` and select the **Create bucket** option:

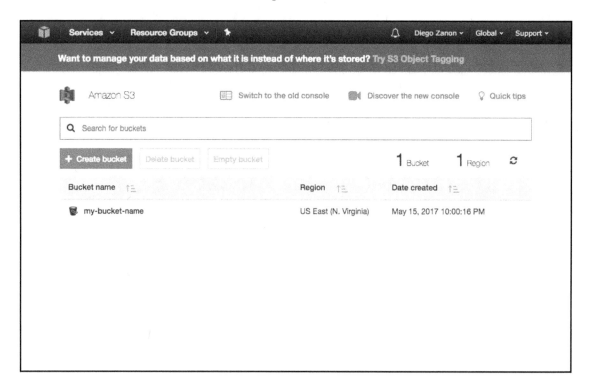

2. We are creating a new bucket to host the website. If you don't have a domain name, you can still use S3 to host the website. You will have to access it from a URL in the following format: `http://my-bucket-name.com.s3-website-us-east-1.amazonaws.com`. If you have a domain name, such as `example.com`, you *must* set the bucket name with the same name as that of your domain, in this case, `example.com`. It is mandatory that you match the domain with the bucket name to allow Route 53 to make the association. As for the region, choose the one that is closer to your target audience:

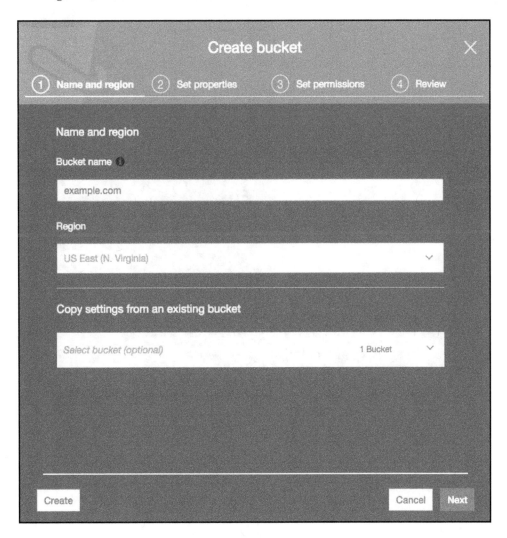

3. The **Set properties** screen allows you to add **Versioning**, **Logging**, and **Tags**. However, these are not required for our sample and can be skipped:

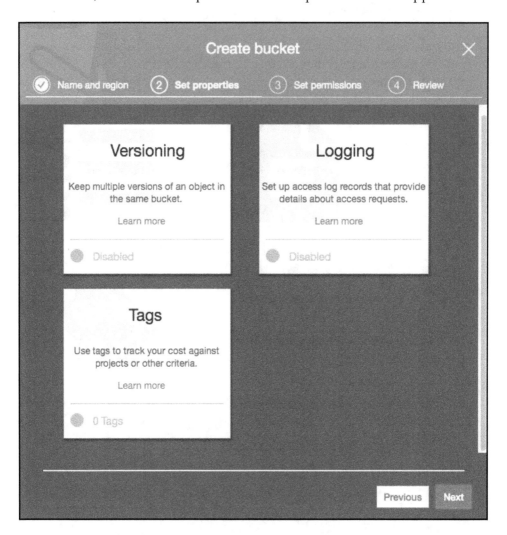

4. In the **Set permissions** screen, under **Manage public permissions**, select the option **Grant public read access to this bucket**. Click on **Next** to continue:

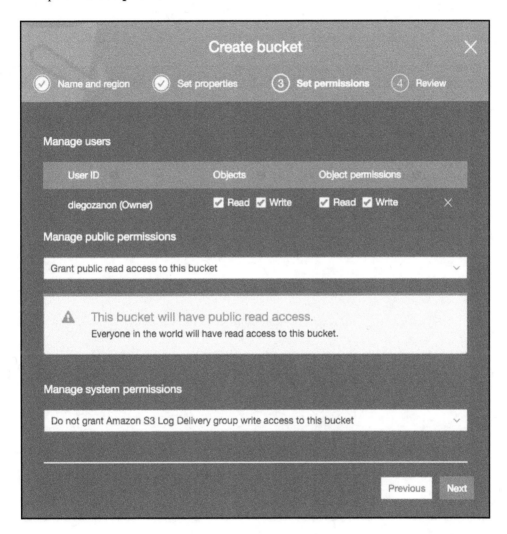

5. Finish by reviewing the selected options and clicking on **Create bucket**.

Enabling web hosting

To enable web hosting in this bucket, perform the following steps:

> 1. Click on your bucket name and select **Properties** from the second tab:

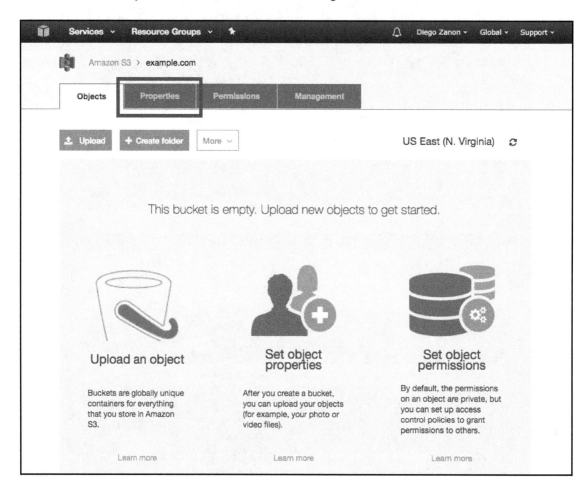

2. Inside the **Static website hosting** card, click on the **Disabled** button to enable the option:

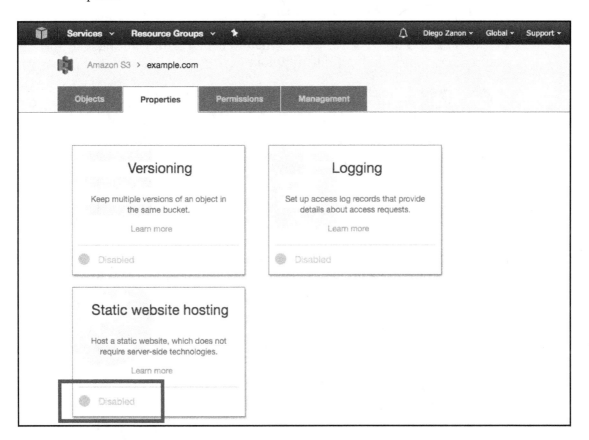

3. Now select the **Use this bucket to host a website** option and set **Index document** and **Error document** with the value index.html. Also, note that you can see the bucket's **Endpoint** address in this image. It's http://example.com.s3-website-us-east-1.amazonaws.com in this example. Write it down because you will need it later during testing and when you configure the CloudFront distribution:

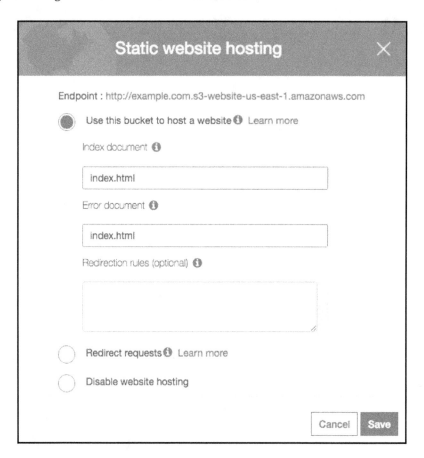

4. Click on **Save** to finish this setting.

Handling errors

There are four common ways to handle errors using S3. I will explain the options you have, but before I do that, let me define what I mean by "handling errors". When a user makes an HTTP request, S3 may fail to get the answer and it will return a status code to explain the failure. An HTTP 500 *Internal Server Error* could be a possible result, but it would be extremely rare and odd. However, S3 returning either a 404 *Not Found* or 403 *Forbidden* error is pretty common.

404 *Not Found* is an error that will be returned when the user browses your website for a page that does not exist. For example, if you have a page named `company.io/about` and the user incorrectly browses `company.io/abot`, S3 won't be able to find the `abot.html` file and will return a 404 error. Another example is when you use a JavaScript framework to create a **Single-Page Application (SPA)**. Although your frontend code knows how to serve the `/about` page, the framework will not create a physical `about.html` file to upload to S3, and a 404 error will be returned even when browsing `company.io/about`.

> We are going to discuss SPA in `Chapter 5`, *Building the Frontend*. For the time being, note that an SPA can serve multiple pages, but there is only one complete HTML file, named `index.html` file.

403 *Forbidden* is an error that happens when the bucket has restricted permissions. If the bucket doesn't allow access to *everyone* or there is a specific file with restricted access, the 403 error will be returned. In my opinion, I prefer to consider *all* the files within the bucket public. If there is a page that shouldn't be public, showing the HTML file should not be a problem. The objective is to protect the *data* and not the *layout*. Setting authorization and data visibility is something that needs to be handled on the server side, not the client side. Also, if there are static files that must remain private, such as photos, you can save them in another bucket instead of reusing the bucket that was created to host the website. These *photos* can be considered *data* and, likewise, need to be controlled by the backend with special care.

Considering that all the files of a bucket will remain public, and that we don't need not worry so much about strange S3 errors, the only problem that we need to handle now is 404 errors.

Using redirection rules

A very common approach to handle 404 errors for an SPA is to add a redirection rule in the **Static website hosting** page using the `ReplaceKeyPrefixWith` option:

```
<RoutingRules>
  <RoutingRule>
    <Condition>
      <HttpErrorCodeReturnedEquals>
        404
      </HttpErrorCodeReturnedEquals>
    </Condition>
    <Redirect>
      <Hostname>
        example.com
      </Hostname>
      <ReplaceKeyPrefixWith>
        #!/
      </ReplaceKeyPrefixWith>
    </Redirect>
  </RoutingRule>
</RoutingRules>
```

With this solution, when the user browses `company.io/about`, the address will be replaced by `company.io/#!/about` and the `index.html` file will be returned. If you have an SPA, it can identify which page needs to be displayed and render it correctly. If the page doesn't exist, it will be able to render a generic 404 page. Also, you can configure HTML5's pushState to remove the hashbang sign (`#!`) after the page loads, but it will make the page to blink.

The drawback of this approach is that you need to choose between a polluted URL with `#!` or experience the page blinking when it is loaded.

Using an error document

Instead of setting a redirection rule, you can set an error document with `index.html`. This is the easiest solution for SPAs. When the user requests an `/about` page that doesn't have a physical `about.html` file to match, the `index.html` file is loaded and the SPA reads the address and understands that it needs to serve the contents of the `/about` page.

This configuration is what we have done in the previous image and it works pretty well without polluting the URL address with `#!` and without blinking the page when loading. However, search engines may refuse to index your website because, when browsing the `/about` page, the result's `body` message will be set using the correct page, but the `status code` will still be set as 404. If the Google crawler sees a 404 error, it will understand that the page doesn't exist and the page content is probably a generic error page.

Delegating to CloudFront

You can set the error document to `index.html`, as in the previous solution, but using CloudFront instead of S3. CloudFront provides a *custom error response* setting that allows you to change the status code of the `response` object. In this case, we can configure CloudFront to act on 404 errors, returning S3's `index.html` file and modifying the `status code` to `200 OK` instead of returning 404.

If you opt for this, the problem is that you will return status code 200 even for pages that doesn't exist.

Prerendering pages

Another issue with the other solutions is that **Search Engine Optimization (SEO)** is not considered, because they require JavaScript to be enabled in the browser to render the correct page. Since most web crawlers can't execute JavaScript code, they will not be able to index the webpage. This problem is solved with prerendering.

In the next chapter, you are going to learn how you can prerender pages. This technique creates physical pages for SPA routes. For example, in an SPA, the `/about` page doesn't have an `about.html` file, but with prerendering, you will be able to create it.

When you prerender all the possible pages and upload the files to S3, there will be no need to worry about 404 errors. If the page exist, S3 will find an HTML file for it. We still need to configure the error document to `index.html` to handle pages that doesn't exist, but we don't need to configure CloudFront to force the status code 200.

Supporting www anchors

A domain name without the **www** anchor text is usually referred to as a *naked* domain. For instance, www.example.com is a domain with the www anchor and example.com is a naked domain. The *canonical* URL is the option that you choose as the main address.

There are pros and cons that you'll need to consider when deciding which address should be your website's main one. One issue with using naked domains is that if your site has cookies, then placing static files in a subdomain, such as static.example.com, will not be optimized because each browser request for static files will automatically send cookies that were created for example.com. If your login happens at www.example.com, you can place static content inside static.example.com without worrying about cookies.

This issue can be mitigated by creating another domain or using a CDN to retrieve the static files. Despite this, the current trend is to drop the www anchor. It looks more modern to brand your tech company as company.io than it does using the old www.company.com format.

Choose your main address, but support both formats. Some people are used to adding www to the address and some of them may forget to include it. In the previous example, we created a domain without the www address. Now we are going to create another bucket, in the www.example.com format, and set the **Static website hosting** configuration with the **Redirect requests** option to target the address without www:

Uploading static files

Uploading is pretty straightforward. Let's perform the following steps to upload static files:

1. First, create a very simple `index.html` file for testing purposes:

```
<!DOCTYPE html>
<html>
    <title>My Page</title>
<body>
    <h1>Hosting with S3</h1>
</body>
</html>
```

2. When you click on the main bucket name, an **Upload** button will be made available. Click on it:

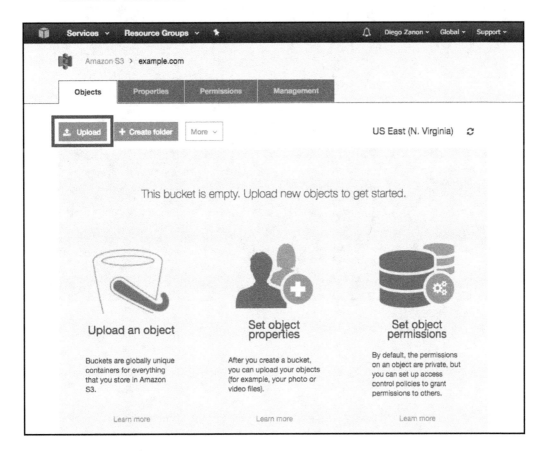

3. The next screen is simple. Click on **Add files**, select the index.html file, and continue by clicking on **Next**:

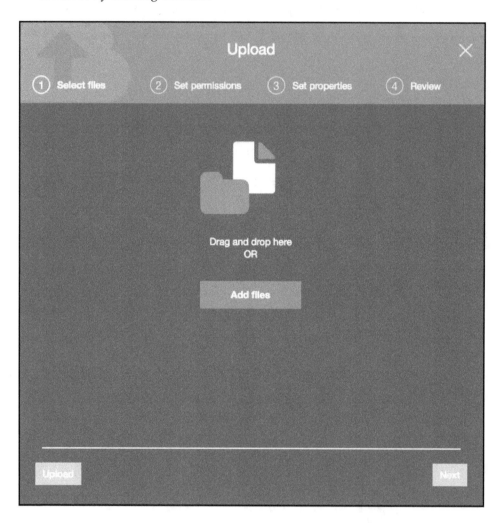

4. At the **Set permissions** step, under **Manage public permissions**, select the option **Grant public read access to this object(s)**:

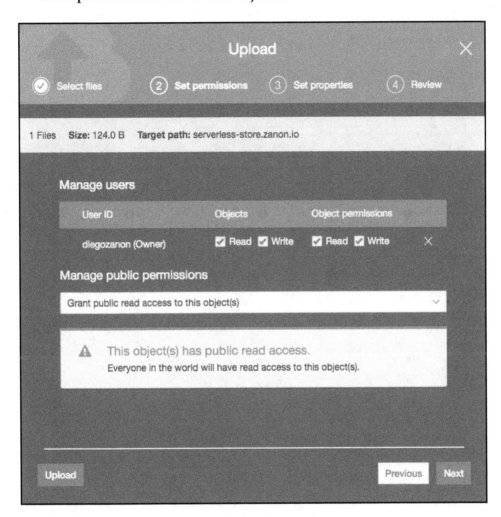

5. At the **Set properties** step, keep the default option for **Storage class** as **Standard** because files will be frequently accessed. Also, set **Encryption** to **None** because all the files will be publicly available, and therefore, adding an extra layer of security is not necessary and will only slow down your responses. As for the **Metadata** fields, you don't need to set them:

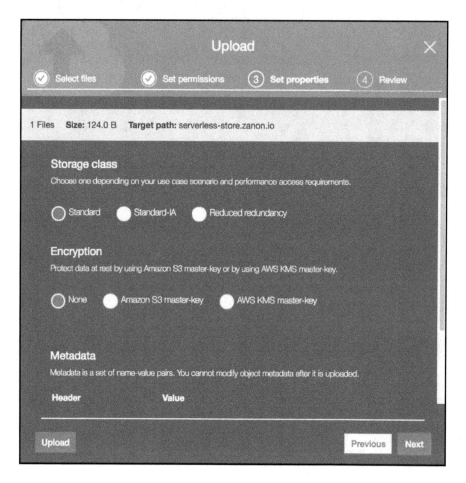

6. Finally, review the options and confirm by clicking on **Upload**.
7. Now you can check whether it is working by browsing the bucket's endpoint, for example, `http://example.com.s3-website-us-east-1.amazonaws.com`.

If it doesn't work on the first try, clear your browser cache and try again because when you test the endpoint before uploading a file, the browser may cache the information indicating that the link is invalid. This may avoid further requests for a short time.

Automating website publishing

We have gone through the necessary steps to upload our site's frontend using the S3 console. It's easy and fast, but it's also pretty easy to automate this task. If you haven't configured the AWS CLI, as instructed in Chapter 2, *Getting Started with AWS*, do so now and see how useful it is to automate the uploading of files. In fact, what we are going to do is synchronize the bucket contents with a local folder. The CLI will upload only the modified files, which will make the upload much faster in future when your site grows.

You can execute the following command to upload your files:

```
aws s3 sync ./path/to/folder s3://my-bucket-name --acl public-read
```

Serving gzip files

The gzip file format is a standard format used on the Web to compress files and improve the download speed by reducing the transferred file sizes. It can lower the bandwidth costs for you and for your users by providing smaller files. This approach has a huge impact on the perceived performance when loading the website.

It is currently supported by every major browser. By default, for every request, the browser will add an Accept-Encoding: gzip header. If the server supports gzip, the file is sent in compressed form.

The following diagram shows an HTTP request without gzip support:

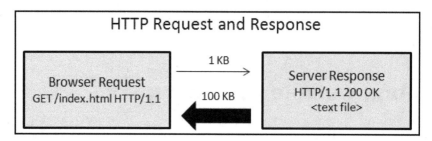

The following diagram shows how much bandwidth you can save with gzip. The compressed response is usually 10 times smaller:

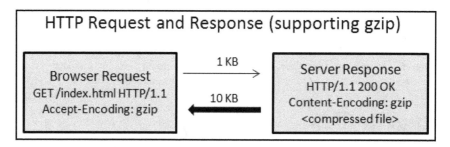

With this format, the server needs CPU time to compress the file and the user's browser needs CPU cycles to decompress the same file. However, with modern CPUs, the time to compress/decompress is much lower than the extra time taken to send the uncompressed file through the network. Even with low-end mobile devices, the CPU is much faster than the mobile network.

However, there is a problem. Since we don't have server-side processing with Amazon S3, there is no option to natively compress files in response to requests. You need to compress them locally before uploading the files and setting the metadata to identify `Content-Encoding` as `gzip`. Thankfully, you can skip the trouble of including this step in the deployment workflow if you use CloudFront. As we are going to see later, CloudFront has an option to automatically compress all your files with gzip.

Setting up Route 53

Route 53 is a DNS management service. You don't need to use it if you want to expose subdomains, such as `www.example.com`, however, it is indeed obligatory if you want to serve your website data under a naked domain, such as `example.com`, hosted on S3 or CloudFront. This is due to the RFC rule: you can't have a CNAME record for your domain root, it must be an A record.

What's the difference? CNAME and A records are both record types that help the DNS system to translate a domain name into an IP address. While CNAME references another domain, an A record references an IP address.

So, if you don't want to use Route 53, you can use your own domain management system, such as GoDaddy, to add a CNAME that will map your `www.example.com` domain to an S3 endpoint, for example, `www.example.com.s3-website-us-east-1.amazonaws.com`. This configuration works fine, but you can't do the same for `example.com` because the IP address of the `example.com.s3-website-us-east-1.amazonaws.com` endpoint changes frequently and your third-party domain controller (GoDaddy, in this example) won't follow the changes.

In this case, you need to use Route 53 because it will allow an A record to be created referencing your S3 bucket endpoint, such as `example.com.s3-website-us-east-1.amazonaws.com`. You just need to say that this endpoint is an alias and Route 53 will be able to track the correct IP address to answer DNS queries.

Creating a hosted zone

If you register your domain address with Amazon, a hosted zone will be automatically created. If you register your domain with another vendor, you will need to create a new hosted zone.

A hosted zone allows you to configure your domain's DNS settings. You can set where your naked domain and subdomains are hosted and configure other parameters, for example, a *mail exchange* record set.

To create a hosted zone, perform the following steps:

1. Browse the Route 53 Management Console at `https://console.aws.amazon.com /route53`. You will see a welcome screen, click on **Get started now**.
2. In the next screen, click on **Hosted zones** in the left menu, followed by the **Create Hosted Zone** button:

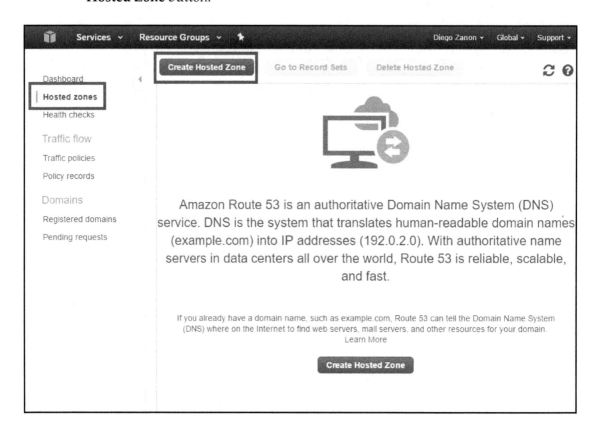

3. Type the domain name and confirm:

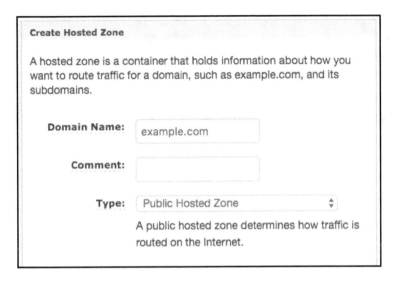

4. A hosted zone will be created with two record types, namely NS (Name Server) and SOA (Start Of Authority):

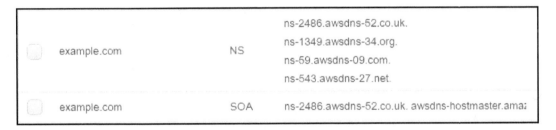

5. If you have registered your domain with another vendor, you must transfer the DNS management to Route 53. This is done by changing your domain registrar Name Servers (NS records) to Amazon's Name Servers.

6. Your registrar may offer a control panel for your domain with an option such as Manage DNS. Find where the Name Servers are located and edit them to use Amazon's servers.

Creating record sets

Now let's create two record sets such as one for `example.com` and another for `www.example.com`. Do this by performing the following steps:

1. Click on **Create Record Set**:

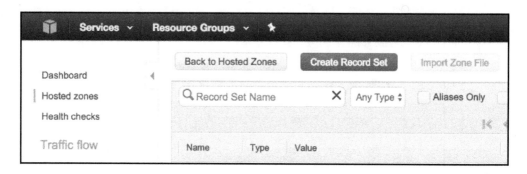

2. In the first record, set the following parameters:
   - **Name**: Leave this field empty
   - **Type**: In this field, select **A - IPv4 address**
   - **Alias**: Check this field with **Yes**
   - **Alias Target**: This field is a drop-down list where you can select the S3 endpoint of your bucket:

3. Create another record set. This time, use the following parameter values:
   - **Name**: Set this field as www
   - **Type**: In this field select **CNAME - Canonical name**
   - **Alias**: Check this field with **No**
   - **Value**: Fill this field input with the S3 bucket's endpoint:

4. Now test your domain name by typing it in your browser address. You will see the index.html file that you have uploaded to the S3 bucket.

If you have transferred DNS control from another vendor to AWS, then because of DNS caching, you may need to wait for some minutes or even hours before the transfer completes. You will only be able to see the files that were hosted on Amazon S3 after the transfer finishes.

Setting up CloudFront

CloudFront serves static files as a **Content Delivery Network** (**CDN**). Having file copies next to your users reduces latency and improves your perceived website speed. Another feature, which we will discuss later, is support for HTTPS requests.

In the next sections, we will create a CloudFront distribution and adjust the Route 53 settings to use CloudFront instead of the S3 bucket.

Creating a distribution

A CloudFront distribution is what makes it possible to associate a DNS configuration (Route 53) with CloudFront to distribute static content. A distribution needs an origin server to know where the files are stored. In our case, the origin will be the S3 bucket that was previously configured.

Let's perform the following steps to create a CloudFront distribution:

1. Browse the CloudFront Management Console at `https://console.aws.amazon.com/cloudfront` and click on **Create Distribution**:

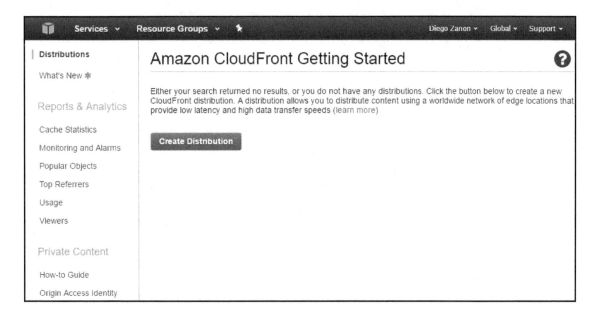

2. The next step is to select the distribution type. For our website, select **Get Started** under the **Web** option:

Select a delivery method for your content.

Web

Create a web distribution if you want to:

- Speed up distribution of static and dynamic content, for example, .html, .css, .php, and graphics files.
- Distribute media files using HTTP or HTTPS.
- Add, update, or delete objects, and submit data from web forms.
- Use live streaming to stream an event in real time.

You store your files in an origin - either an Amazon S3 bucket or a web server. After you create the distribution, you can add more origins to the distribution.

Get Started

RTMP

Create an RTMP distribution to speed up distribution of your streaming media files using Adobe Flash Media Server's RTMP protocol. An RTMP distribution allows an end user to begin playing a media file before the file has finished downloading from a CloudFront edge location. Note the following:

- To create an RTMP distribution, you must store the media files in an Amazon S3 bucket.
- To use CloudFront live streaming, create a web distribution.

Get Started

Cancel

3. The next screen is a big form that we need to fill out. In the first fieldset, **Origin Settings**, the **Origin Domain Name** option will provide a drop-down list of S3 endpoints.

 You should not use the endpoints provided here because some S3 configurations, such as redirects or error messages, won't be available when using this address.

Instead, use the endpoint that is available in the bucket properties inside the **Static Website Hosting** settings. The difference between these S3 endpoints is that the suggested endpoint doesn't have the bucket region (for example, `example.com.s3.amazonaws.com`) and the endpoint that we will use does have the region (for example, `example.com.s3-website-us-east-1.amazonaws.com`). **Origin ID** will be set automatically after you provide **Origin Domain Name**. Leave **Origin Path** and **Origin Custom Headers** empty:

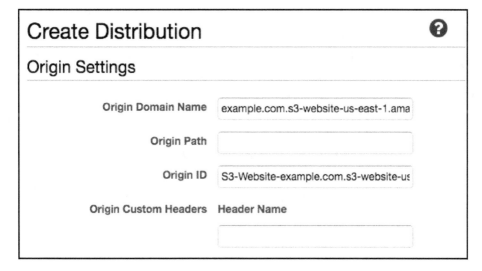

4. In **Default Cache Behavior Settings**, set the following parameters:
   - **Viewer Protocol Policy** as **HTTP and HTTPS**
   - **Allowed HTTP Methods** as all the HTTP verb options
   - **Cached HTTP Methods** with **OPTIONS** checked
   - **Object Caching** as **Use Origin Cache Headers**

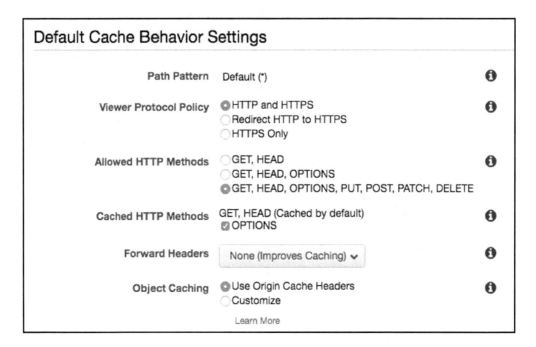

5. Leave the rest of the fields in this section with their default values, except the
    Compress Objects Automatically option. This feature is used to compress the
    files on demand using gzip. As already discussed in this chapter, Amazon S3
    doesn't offer automatic compression, but CloudFront does. You just need to set
    the **Yes** option:

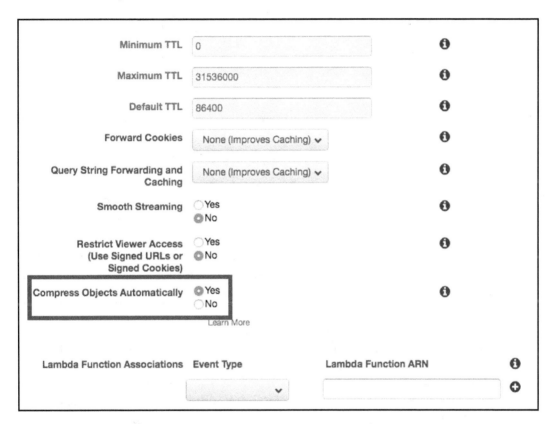

6. In **Distribution Settings**, set the following parameters:
    - Set **Price Class** with the option based on your target audience and the
      costs that you are willing to pay (better performance means higher
      costs).
    - Set **Alternate Domain Names (CNAMEs)** with the naked domain and
      the www domain, separated by commas.

- In **SSL Certificate**, choose **Default CloudFront Certificate (*.cloudfront.net)**. We will return to this option later once we issue our own certificate.
- Leave the rest of the fields with their default values.

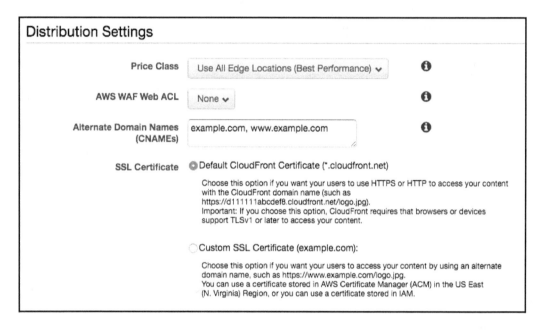

7. Now click on **Create Distribution**.
8. CloudFront needs a few minutes to replicate the distribution configuration between all the edge points, but you can follow the status in the CloudFront console main page. After it finishes, it will display the status as **Deployed**. In the following screenshot, you can see the CloudFront distribution address. Copy this link to your browser and test to check whether it is working:

Handling CloudFront caching

By default, CloudFront will cache all the files for 24 hours. It means that if you modify the files in your S3 bucket, you won't see any changes when browsing through a CloudFront distribution. Forcing a cache reset in your browser will not help because it's server-side caching. So, what's the recommended practice to handle caching? You have the following two options for this:

1. **Server side**: Create a cache invalidation request
2. **Client side**: Add suffixes to all the static files when changing their contents

Invalidating server-side cache

Creating a cache invalidation request to CloudFront takes some minutes to process because CloudFront will need to contact all the edge locations and request them to clear their individual caches.

Since this will be a recurring task, I don't recommend that you use the CloudFront console. It's better to use the CLI. However, CLI support for CloudFront is currently only available at the preview stage. So you may need to enable it by running the following command:

```
aws configure set preview.cloudfront true
```

To create a cache invalidation request for all files (path /*), execute the following command:

```
aws cloudfront \
  create-invalidation --distribution-id=DISTRIBUTION_ID --paths "/*"
```

You can find `DISTRIBUTION_ID` of your CloudFront distribution by looking at the CloudFront console or running the following CLI command:

```
aws cloudfront list-distributions
```

 You can add `--query DistributionList.Items[0].Id` to the previous command in order to only output the distribution ID of the first distribution.

This solution requires a long time for the invalidation to take effect, and it doesn't solve the problem of client-side caching.

Invalidating client-side cache

When you browse a web page, the browser will cache all the files that were downloaded to display the page (HTML, CSS, JavaScript, images, and so on) and avoid requiring the same files in the near future to improve performance. However, if you modify the contents of one file, how can you tell the browser to dispose of the previous cached content? You can't create an invalidation request because this time the cache is at the client side, not server side, but you can force the browser to make a new request by changing the name of the file that has been modified. For example, you can change the file name from `script.js` to `script.v2.js` and use its new name inside the HTML page:

```
<script src="script.v2.js"></script>
```

Another option is to add a query string to the filename when declaring it inside the HTML page, such as the following:

```
<script src="script.js?v=2.0"></script>
```

In this example, the filename was not changed, but the reference was changed, and this is enough for the browser to consider the previous cache invalid and make a new request to get the updated content.

The problem of both strategies is that you can't cache the HTML page. All other data can be cached, except the HTML page. Otherwise, the client will not understand that it should download a newer version of a file dependency.

To upload HTML files in such a way that they will never be cached, you must set the `Cache-Control` header to `no-cache` when uploading the files. In our website, after syncing a local folder with your bucket, upload the `index.html` file again, but this time, use the `cp` (copy) command and add the `Cache-Control` header:

```
aws s3 cp index.html s3://my-bucket-name \
    --cache-control no-cache --acl public-read
```

This strategy works pretty well, but it requires you to automate your build process to change the filenames or query string parameters for all changed files. In the next chapter, we are going to build a React app using the "Create React App" tool. Thankfully, this tool is already configured to change the filenames of all the deployments. It adds random strings, as in the `main.12657c03.js` file.

Updating Route 53 to use CloudFront

Our current record sets use S3 buckets. You just need to go back to Route 53 and replace it with the new CloudFront distribution. For the naked domain, which uses the A record type, you need to select the **Alias** option as **Yes** and the CloudFront distribution in the drop-down menu.

For the www domain, which uses the CNAME record type, select the **Alias** option as **No**. In this case, copy the CloudFront distribution address available in the A record and paste it into the box of the CNAME record.

Supporting HTTPS

Unfortunately, Amazon S3 does not support HTTPS connections, it only supports HTTP. We have set the Route 53 record sets to use a CloudFront distribution, but we haven't enabled support to HTTPS in CloudFront yet.

But why should we support HTTPS? There are many reasons nowadays. Let's list some of them:

- We are building an online store. We need to handle logins and payment transactions. Doing such things without an encrypted connection is not safe. It's too easy to eavesdrop the network and steal sensitive data.
- HTTP/2 is the newest protocol and is much faster than the old HTTP/1.1 version. Currently, *all* major browsers that support HTTP/2 *require* HTTPS. It is not possible to support HTTP/2 over an unencrypted HTTP connection.
- HTTP/2 with encryption is faster than HTTP/1.1 without encryption. Troy Hunt shows an interesting demo at this link: `https://www.troyhunt.com/i-wanna-go -fast-https-massive-speed-advantage`. In his test, loading a website with hundreds of small files was 80 percent faster with HTTP/2 over TLS due to the multiplexing feature of the newer protocol.
- Another good reason is privacy. Using HTTPS everywhere helps to keep your browsing data safe. It's not enough because the domain names of the sites that you visit will continue to be exposed, but it helps a lot. The pages that you visit and the things that you read or write will not be (easily) compromised because data will always be transferred with encryption.

If you are convinced and want to support HTTPS, follow these steps:

1. Create a mail exchange record in Route 53.
2. Request a free SSL/TLS certificate to AWS.
3. Edit the CloudFront distribution to use this new certificate.

The first step, to create a mail account, is necessary because AWS will only issue a free SSL/TLS certificate if you prove that you own the domain, and this verification is done by following a link sent to the `admin@example.com` e-mail address.

Creating a mail exchange record

We need a service that will handle e-mail messages before we request our free certificate to AWS. I suggest Zoho Mail as a free option (up to 5 GB space). In this section, we will see how to configure this service by performing the following steps:

1. First, browse `www.zoho.com/mail` and sign up for a free *business* e-mail account. This account will be associated with your domain. When selecting the administrator account, choose the name `admin`. This name is important because AWS will check your domain ownership by sending a confirmation e-mail to `admin@example.com`.

2. After you create your account, you will be requested to confirm the ownership of the associated domain. There are a few options to prove your ownership, and I prefer using the CNAME method. In the **Select your domain's DNS Manager (DNS Hosting provider) from the list** option, choose **Others..** because AWS is not listed. Now, select **CNAME Method**, and the **CNAME** and **Destination** will be presented. You need to configure a new temporary Route 53 record set with this pair and finish clicking on the **Proceed to CNAME Verification** button:

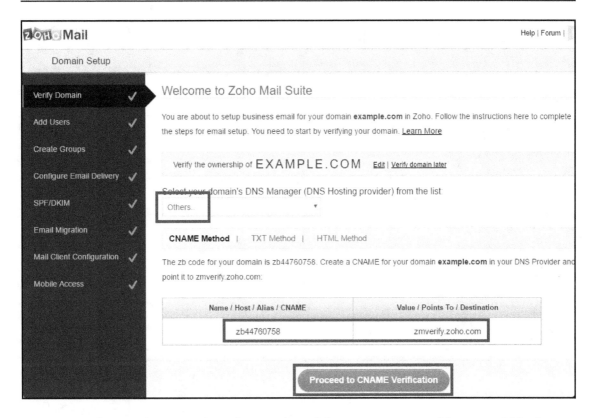

3. After verifying, confirm the creation of the `admin` account. You can add in the sequence other users.

4. The next step is to configure MX (mail exchange) records in Route 53. Copy the values that are presented by Zoho:

5. Go back to Route 53. Delete the CNAME record set that was created to verify your Zoho account because it is no longer necessary. Now you need to create a new record set of the type MX using the values from the preceding screenshot:

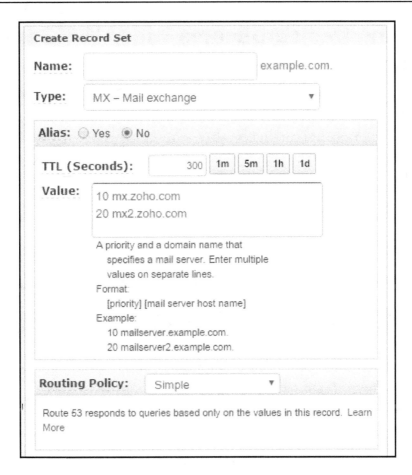

6. We are done. You can test whether it is working correctly by sending an e-mail to this new address and by checking your Zoho e-mail account for received e-mails.

Requesting free certificates with AWS Certificate Manager

Let's see how to request free certificates with AWS Certificate Manager by performing the following steps:

1. Request a TLS certificate at `https://console.aws.amazon.com/acm/home?regio n=us-east-1`.

 You need to be on us-east-1 because CloudFront only uses certificates from this region.

2. On the welcome screen, click on **Get started**. In the next screen, type your naked domain name and the www version and click on **Review and request:**

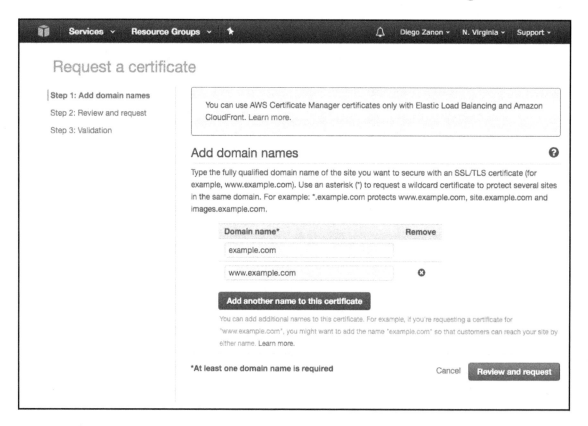

3. In the following screen, you just need to click on **Confirm and request**. Amazon will try to prove your domain ownership by sending an e-mail to admin@example.com. If you have configured your e-mail account correctly in the previous section, you will receive an e-mail in your Zoho inbox.
4. The e-mail has a confirmation link that you must click on to prove your ownership. After that, Amazon will issue a new TLS certificate that will be available for your account.

 You don't need to worry about the certificate expiration date. AWS will renew it automatically when necessary.

Configuring CloudFront to support HTTPS connections

The last step to support HTTPS is to edit the CloudFront distribution to use the new certificate. To perform this task, take a look at the following steps:

1. Browse the CloudFront Management Console at https://console.aws.amazon.com/cloudfront and open your distribution.
2. Under the **General** tab, click on the **Edit** option.

3. Click the **Custom SSL Certificate (example.com):** option and select your domain certificate using the drop-down button:

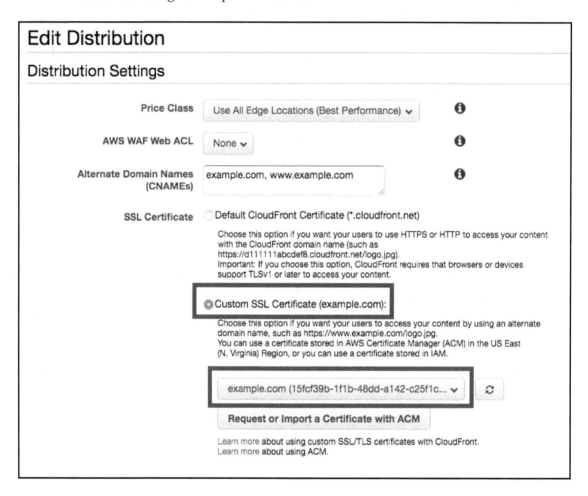

4. Save to return to the previous page, then click on the third tab, **Behaviors**, and click on **Edit** to edit the existing behavior.

5. Now we can change the **Viewer Protocol Policy** parameter to **Redirect HTTP to HTTPS** to force the users to always use HTTPS:

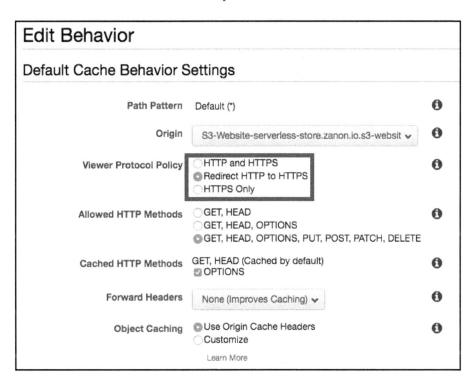

6. After changing these settings, CloudFront will automatically deploy the new configuration to all the edge nodes.
7. After waiting for some minutes, you can browse your domain to confirm HTTPS support.

Summary

In this chapter, you learned how to configure S3, CloudFront, and Route 53 to host a serverless frontend solution. Now you have your site distributed all around the world for reduced latency and increased speed along with HTTPS support to make the Web more safe and private.

In the next chapter, we are going to build the frontend of our serverless store application using React as an SPA.

5
Building the Frontend

In this chapter, we will build the web pages of our demo application. The objective here is not to teach frontend development, but to demonstrate that you can use modern tools along with serverless. For this demo, we will use React, but you could use Angular, Vue.js, or any other tool, and still take advantage of the serverless features. Also, we will discuss the pros and cons of SPA from a serverless perspective and let's take a look at how we can prerender SPA pages for better **Search Engine Optimization** (**SEO**).

In this chapter, we will cover the following topics:

- How to use React to build our web pages
- Pros and cons of Single-Page Applications
- Prerendering pages for a better SEO

After this chapter, you'll have built the frontend of our serverless online store.

Getting started with React

Teaching frontend tools is not the objective of this book, but we need to build something useful to see how serverless deals with modern frontend development. We will use React here because it is currently one of the most popular tools. If you don't know what React is or how to use it, I'll guide you to understand the basic concepts.

React principles

The first thing you should note is that React is a library and not a framework. The difference is that a library provides a set of functionalities to solve a *specific* problem, and a framework provides a set of libraries centered on a particular methodology.

React is only responsible for the view layer of your application. That's the problem React solves. If you need to make Ajax calls or handle page routes, you need to add other libraries. When you develop with React, you need to think in components. Your user interface is a composition of simple components, where each one of them has an inner state and an HTML definition. When using React, you don't manipulate the web page directly. You change the component's state and React will render it again to match the current state. This approach promotes predictability. For a given state, you always know how the component will render. This is very important for testing and maintaining complex applications.

Another important concept is the virtual DOM. The **Document Object Model (DOM)** is a representation of all nodes of an HTML page. If something changes on a page and you need to render a different view, the DOM needs to be manipulated. The problem is when you have hundreds of nodes. Recreating the entire view has a performance cost that can be perceived by the user.

The virtual DOM is an abstract version of the real DOM. React tracks the state of all components and knows when one of them was modified. Instead of rerendering the entire view, it compares the modified virtual DOM with the real DOM and makes a small patch containing only the differences. This patch is applied with a much better performance.

In summary, you need to know that React is a **library** with the specific purpose of handling the **view layer,** it is based on **components**, where each one of them has an internal **state** and a **view** definition, and you can't modify the DOM directly because that's the responsibility of the virtual DOM.

The Flux pattern

Flux is a pattern for application-state management, and Redux is the most popular Flux-inspired implementation. If you are building a complex React application, you should learn Redux or another Flux-like framework. However, *You Might Not Need Redux*, as Dan Abramov, the creator of Redux, has blogged about (`https://medium.com/@dan_abramov/you-might-not-need-redux-be46360cf367`): *"People often choose Redux before they need it."*

Redux is a great framework, but it adds complexity to your project. As we are building a small frontend application, we will not use it here, and this decision makes sense for applications that have a short component tree. Again, the objective of this book is to focus on serverless and not on frontend development, so Redux is out of scope for us. In a real-world application, you need to consider the pros and cons. Most of the time, you will choose to use Redux, but not always.

React hello-world

React promotes the usage of JSX, a syntax that mixes JavaScript with XML. You don't need to use JSX, but you *should* use it to improve the readability of the code. For example, take a look at the following JSX:

```
class HelloReact extends React.Component {
  render() {
    return <div>Hello, {this.props.name}!</div>;
  }
}

ReactDOM.render(
  <HelloReact name="World"/>,
  document.getElementById('root')
);
```

This example defines a `<HelloReact />` HTML element and the rendered output will use the value of the `name` property. If the input is `World`, the rendered result will be `<div>Hello, World!</div>`.

However, the browser can't execute this code because JSX doesn't have native support. You need to use a JSX transpiler that will translate this example into the following JavaScript code:

```
class HelloReact extends React.Component {
  render() {
    return React.createElement(
      "div", null,
      "Hello, ", this.props.name, "!"
    );
  }
}

ReactDOM.render(
  React.createElement(HelloReact, { name: "World" }),
  document.getElementById('root')
);
```

Mixing JavaScript code with HTML sounds strange, but we can get used to it. In the end, most people find it more enjoyable and easier to maintain.

To make this piece of code work, we need to add two dependencies such as React and ReactDOM. The former is the core, which lets us create components, and the latter is the library that renders the components and attaches them into an HTML node.

You can find these dependencies at `https://unpkg.com/react/` and `https://unpkg.com/react-dom/`. You will find the necessary files inside the `dist` folder.

The following code is a working hello-world example:

```html
<!DOCTYPE html>
<html>
  <head>
    <title>Hello, World!</title>
  </head>
  <body>
    <div id="root"> <!-- this is where we'll hook React -->
    </div>
    <script src="react.min.js"></script>
    <script src="react-dom.min.js"></script>
    <script type="text/javascript">
      class HelloReact extends React.Component {
        render() {
          return React.createElement(
            "div", null,
            "Hello, ", this.props.name, "!"
          );
        }
      }

      ReactDOM.render(
        React.createElement(HelloReact, { name: "World" }),
        document.getElementById('root')
      );
    </script>
  </body>
</html>
```

Building a shopping cart

To understand React, we need to see how props and states work, and how we can compose an interface with different components. For a practical example, we will build a shopping cart. This example will be the foundation of our **Serverless Store** and the objective now is to achieve the following result:

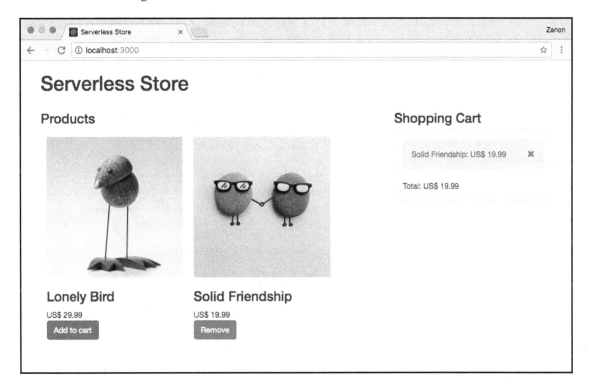

Preparing the development environment

One of the criticisms of React is the need of external tools for development. In fact, one can use plain JavaScript, but as we saw, JSX is easier to understand. So, the first tool that you need to add to your project is a JSX transpiler.

When you browse a React project or any other modern web project, you will also find that people use many other tools such as Babel (ES6 to ES5 transpiler), Webpack (module bundler), ESLint (code analysis), and others. Also, each tool has many competitors. You may prefer to use Browserify instead of Webpack, for example. Understanding and configuring these tools takes a long time. If you are learning React, you need to understand first how React works and not how the environment is configured.

With this in mind, the tool **Create React App** offers an opinionated configuration that uses well-established tools and practices. You don't need to worry about the environment anymore, you just follow what others have suggested.

Take a look at the following steps to start a new project using this tool:

1. Install the Create React App tool using the following npm command:

   ```
   npm install create-react-app@1.3.1 --global
   ```

 The @1.3.1 term means that it will download the exact version that was used for this book's examples. If you prefer, you can remove this @1.3.1 restriction to get the latest features, but that may introduce breaking changes to the examples.

2. Now, create a new application using the following command:

   ```
   create-react-app react-shopping-cart
   ```

3. Change the directory to the new folder and start the application using the following command:

   ```
   cd react-shopping-cart
   npm start
   ```

4. You can see the application running at `http://localhost:3000`, as shown in the following screenshot:

Organizing the solution

This application will create the following structure:

```
node_modules
public
   |- favicon.ico
   |- index.html
   |- manifest.json
src
   |- App.css
   |- App.js
   |- App.test.js
   |- index.css
   |- index.js
   |- logo.svg
   |- registerServiceWorker.js
.gitignore
package.json
README.md
```

The `public/manifest.json` and `src/registerServiceWorker.js` files are used to support **Progressive Web App** (**PWA**), which is a great feature to build fast and more reliable web pages as it caches static assets and allows offline access. However, PWA is not so useful for an online store and is out of scope of this book, so it will be removed from the examples.

We will make the following changes here to adapt the example to our project:

1. **Remove PWA support**: Delete the `public/manifest.json` and `src/registerServiceWorker.js` files.

2. **Remove src files that won't be used**: Delete the files `App.css`, `App.js`, `App.test.js`, `index.css`, and `logo.svg`

3. **Create folders**: Under `src/`, create the `css/`, `components/`, and `images/` folders.

4. **Add components**: Under `components/`, add the files `App.js`, `ShoppingCart.js`, `ShoppingCartItem.js`, `Product.js`, and `ProductList.js`.

5. **Add CSS**: Under `css/`, create a file named `site.css` that will serve as our custom styles.

6. **Add images**: Add two images that will be used as our products. I've used free images (Creative Commons CC0) from Pixabay (`https://pixabay.com`).

You can browse the Packt resources for this chapter (`https://github.com/PacktPublishing/Building-Serverless-Web-Applications`) to see the final result. This project is available under a folder named `react-shopping-cart`.

Now you should have the following project tree:

```
node_modules
public
   |- favicon.ico
   |- index.html
src
   |- components
      |- App.js
      |- Product.js
      |- ProductList.js
      |- ShoppingCart.js
      |- ShoppingCartItem.js
   |- css
      |- site.css
```

```
|- images
    |- <images>
|- index.js
.gitignore
package.json
README.md
```

Before starting to code the components, we need to make a few changes in the `index.js` file to match the new project tree. Use the following code:

```
import React from 'react';
import ReactDOM from 'react-dom';
import App from './components/App';
import './css/site.css';

ReactDOM.render(
  <App/>,
  document.getElementById('root')
);
```

For a responsive website, I've included the Twitter Bootstrap 3 (`https://getbootstrap.com`) styles in the `public/index.html` file:

```
<!doctype html>
<html lang="en">
  <head>
    <meta charset="utf-8">
    <title>Serverless Store</title>
    <link rel="shortcut icon" href="%PUBLIC_URL%/favicon.ico">
    <link rel="stylesheet" href="bootstrap.min.css">
  </head>
  <body>
    <div id="root"></div>
  </body>
</html>
```

Composing components

The user interface is a composition of components. To make this clearer, the following diagram shows how we will compose our components to create the application design:

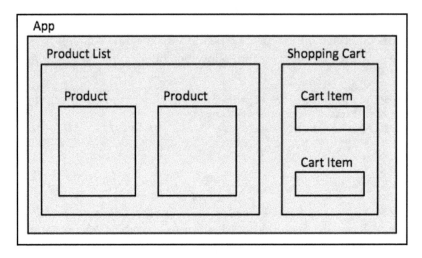

The **App** component holds the entire view and is responsible for positioning the **Product List** and **Shopping Cart** components. The **Product List** component has a list of **Product** components, and the Shopping Cart will list the selected products as **Cart Item**.

In React, there is no interaction between components, except by passing properties from parent to child components. These properties are called props. The child can't pass data to the parent unless the parent gives a handler function as a property and the child executes this handler when an event occurs. For example, the parent can give a `handleClick` function that will be triggered by the child when a button is clicked.

Due to the restriction that you can have only parent-child interactions, the Product List and Shopping Cart components need a common parent. When a product is selected, it will trigger a function in Product List, which in turn will trigger another in the App component. This handler will change the App component's state, and by consequence, the state of the Shopping Cart component will also be changed because the App component will be defined to pass data to the cart through `props`.

Implementing a component

In the following code extract, the skeleton of a component is presented. This format will be used to implement all components. To focus on the content, further examples will show only the `constructor()` and `render()` implementations. Full code examples can be downloaded from the Packt resources associated with this book:

```javascript
// import React and other dependencies
import React, { Component } from 'react';
import AnotherComponent from './AnotherComponent';

// define the Component as a class
class MyComponent extends Component {
  // optional method
  constructor() {
    super();
    this.state = {
      // state
    };
  }

  // this method must be implemented
  render() {
    return (
      // HTML definition
    );
  }
}

// export the component, so it can be used by others
export default MyComponent;
```

The App component

The App is a component with the responsibility of organizing the page's layout. It uses Bootstrap's grid system to position the two other main components such as Product List and Shopping Cart. It should be rendered with the following:

```javascript
render() {
  return (
    <div className="container">
      <div className="row">
        <div className="col-md-12">
          <h1>Serverless Store</h1>
        </div>
      </div>
```

```
    <div className="row">
      <div className="col-md-8">
        <h3>Products</h3>
        <ProductList
          products={this.state.products}
          onSelect={this.handleSelect}/>
      </div>
      <div className="col-md-4">
        <h3>Shopping Cart</h3>
        <ShoppingCart
          selectedProducts={
            this.state
              .products
                .filter(p => p.isSelected)
          }
          onDeselect={this.handleDeselect}/>
      </div>
    </div>
  </div>
);
}
```

 When using JSX, you add a class to an HTML element with the
className property, for example:
`<div className="container"></div>`

In this code, we can see the Product List component being set with two properties such as
`products` and `onSelect`:

```
<ProductList
  products={this.state.products}
  onSelect={this.handleSelect}/>
```

The `products` property will receive a list of products that is controlled by the state of the
App component. The `onSelect` property will receive a handler function, which will be
used by the children to trigger the parent component when a product is selected.

We can also see that the Shopping Cart component has two properties such as
`selectedProducts` and `onDeselect`:

```
<ShoppingCart
  selectedProducts={
    this.state
      .products
      .filter(p => p.isSelected)
  }
  onDeselect={this.handleDeselect}/>
```

The `selectedProducts` property will receive a list of products that were selected, while
the `onDeselect` property defines a handler function that should be triggered by the
Shopping Cart component when a product is deselected.

So, in this component, the App component is sharing its state with the Product List and the
Shopping Cart components, thus App is responsible for defining the products objects and
for keeping track of the selected products. The initial list of products is defined in the
following piece of code:

```
import lonelyBird from '../images/lonely-bird.jpg';
import solidFriendship from '../images/solid-friendship.jpg';

const products = [{
    id: 1,
    name: 'Lonely Bird',
    image: lonelyBird,
    price: 29.99,
    isSelected: false
}, {
    id: 2,
    name: 'Solid Friendship',
    image: solidFriendship,
    price: 19.99,
    isSelected: false
}];
```

The preceding code snippet is a simplified example. In the next chapter,
we will retrieve this list from a Lambda function.

The initial state is defined inside the class constructor. Also, you need to bind the component's `this` instance to the callback functions. Otherwise, `this.state` will not be found when the function gets called inside another component:

```
constructor() {
    super();
    this.state = {
      products: products
    };

    // bind the component's "this" to the callback
    this.handleSelect = this.handleSelect.bind(this);
    this.handleDeselect = this.handleDeselect.bind(this);
}
```

The `handleSelect` function should be defined inside the class and it will receive a product as an argument to set its `isSelected` state:

```
handleSelect(product) {
    // create a copy of the products array
    const products = this.state.products.slice();

    // find the index of the product to modify
    const index = products.map(i => i.id).indexOf(product.id);

    // modify the selection state
    products[index].isSelected = product.isSelected;

    // make React aware that the state has changed
    this.setState({products: products});
}
```

There are a couple of things to observe in this example: `slice()` was used to create another array, instead of mutating the current array, and `setState()` was used instead of directly changing the reference to `products`. This is because working with immutable objects has performance benefits. It's easier to identify a modified object by checking whether its reference has changed than by looking into all of its property values. Regarding `setState()`, it is used to make React aware of the need to rerender the component.

To finish, as the `handleSelect` function is taking the `isSelected` property and setting the state, regardless of whether the property is true or false, we can use the `handleSelect` function to define the `handleDeselect` function:

```
handleDeselect(product) {
    this.handleSelect(product);
}
```

The Product List component

This component accesses the data provided by its parent through the `props` variable. It will use the `products` array to iterate and create a new Product component for each item of the array. Also, it will set the `onSelect` handler with the function passed by its parent:

```
render() {
  const onSelect = this.props.onSelect;
  const productList =
    this.props.products.map(product => {
      return (
        <div key={product.id}
             className="product-box">
          <Product
            product={product}
            onSelect={onSelect}/>
        </div>
      )
    });

  return (
    <div>
      {productList}
    </div>
  );
}
```

The Product component

This component is responsible for rendering the details of the product, such as the image, description, price, and a button that allows the user to add the product to the cart. As you can see, the `onClick` event of the button will change the `isSelected` state and trigger the `onSelect` function:

```
render() {
  return (
    <div>
      <img src={this.props.product.image}/>
      <div>
        <h3>{this.props.product.name}</h3>
        <div>US$ {this.props.product.price}</div>
        <div>
          <button onClick={() => {
            const product = this.props.product;
            product.isSelected = !product.isSelected;
            this.props.onSelect(product);
```

```
        }}>
          {this.props
              .product
                  .isSelected ? 'Remove' : 'Add to cart'}
        </button>
      </div>
    </div>
  </div>
 );
}
```

The Shopping Cart component

The Shopping Cart component is responsible for rendering the selected products and showing the total value. Let's take a look at the following code snippet to see how this is done:

```
render() {
  const onDeselect = this.props.onDeselect;
  const products =
    this.props.selectedProducts.map(product => {
      return (
        <ShoppingCartItem key={product.id}
                          product={product}
                          onDeselect={onDeselect}/>
      )
    });
  const empty =
    <div className="alert alert-warning">
      Cart is empty
    </div>;

  return (
    <div className="panel panel-default">
      <div className="panel-body">
        {products.length > 0 ? products : empty}
        <div>Total: US$ {this.getTotal()}</div>
      </div>
    </div>
  );
}
```

The `getTotal` function uses a `map/reduce` operation to get the aggregated total value. The `map` operation will transform the input, creating an array of numbers, and `reduce` will sum all values:

```
getTotal() {
  return this.props
            .selectedProducts
            .map(p => p.price)
            .reduce((a, b) => a + b, 0);
}
```

The Cart Item component

The last component is the Cart Item. For each selected product, a cart item will be added to the Shopping Cart component. This component is rendered with the product name and value, along with a Glyphicon for an X mark icon. Glyphicon is a set of icons that are available through Bootstrap.

Also, when the user clicks on the icon, we need to trigger the `onDeselect` function. Take a look at the following code snippet to see how it is done:

```
render() {
  const product = this.props.product;
  return (
    <div>
      <span>
        {product.name}: US$ {product.price}
      </span>
      <a
        onClick={() => {
          product.isSelected = false;
          this.props.onDeselect(product);
        }}>
        <span className="glyphicon glyphicon-remove">
        </span>
      </a>
    </div>
  );
}
```

Publishing our demo

Publishing the static files requires a processing phase due to the fact that we have used JSX to build the React demo. In this case, the Create React App module will help us again.

Take a look at the following steps to learn about publishing our demo:

1. Before publishing, we need to test it locally to confirm that everything is working as expected, which can be done using the following command:

   ```
   npm start
   ```

2. Now we can prepare our frontend project to be published using the following command:

   ```
   npm run build
   ```

3. The resulting files will be processed, minimized, and bundled. You can find all files inside the `build` folder. Now upload them to Amazon S3 using the following command:

   ```
   aws s3 sync ./build s3://my-bucket-name --acl public-read
   ```

4. Now, reupload the `index.html` file, adding the `Cache-Control: no-cache` header just to this file using the following command:

   ```
   aws s3 cp ./build/index.html s3://my-bucket-name \
      --cache-control no-cache --acl public-read
   ```

Making Ajax requests

React is responsible for just the view layer. React is *not* concerned with how data is fetched from the server. So, there are no restrictions and you can retrieve the server data using many different approaches. Redux offers a pattern using *Async Actions* and Relay, which is another JavaScript framework, uses *GraphQL* to handle data.

In our sample application, we will use the simplest approach: the *Root component*. This pattern is simple and can be very useful for small projects where you have a shallow component tree. What we will do is to concentrate all Ajax requests in a single component and the best option for this is to use the Root component because it's the only component that can communicate with all the others.

When the Root component retrieves some data from the server, the children components will be updated through *properties,* and React, as expected, will render again only the ones that were changed. And whenever a component needs to perform an action, it will execute a function that was passed as a property by the parent component. This information will go up until it reaches the root level, where it can be sent to the server.

In our examples, we will consider the App component as the Root component. The `index.js` file is technically the root since it is the first to load, but `index` is only responsible for appending the React application to the HTML page. As the App component is loaded by `index` and App is a common parent for all other components, it will be defined as our root.

Retrieving data from the server

In the following example, we will build a page that will request a list of products on load. This request will be done in the Root component, but we need to define where exactly it will be executed. The `render` function is *never* a good choice because `render` is always considered as a *pure function*: for a given input, the output will always be the same, which means that side effects are not allowed.

Excluding `render`, we have two candidates: `componentWillMount` and `componentDidMount`, both of them execute *just once* and before (`componentWillMount`) or after (`componentDidMount`) the first `render` execution. Since the asynchronous call will take some time to execute, and the component rendering will take place before the result is received, it doesn't help to use the `componentWillMount` option. The first rendering will always be done with empty data. So, it makes more sense to use the `componentWillMount` function to set the initial state as empty (and avoid undefined values in your properties) and the `componentDidMount` function to fetch data from the server.

Another question is whether the initial state should be set in the `constructor` function or the `componentWillMount` function. They are technically equivalent, but it is much more common to use the `constructor` function for this task. In practice, `componentWillMount` is hardly used at all.

The last thing to decide is: which Ajax library will be used? I like to use **axios** for this task, but if you prefer, you can use another library for this such as **Fetch** or **SuperAgent**. Some people like to use **jQuery** for Ajax calls, but adding a full-featured library for just one task doesn't make much sense.

To install axios, run the following command:

```
npm install axios --save
```

To include axios in a component, add the following import:

```
import axios from 'axios';
```

The first part of the example shows how the initial state is defined inside the constructor. It sets an empty array of products and a Boolean variable, `ready`, with the value `false`. This Boolean will be set to `true` once the request completes. Using this approach, we can control the rendering state and display a loading icon while the page is still fetching data:

```
constructor() {
  super();

  // empty initial state
  this.state = {
    products: [],
    ready: false
  };
}
```

Checking the `ready: false` state, we can display a `glyphicon-refresh` icon instead of the list of products:

Take a look at the `componentDidMount` implementation in the following code snippet. The API address is used to trigger a Lambda function:

```
componentDidMount() {
  const apiAddress =
    'https://abc123.execute-api.us-east-1.amazonaws.com';
  const stage = 'prod';
  const service = 'store/products';
  axios
    .get(`${apiAddress}/${stage}/${service}`)
    .then(res => {
```

```
    this.setState({
      products: res.data.products,
      ready: true
    });
  })
  .catch(error => {
    console.log(error);
  });
}
```

After getting the results, we set the `ready` state with the `true` value and the list of products with what we have received:

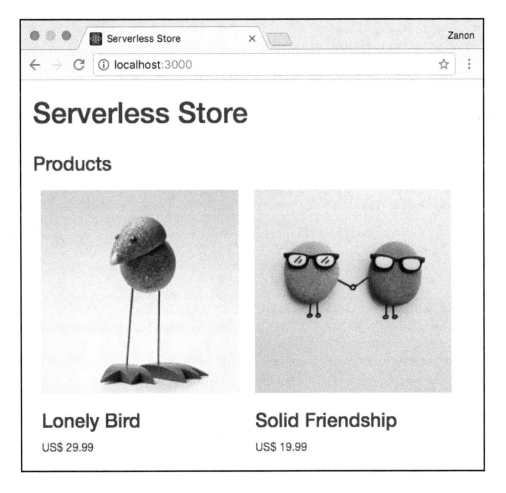

Sending data to the server

In the previous example, we have placed the Ajax request inside the `componentDidMount` function because we wanted the data on page load. However, in the following example, the Ajax request will be executed when a button is clicked, so we don't have the same restriction. Take a look at the following steps, which describe the process step-by-step:

1. The request will be defined as a function of the component:

```
handleSave (products) {
  axios
    .post(`${apiAddress}/${stage}/${service}`,
        products) // data to send
    .then(res => {
      this.setState({
        products: this.state.products,
        hasSaved: true
      });
    })
    .catch(error => {
      console.log(error);
    });
}
```

2. The `handleSave` function is passed through properties to the children components:

```
<ShoppingCart
  products={this.state.products}
  hasSaved={this.state.hasSaved}
  onSave={this.handleSave}/>
```

3. And, to finish, the children will trigger the `save` function when a button is clicked. After the request finishes, the parent component will change the state of the `hasSaved` property to `true`, and we can use this value in the children components to display a message:

```
return (
  <div>
    {products}
    <div>Total: US$ {this.getTotal()}</div>
    <button
      onClick={() => {this.props.onSave();}}>
      Save
    </button>
    {this.props.hasSaved ? <div>saved</div> : ''}
```

```
        </div>
    );
```

4. After saving, the word **saved** will appear under the button:

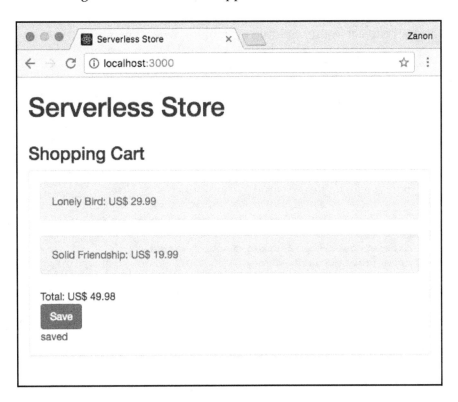

Handling the page routes

Later in this chapter, we will discuss the pros and cons of SPA, but first we will take a look at how to build one. An SPA is an application that loads just one HTML file, but it will dynamically update that page while the user interacts with it. Also, the content will render differently to match the URL. For example, browsing the example.com address will render the Home component, while browsing example.com/about will render the About component.

To implement this, we will use the React Router module. Let's take a look at the following steps to build an SPA:

1. Create a new application using the Create React App tool, or modify the previous Shopping Cart application.
2. Install the React Router module by running the following:

```
npm install react-router-dom@4.x --save
```

 The @4.x term means that it will download a version that is compatible with the one used for this book's examples.

3. The App.js file will be modified to define the application routes. First, we need to import the React Router module components:

```
import React, { Component } from 'react';
import {
  BrowserRouter as Router, Route, Switch
} from 'react-router-dom';
```

4. Next, we need to import our App components. In this example, we will use the following components:
   - Header: This is the component that will render the text "Serverless Store" for all pages
   - Footer: This is the component that will render a footer text for all pages
   - ProductList: This is a list of products, where each product links to the Product component
   - Product: This component gives details of a specific product
   - ShoppingCart: This is a list of products that were selected by the user
   - NoMatch: This is a component that will render the text "Page not found"

5. The App component will render the page using the following components:
   - Router: This is the Root component for the page routing.
   - Switch: This renders the first child route that matches the URL path. If there is no match, it will render the NoMatch component.

- `Route`: This renders the component for the specified path.

Let's take a look at the preceding mentioned components in the following code snippet:

```
render() {
  return (
    <Router>
      <div>
        <Header/>
        <Switch>
          <Route path="/" exact component={ProductList}/>
          <Route path="/product/:id" component={Product}/>
          <Route path="/shopping-cart" component={ShoppingCart}/>
          <Route component={NoMatch}/>
        </Switch>
        <Footer/>
      </div>
    </Router>
  );
}
```

6. Run the application and test the URLs. If it doesn't match any path, the `NoMatch` component will be rendered and it will display the **Page not found** message:

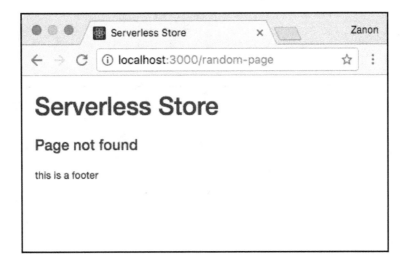

Linking pages

Linking one page to another is done using the React Router's Link component:

```
import { Link } from 'react-router-dom';
```

Link is just a wrapper for the HTML anchor element. In the following example, the implementation of the Product List component shows how to link to a page of a specific Product:

```
render() {
  return (
    <div>
      <ul>
        <li>
          <Link to='/product/1'>
            Product 1
          </Link>
        </li>
        <li>
          <Link to='/product/2'>
            Product 2
          </Link>
        </li>
      </ul>
    </div>
  );
}
```

This component will be rendered as follows:

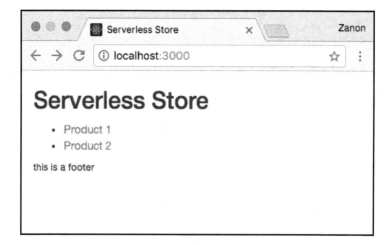

Using the query parameters

When we have declared the routes of our application, we have defined the route of the Product component as follows:

```
<Route path="/product/:id" component={Product}/>
```

The colon sign defines the parameter that can be used by the related component. In this case, :id defines a parameter with the name id, which can be used as follows:

```
render() {
  return (
    <div>
      <h4>
        Product Details for ID: {this.props.match.params.id}
      </h4>
    </div>
  );
}
```

This Product component will render as shown in the following screenshot:

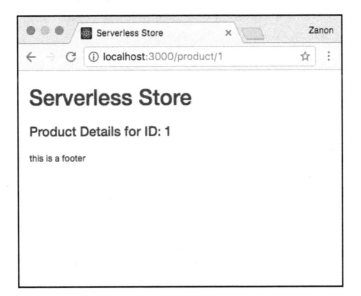

Note that the localhost:3000/product/1 path defined an id parameter with value 1.

Single-Page Applications

In a traditional multipage website, each URL loads a different HTML page. If you are at the example.com page and need to navigate to example.com/about, the entire view will blink with a page reload because it will need to be rendered again. The problem is that, usually, a page reload is a waste of time since both pages share similar content, such as the page header and footer. Also, CSS and JavaScript dependencies may be exactly the same.

In a Single-Page Application, there is a base HTML file that will be loaded for every URL and, depending on the given URL, the inner content will be dynamically loaded to match the address. Also, the URL browsing is controlled at the client-side using JavaScript. Changing from one URL to another will not cause a full page reload. Instead of loading an entire new file, a request is made to the server to retrieve only what is necessary for the new address and just a part of the page will be rendered again.

Pros and cons of Single-Page Applications

SPA is a modern approach that has the objective to provide a better user experience, but it's not perfect. There are pros and cons that you need to know before using it. While this topic can be extensive, we will highlight only the most relevant.

Pros

Let's list the main benefits of this approach:

- **No page refresh**: This is an obvious benefit. When the user changes to another view, the page will not blink. The browsing experience becomes more pleasant with a fluid navigation.
- **Decoupling**: You have a better separation of frontend and backend code.
- **Reduce the server-side code**: We are building a serverless website, so we must consider that cold start delays at the backend may impact the user experience. In SPA, there is much more logic at the client side to make the dynamism feasible, and we can use this approach to reduce the size of the server-side code and improve the performance by reducing the number of requests to the backend.

Cons

SPA has a few drawbacks, we can consider the following cons:

- **Larger file sizes**: As we have more logic at the client side, the applications usually have larger JavaScript dependencies. This is a big problem, especially with mobile clients with poor network conditions. The first load of the site will take more time.
- **Requires JavaScript**: There is yet a small percentage of users that disable JavaScript due to security reasons. If you have a simple site that doesn't need any fancy features, your SPA is forcing JavaScript support that would otherwise be optional.
- **Search Engine Optimization**: An SPA application relies heavily on JavaScript. Google crawlers can execute some JavaScript code in special conditions, but Bing and others won't execute. If we want the search engines to correctly index our website, we need to prerender the content especially for them.

Considerations

Some may argue that a low-end mobile device may have a poor performance with SPA because of the increased amount of JavaScript code. While that might have been true in the past, it may not be the reality at present and won't be in the future. Nowadays, even low-end devices have a powerful CPU that can perfectly execute most operations seamlessly. The real issue with mobile devices is not the computational power, but the network performance to download a larger size of code.

In this book, we will stick with SPA, and the main reason is that it fits well with the serverless approach. SPA is a modern approach to offload to clients some of the computing costs needed to run a website.

Lambda is cheap, but not free. On the other hand, client-side executions are limitless. Using the premise that more logic at the client won't significantly hurt the performance, I prefer avoiding making Lambda requests to handle the application state. Lambda should be used only to retrieve or save data and not to control UI logic.

However, as with most things in our field, each case should be treated separately. You may benefit from a multipage application and there is nothing wrong with it. With multipage, you just need to configure the Lambda function to return HTML content instead of JSON data, as we saw in an example in `Chapter 3`, *Using the Serverless Framework*.

Prerendering pages

In our frontend approach, the layout is entirely composed by JavaScript code using React components. Prerendering a web page means executing this JavaScript code and saving the output HTML file.

As discussed in the previous section, to improve **Search Engine Optimization** (**SEO**), we need to prerender pages because the majority of crawlers can't execute JavaScript code, and the ones that can, such as Google, won't execute all kinds of code.

Using PhantomJS

PhantomJS is a headless web browser, based on WebKit, which can be used to make HTTP requests and save the HTML output. It is not a Node.js module, but it can use Node.js modules. It runs in its own process, which is not the same as a Node runtime. You can download it from the official site: `http://phantomjs.org`.

As we discussed in the previous chapter, you can configure the S3 bucket to return the `index.html` page whenever an error of HTTP 404 *Not Found* occurs. So, when the user browses the address `example.com/page1`, S3 will look for a `page1.html` file. It will not find it, but it will load the `index.html` file instead. As we have developed an SPA, it will be able to render the contents of the corresponding `page1` file, keeping the browser address as `example.com/page1`.

When we prerender the `page1` file, the output HTML must be uploaded to the S3 bucket. This means that the next time we try to fetch the address `example.com/page1`, S3 will find a `page1.html` file and load it directly. Loading a prerendered page for a real user is not a problem, it's even better from a performance perspective. This user will load the HTML with the React dependencies. After a few instants, the React application will take control and further requests will be handled as a normal SPA.

The script to prerender a page is quite simple. You can follow this example:

```
const fs = require('fs');
const webPage = require('webpage');
const page = webPage.create();

const path = 'page1';
const url = 'https://example.com/' + path;

page.open(url, (status) => {
```

```
  if (status != 'success') {
    console.log('Error trying to prerender ' + url);
    phantom.exit();
  }

  const content = page.content;
  fs.write(path + '.html', content, 'w');

  console.log("The file was saved.");
  phantom.exit();
});
```

To test, add the PhantomJS binary to PATH and execute the following command:

```
phantomjs prerender.js
```

One of the problems of this approach is that you need to keep track of all the pages of your application. If a new page is added, you need to remember to include it in this list of pages to process. Also, you need to prerender your application's root file (index.html) and replace it in the S3 bucket.

Serving the output HTML file will make the content visible for all web crawlers.

Using the Lambda functions for prerendering

If your application is a static website, you can prerender all pages just once. However, for dynamic applications such as our Serverless Store, we need to have a routine of prerendering pages to avoid serving outdated content to crawlers. For example, the https://serverless-store.com/products/lonely-bird page shows the details of the **Lonely Bird** product. If the product is modified or deleted, we need to apply the changes to the /products/lonely-bird.html file. You have the following two options for this:

- Whenever some content is modified, trigger a Lambda function to update the page
- Schedule a Lambda function to execute daily to update all pages

In both cases, Lambda functions will be used, but how to call the PhantomJS binary if it is not a Node module? For this, we can install the `phantomjs-lambda-pack` Node module, which provides binary files compatible with Amazon Linux AMI machines to run on Lambda. It can be used as a Node module because it will spawn a child process to execute PhantomJS.

The `prerender.js` file that is loaded in the next example is the code implemented in the previous section. It must be placed in the same folder as the `serverless.yml` file.

The following code can be used as our Lambda handler:

```
const phantomjsLambdaPack =
  require('phantomjs-lambda-pack');
const exec = phantomjsLambdaPack.exec;

exports.handler = (event, context, callback) => {
  exec('prerender.js', (err, stdout, stderr) => {
    console.log(err, 'finished');
    callback(err, 'finished');
  });
};
```

 This PhantomJS wrapper requires the Lambda function to use at least 1,024 MB of RAM and a timeout of 180 seconds. So, instead of requiring one Lambda function for each page, it's better to call the Lambda to handle multiple pages.

Rendering on the fly

Instead of prerendering a web page, you can also render it on the fly. You need to detect that the request was made from a crawler and execute some logic to render the HTML page. Detecting a crawler can be done by checking the user-agent string and comparing it with a known list of common crawlers. This method works, but requires periodic maintenance and will not cover all crawlers, just the most popular.

There is a website, `https://prerender.io`, which offers a service to prerender sites on the fly when a crawler is detected. You install a middleware in your server and it will be responsible for checking the requests to find crawlers and provide them a cached prerendered version of your page. As we don't have a server, and we are using CloudFront/S3 to host the frontend, we can't execute code on demand.

To solve problems like this one, AWS released a new service named **Lambda@Edge**, which is currently in preview phase. This service will execute Lambda functions in edge locations in response to *all page requests*. AWS promised a very short latency to execute those Lambda functions, and you can use it to prerender on the fly if an agent is a crawler. You can also use it for other use cases such as modifying response headers or adding content depending on the agent, IP address, or referrer.

Rendering on the fly has the obvious drawback that it will be slower to answer the requests, but as the Lambda function has direct access to the database, the rendered page will always be updated.

Building an online store

We will use the previous Shopping Cart demo to begin our application. Now, we know how to set page routes and how to make Ajax requests, so we have everything to continue. One important difference is that the Shopping Cart component will be in a different page than the Product List component. Also, we need to create other pages. The following is a list of the pages:

- **Home page**: This presents a list of all available products where the user can add them to the Shopping Cart component
- **Product details**: This is a dedicated page that provides more details of a specific product where users can see and add new comments
- **Shopping Cart**: This shows all of the selected products and is responsible for handling payments
- **Signup page**: This handles account creation
- **Login page**: This allows the user to log in
- **Page not found**: This is a page that will be displayed when the address doesn't exist
- **Error page**: This is a page that will be displayed when an error occurs

This book will not cover all the code for the online store sample. There are too many parts that are simple to implement or are unrelated to the serverless concept. You can find the entire code in the Packt resources associated with this book or on my GitHub repo: `https://github.com/zanon-io/serverless-store`. For a running demo, access: `https://serverless-store.zanon.io`. Instead of dumping all the code here, we are focusing on the important parts. The following sections will describe what each page implements along with a screenshot of the result.

The Navbar component

The Navbar component is like the header component that should appear for all pages. For its implementation, let's perform the following steps:

1. First, we need to install two Node modules: `react-bootstrap` and `react-router-bootstrap`. Install them using the following npm command:

```
npm install react-boostrap --save
npm install react-router-bootstrap --save
```

2. Import the necessary components using the following code:

```
import {
  Navbar, Nav, NavItem
} from 'react-bootstrap';
import {
  IndexLinkContainer, LinkContainer
} from 'react-router-bootstrap';
```

3. Implement the Navbar component to set the links using the following code:

```
<Navbar>
  <Nav>
    <IndexLinkContainer to="/">
      <NavItem>Home</NavItem>
    </IndexLinkContainer>
    <LinkContainer to="/shopping-cart">
      <NavItem>Shopping Cart</NavItem>
    </LinkContainer>
  </Nav>
  <Nav pullRight>
    <LinkContainer to="/signup">
      <NavItem>Signup</NavItem>
    </LinkContainer>
    <LinkContainer to="/login">
      <NavItem>Login</NavItem>
    </LinkContainer>
    <NavItem>
      <span className="glyphicon glyphicon-bell">
      </span>
    </NavItem>
  </Nav>
</Navbar>
```

We will get the following result:

The last item is a notification icon. We will implement it in Chapter 9, *Handling Serverless Notifications*.

The Home page

The **Home** page will render the Product List component that we have defined in this chapter. One important observation is how the page router will select this component. Previously, we used the following code:

```
<Route path="/" exact component={ProductList}/>
```

However, we need to pass some properties from the App component to the Product List component, since the App component is responsible for managing the application state. In this case, we need to use the render attribute:

```
<Route path="/" exact render={
  () => <ProductList
        products={this.state.products}
        onSelect={this.handleSelect}/>
}/>
```

The same applies for all other components that need to share their state with the App component.

Take a look at the result in the following screenshot:

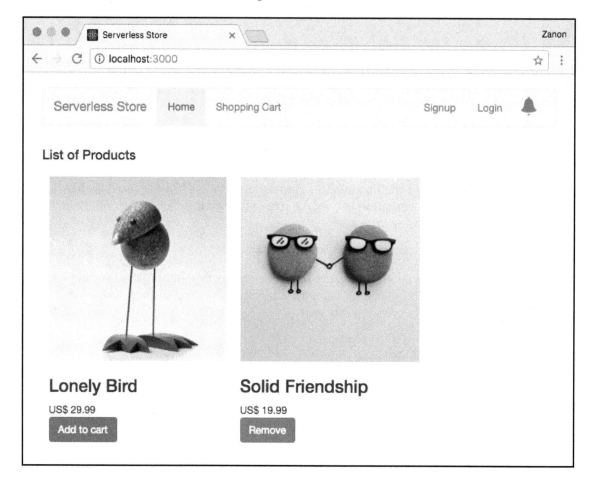

The product details page

The product details page will be accessed by clicking on the image of a product. On this page, the user will be able to see the product and customer reviews:

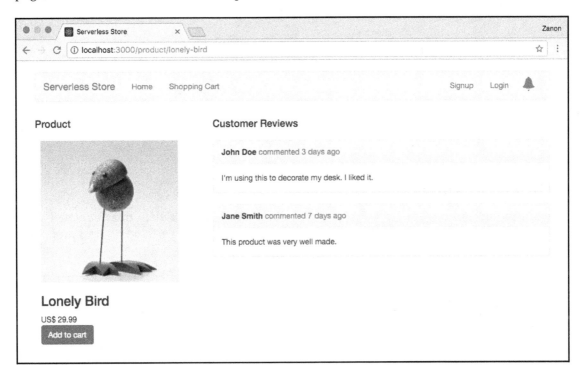

The *customer reviews* feature will be implemented later in this book, in `Chapter 9`, *Handling Serverless Notifications*.

To display the product details page, we need to add a link in the product image using the `Link` tag, as shown in the following code snippet:

```
<Link to={`/product/${this.props.product.id}`}>
  <img src={this.props.product.image}/>
</Link>
```

Another change that is required is how the page route will be able to identify which product to render. In this case, we will modify the Route component to render the Product component using the URL parameter available at the props.match.param object:

```
<Route path="/product/:id" render={
  (props) => <Product
               product={
                 this.state
                   .products
                   .find(x =>
                     x.id === props.match.params.id)
               }
               onSelect={this.handleSelect}/>
}/>
```

The Shopping Cart page

The **Shopping Cart** page will be implemented like we did previously in this chapter. The only modification here is the addition of a checkout button, which will be used to process the request:

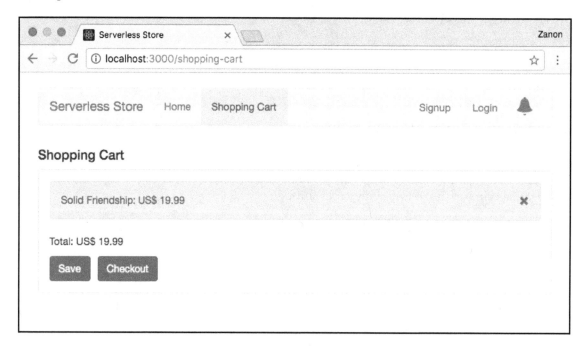

However, handling payments is a complex feature for a restricted audience, thus it will not be discussed here. If you need a serverless service for this, I recommend that you take a look at Stripe (`https://stripe.com`).

When the user clicks on this button, we will display a modal, as shown in the following screenshot:

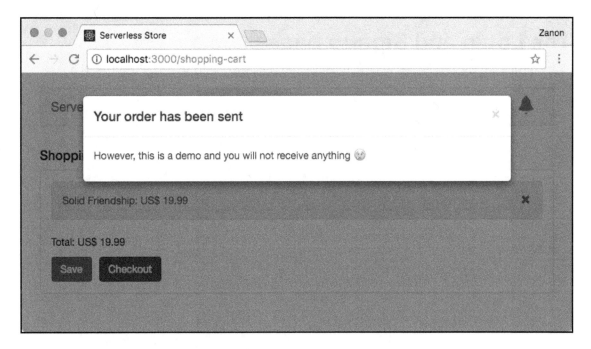

This modal is implemented using the `react-bootstrap` component, as shown in the following example:

```
<Modal show={this.state.showModal} onHide={this.closeModal}>
  <Modal.Header closeButton>
    <Modal.Title>Your order has been sent</Modal.Title>
  </Modal.Header>
  <Modal.Body>
    <p>However, this is a demo...</p>
  </Modal.Body>
</Modal>
```

In the following code snippet, `closeModal` is a method to set the `showModal` state to `false`:

```
closeModal() {
  this.setState({ showModal: false });
}
```

The Login and Signup pages

The **Login** and **Signup** pages will be implemented as simple forms, as shown in the following screenshot:

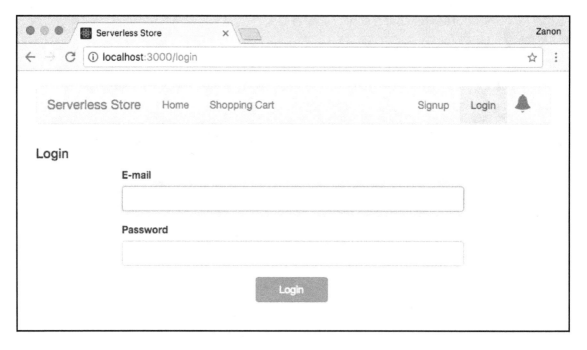

The only difference between them is that the **Signup** page has an extra field to request the user to type the password a second time for confirmation.

Both features will be implemented in Chapter 8, *Securing the Serverless Application*.

The error pages

We have to support two types of errors: HTTP 404 *Not Found* and HTTP 500 *Internal Server Error*. The Not Found status code will be rendered when the URL doesn't match any page and Internal Server Error is a page that we can display when an error occurs in the backend. Both pages will be implemented to show an error message.

Take a look at the error page in the following screenshot:

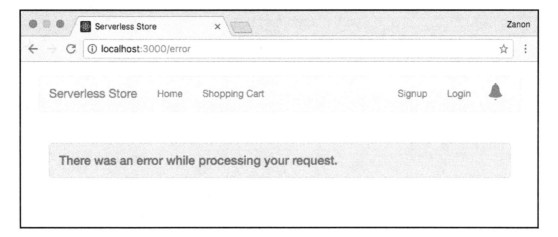

Take a look at the page not found in the following screenshot:

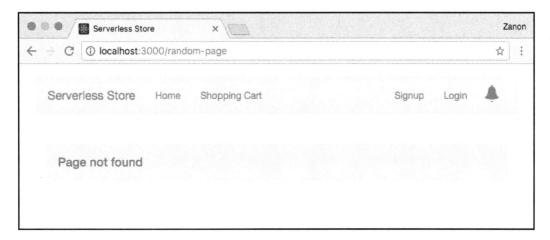

Summary

In this chapter, we have covered the basics of React to demonstrate how to use modern tools to build a serverless frontend. We discussed SPA and how to prerender pages to improve SEO. We have finished defining how to build the frontend of our Serverless Store.

In the next chapter, we will build the serverless backend of the online store, learning more about serverless architectures and RESTful APIs.

6
Developing the Backend

Developing the backend without servers is the main drive of the serverless concept and what makes it so interesting. In this model, a paradigm shift is to break the project into small pieces of logic that can be deployed separately instead of one single bloated application. How to architecture this separation is covered in this chapter. Also, we will continue the development of our serverless online store building the backend using the REST principles.

In a nutshell, we will cover the following topics:

- An overview of serverless architectures
- Organizing the project's code
- How to create RESTful services

After this chapter, you'll have built the backend of our serverless online store.

Defining the project architecture

In this section, we will cover four different architectural approaches for serverless projects:

- **Nanoservices**: This is where **each functionality** has its **own Lambda** function
- **Microservices**: This is where **each Lambda** handles **all HTTP verbs** of a single resource
- **Monolith**: This is where **one single Lambda** function handles **all functionalities**
- **Graph**: This uses the **GraphQL** standard, which is an alternative to REST APIs

As we will see, each architectural approach has its pros and cons and there is no *silver bullet*. You need to weigh the benefits and choose what you think is the best for your specific use case. Let's see more about them.

Monolith versus Microservices

The first thing that we need to think about when choosing a serverless architecture is if the application will execute with just one Lambda function (**Monolith** or **Graph**) or if it will have multiple Lambdas (**Microservices** or **Nanoservices**). The number of Lambda functions represents how many deployment units it has.

A monolith is a self-contained application where all functionalities are developed in a single solution and a modification in one piece of the code requires a new deployment of the whole solution.

The microservices architecture is the opposite. You have multiple units that can be deployed separately, where each one is responsible for a distinct part of the whole solution. To follow the microservices architecture, you need to add modularity to the application. You break a large application into a set of small services that can communicate with each other through HTTP requests.

Microservices uses the concept of bounded context. For example, in an online store, we have a context for **sales**, which represents all business rules related to selling products, and another context for **support**, which involves the features related with customer service. We can separate those concerns considering that they have different business rules and are able to evolve independently. Modifications in a support rule must not impact a sales feature, so you can deploy one service without deploying the other, which makes it easier for different teams to work in different contexts at the same time.

In general, microservices offer the following benefits:

- Better separation of concerns and modularity
- Independent and frequent deployment
- Easier parallel development using separated teams

As with everything else, it is accompanied with some drawbacks, which are as follows:

- More DevOps effort (which is mitigated by the Serverless Framework)
- A distributed system adds complexity
- Integration tests between multiple services are harder

Nanoservices

A nanoservice is the smallest part that you can extract from a monolithic application. You can split a monolith into multiple microservices, but those microservices can also be split into multiple nanoservices.

For example, you can have a **users** microservice that is responsible for handling all operations related with users such as create, retrieve, update, delete, password recovery, and others. *Retrieving* a user is a single functionality that can be very simple, implemented with less than 10 lines of code. If you create a Lambda function just for this piece of logic, you are creating a nanoservice.

The following diagram shows that each exposed functionality has its own Lambda function and an HTTP endpoint:

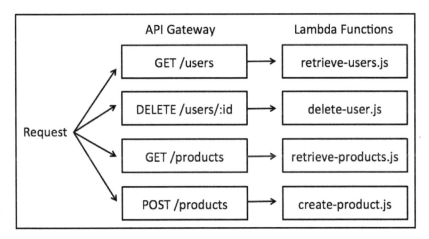

To build an application like this, we need to configure the `serverless.yml` file giving each function its own endpoint:

```
functions:
  retrieveUsers:
    handler: handlers.retrieveUsers
    events:
      - http: GET users
  deleteUser:
    handler: handlers.deleteUser
    events:
      - http: DELETE users
  retrieveProducts:
    handler: handlers.retrieveProducts
    events:
```

```
      - http: GET products
  createProduct:
    handler: handlers.createProduct
    events:
      - http: POST products
```

Due to simplicity, this example has ignored the OPTIONS verb that would be required in this solution because the browser, in cross-origin requests, preflights an OPTIONS request to check the CORS headers before executing POST, PUT, PATCH, and DELETE. We'll cover more about this later in this chapter.

For this architecture, we can list the pros and cons as follows:

Pros:

- Separation of concerns allows you to modify one feature without affecting other parts of your system. Autonomous teams will also benefit from a minimized number of conflicts.
- Debugging problems is much easier when a function has a single responsibility.

Cons:

- Performance can be slower. Since some functions will be rarely triggered, cold start delays will be more frequent.
- In a big project, you can end up with hundreds of functions! A huge number of logical parts may cause more harm than benefit.

Microservices

The microservices pattern adds modularization of functionalities related to the bounded context of an application. In this architecture, each Lambda function handles all HTTP verbs of a single resource. It generally results in having five endpoints (**GET, POST, PUT, DELETE, OPTIONS**) per function:

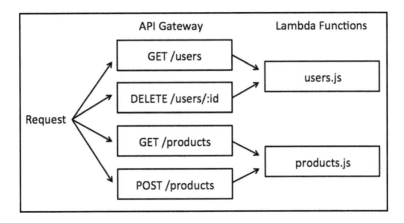

The preceding system can be defined by the `serverless.yml` file as two bounded contexts, where all HTTP verbs of a given context reference the same Lambda function:

```
functions:
  users:
    handler: handlers.users
    events:
      - http: GET users
      - http: DELETE users
  products:
    handler: handlers.products
    events:
      - http: GET products
      - http: POST products
```

This architecture has the following pros and cons:

Pros:

- Results in a reduced number of Lambda functions to manage
- With less cold starts, performance can be slightly better than nanoservices

Cons:

- Debugging is a little bit more complicated, since each function has more options and possible outcomes
- Requires implementing a routing mechanism to handle each request correctly

This routing mechanism can be implemented with a simple `switch...case` statement using the Lambda event to find the HTTP method and the REST resource:

```
module.exports.users = (event, context, callback) => {

  switch(`${event.httpMethod} ${event.resource}`) {
    case 'GET /users':
      users.retrieveUsers(callback);
      break;
    case 'DELETE /users':
      let id = JSON.parse(event.body).id;
      users.deleteUser(id, callback);
      break;
    default:
      // handle unexpected path
  }
};
```

Monolith

The monolith pattern uses just one Lambda function to handle all functionalities of our application. In this case, we have all of the application's endpoints triggering the same Lambda function:

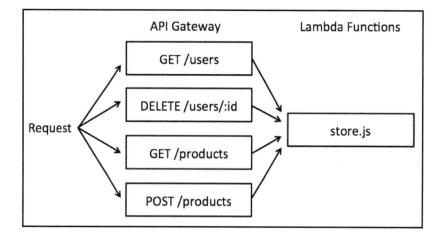

The preceding example can be represented as follows:

```
functions:
  store:
    handler: handler.store
    events:
      - http: GET users
      - http: DELETE users
      - http: GET products
      - http: POST products
```

A monolith architecture is not necessarily bad. For small applications that need to minimize cold delays, it can be indeed the best option. Let's now look at the pros and cons.

Pros:

- When all endpoints use the same Lambda function, the code will be constantly cached and cold starts will hardly happen
- Fast deployments as there is just one resource

Cons:

- Requires building a complex routing system to handle each request, for big applications, it can be transformed in a *big ball of mud*
- If the code base grows too much with too many dependencies, the performance of a single execution will be reduced
- Debugging problems will be much more difficult
- It's much harder to provision memory and set timeouts since each code path has a distinct execution

Graph

The Graph pattern is based on the GraphQL standard that was proposed by Facebook. It is an emerging technology with the objective to provide an alternative to RESTful APIs. Since it is growing in popularity among serverless projects, it deserves a section in this book.

In this pattern, we have just one Lambda function with a single endpoint. This endpoint is a query that will trigger the GraphQL to fetch the corresponding data in any form that the client needs:

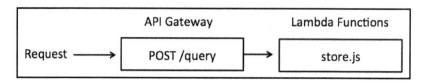

 Having just one endpoint is not a restriction. You can have multiple endpoints, but the objective of this pattern is to reduce the number of interfaces.

The `serverless.yml` file is very simplified:

```
functions:
  store:
    handler: handler.store
    events:
      - http: POST query
```

Here, we will see a simple example of how to build a GraphQL API inside a Lambda function. Let's take a look at the following steps:

1. Install the GraphQL module (`npm install graphql --save`) and require it inside the `handler.js` function:

```
const { graphql, buildSchema } = require('graphql');
```

2. The next step is to describe how your data is organized. In the following example, we have a `ShoppingCart` entity which contains a list of `Products` that the user wants to buy. The object key is the property name and the value is its data type. The schema is a string input that will be compiled by the `buildSchema` function:

```
const schema = buildSchema(`
  type Query {
    cart: ShoppingCart
  }

  type ShoppingCart {
    products: [Product],
    promotionCode: String,
    discountPercentage: Int
```

```
    }

    type Product {
       name: String,
       code: String,
       quantity: Int,
       price: Int
    }
`);
```

The `decimal` data type is not a built-in data type, but you can count money in pennies instead of dollars with the `integer` type. GraphQL offers the `float` data type, but it is not reliable for handling currencies.

3. Now, take a look in this JSON object that follows the defined schema:

```
const data = {
  "cart": {
    "products": [
      {
        "name": "Lonely Bird",
        "code": "FOO",
        "quantity": 1,
        "price": 2999
      },
      {
        "name": "Solid Friendship",
        "code": "BAR",
        "quantity": 1,
        "price": 1999
      }
    ],
    promotionCode: null,
    discountPercentage: 0
  }
};
```

In this example, the entire dataset will be provided as an input to the `graphql` function through the `data` variable. However, in a real-world application, it would not be feasible to load the entire database to memory. What is done in this case is to define a resolver function in the schema definition that tells the GraphQL engine how to fetch the required data, which means how to query the database.

4. After defining how your data is structured and where it is, you can use `graphql` to query the data. This query will be defined by the client and will be available in the `event` input of the Lambda function. For example, consider this query sent by the client:

```
const query = `{
  cart {
    products {
      name
      quantity
      price
    }
    discountPercentage
  }
}`;
```

 In this query, the client wants to know the list of selected products, but there is some information that the client is not interested in. For example, the client doesn't want to know the `code` of the products or whether there is a `promotionCode` associated with this cart.

5. To use it in a Lambda function, call the `graphql` function passing the `schema`, `query`, and `data` arguments:

```
module.exports.store = (event, context, callback) => {

  const query = JSON.parse(event.body);

  graphql(schema, query, data).then((resp) => {

    const response = {
      statusCode: 200,
      body: JSON.stringify(resp)
    };

    callback(null, response);
  });
};
```

6. A request to this function would return the following JSON object:

```
{
  "data": {
    "cart": {
      "products": [
        {
          "name": "Lonely Bird",
          "quantity": 1,
          "price": 2999
        },
        {
          "name": "Solid Friendship",
          "quantity": 1,
          "price": 1999
        }
      ],
      discountPercentage: 0
    }
  }
}
```

What makes GraphQL powerful is its simple syntax, that allows the client to request exactly what it needs and receive that data in the format that it expects. In this model, a single request can bring data from multiple resources. It can be an interesting alternative to RESTful APIs, but it also has its limitations. Ignoring the pros and cons related to REST, the following list compares the Graph pattern as a solution for a serverless architecture:

Pros:

- The Graph query can be a better replacement for the routing mechanism of the monolithic approach
- When all endpoints use the same Lambda function, the code will be constantly cached and cold starts will hardly happen
- Fast deployments as there is just one function and one endpoint

Cons:

- The Lambda size may hurt the performance if the code base grows too much with too many dependencies
- It's much harder to provision memory and set timeouts since each query has a distinct execution

GraphQL has many other features and requires extensive material, which is not the focus of this book. For a start, you can learn more at http://graphql.org/learn.

Naming differences

The Serverless Framework's team shares a similar view of the serverless architectures, which you can check out at `https://serverless.com/blog/serverless-architecture-code-patterns`.

However, what I call "nanoservices", they call "microservices". In my opinion, microservice is not a good term to describe the architecture style where every single feature is considered as one microservice. The concept of microservices was created to designate monolithic applications that were broken down into a few distinct pieces to better handle the management and evolution of features. When you have too many pieces, the principles do not apply so easily. Fortunately, the Serverless Framework makes it easier to handle dozens of services, but for a traditional application, when a microservice is too fine-grained, the overhead of maintenance and communication overweighs its benefits and, for the purpose of differentiation, it is called here a nanoservice.

Also, note that they have named the pattern that I call "microservices" as "services". You can name these patterns as you prefer, but understand that those terms can be confusing.

The following diagram illustrates the difference between **Monolith**, **Microservices**, and **Nanoservices** architectures in my point of view:

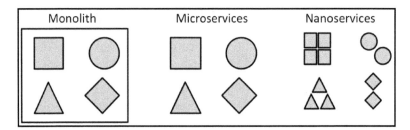

Developing the backend

After this overview of architectures, we can start building the backend. In this sample, which is only an experiment, I've opted for the monolith architecture because it reduces the cold start delays and our backend logic is very small. In your solution, you need to think about the use cases and weigh the benefits and drawbacks of each option.

Defining the functionalities

In the previous chapter, we developed the frontend and hardcoded some data to display static pages. Now, we are going to create the backend to expose the necessary information that will be used by the frontend. Take a look at the following frontend views and what functionalities they will need from the backend:

1. **Home page**: This page requires a list of all available products to display
2. **Product details**: This page requires the detailed information about a product, including the list of user comments
3. **Shopping Cart**: This page needs to display the selected products and allow the user to save or checkout the cart
4. **Signup page**: The logic of this page will be implemented in Chapter 8, *Securing the Serverless Application*
5. **Login page**: The logic of this page will also be implemented in Chapter 8, *Securing the Serverless Application*
6. **Page not found**: There is no need to request the backend when the URL is invalid
7. **Error page**: This page won't make any additional request to the backend when an error occurs

Besides those pages, we have a Navbar component that will be displayed for all pages and it has a notification icon. We are going to implement this feature in Chapter 9, *Handling Serverless Notifications*.

In a nutshell, we need to implement now the following functionalities:

1. Retrieve all available products to sell
2. Retrieve the details of a specific product
3. Retrieve the list of selected products of the user's Shopping Cart
4. Save the list of selected products
5. Checkout a Shopping Cart

To make it simpler, second and third features will be provided in the result of the first feature, which means that when the user requests the list of all available products, the response object will bring all information about each product, as well as the information on whether the user has added the product to the Shopping Cart.

Organizing the code

Choosing how to organize the files of a project is a personal choice. You just need to place the files using meaningful names that will make it easier to find them later. In this project, I've used the following structure:

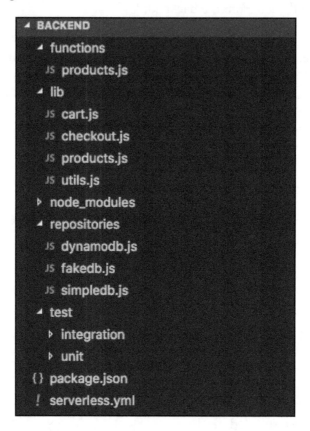

Here's a brief description about each folder shown in the preceding screenshot:

- `functions`: These are the Lambda functions that will be directly deployed to AWS. We have just one function because our application is a monolith. This function will handle all things related to products. We don't need a Lambda function to handle user creation/authentication because we are going to use Cognito for this task.
- `lib`: This is the common application logic that can be used by different Lambda functions.

- `node_modules`: These are Node dependencies that were installed in this project folder and are referenced by the `package.json` file. They will be zipped to be used by the Lambda functions.
- `repositories`: This folder holds the infrastructure code to connect with the database and define the queries. It will be implemented in `Chapter 7`, *Using a Serverless Database*. In the screenshot, you can see that we are going to implement queries for SimpleDB and DynamoDB. The FakeDB will be used in this chapter to provide hardcoded data for testing.
- `test`: This folder holds the unit and integration test files. It will be implemented in `Chapter 10`, *Testing, Deploying, and Monitoring*.

Referencing Lambda functions in other folders

When you create a new service with the Serverless Framework, it will create a `serverless.yml` file to reference a sample function:

```
functions:
  hello:
    handler: handler.hello
```

What you should note here is that `handler.hello` means that the Serverless Framework will try to find a `handler.js` file in the *same directory* as your `serverless.yml` file and look for an exported `hello` function. When you have a big project, you may prefer to separate your handler functions in subfolders. The syntax is pretty straightforward, `foldername/file.function`.

Consider the following example:

```
functions:
  hello:
    handler: subfolder/handler.hello
  goodbye:
    handler: lambdas/greetings.bye
```

In this project, I've used the following code:

```
functions:
  products:
    handler: functions/products.handler
```

Using multiple services

Another thing that you should note is that the Serverless Framework will create a ZIP folder only with the contents that are in the same level of the serverless.yml file or lower. It is not possible to include dependencies of upper levels. The implication is that if your project uses two different services, each one of them with a distinct serverless.yml file, you can't share dependencies directly between them.

The following screenshot illustrates an example of a project with this issue:

The greetings.js file is a simple Node.js module with just one line of code:

```
module.exports.saySomething = () => 'hello';
```

Both the handler.js files from service1 and service2 were implemented to return a message using the greetings module:

```
const response = {
  statusCode: 200,
  body: JSON.stringify({
    message: greetings.saySomething()
  })
};
```

The only difference between them is how the greetings module is loaded. In the first service, as it is in the same level, we load using the following code:

```
const greetings = require('./greetings');
```

In the second service, we need to reference the `service1` file:

```
const greetings = require('../service1/greetings');
```

If you test the `service2` function locally (`serverless invoke local --function hello`), it will run without problems, but it will fail if deployed to AWS because the ZIP file will not be published with the dependency.

The following are two solutions for this problem:

- Avoid using several services. Aggregate them into a single service and place the merged `serverless.yml` file in the project root.
- Use local npm packages to manage common dependencies.

Although I prefer the first option, the second option is also valid. To create a local npm package, browse to the folder that contains the common dependencies and run the following command:

npm pack

This command will create a zipped package with the exact same format that would be created for a public npm module.

Now, in the folder that contains your serverless service, install the package locally using the following command:

npm install ../path/to/pack.tgz

 You need to repeat this process every time that the common dependency is modified. If it is constantly updated, you would need to include this stage into your build workflow.

Setting the endpoints

As we already know, we need to create the API Gateway endpoints to expose to the world our serverless functions. This is done in the `serverless.yml` file, and the following example shows how to create the endpoints for the serverless store:

```
functions:
  products:
    handler: functions/products.handler
    events:
      - http: GET products
```

```
- http: POST cart      # create the cart (new order)
- http: OPTIONS cart
- http: PUT checkout   # update the order (status = sent)
- http: OPTIONS checkout
```

Setting an OPTIONS endpoint is mandatory in cases where you want to support the POST, PUT, PATCH, or DELETE verbs in a cross-origin request. The reason is a security measure used by browsers, that is, before making an HTTP request that can modify the resource, it preflights a request with OPTIONS to check whether CORS is enabled and whether the HTTP verb is allowed.

RESTful APIs

If you are not already familiar with RESTful APIs, you should know at least the following common HTTP verbs and how they are used:

- GET: This is used to request data to the server
- POST: This is used to create or modify resources:
    - POST/resource: Without an ID, a new element will be created
    - POST/resource/id: If you know the ID and pass it in the request, the element will be updated, however, it is typically used only to create and not to update resources
    - POST/resource/new-id: If there is no resource for a given ID, this request must return an error
- PUT: This is used to create or modify the following resources:
    - PUT/resource: This should return an error because the ID is expected
    - PUT/resource/id: This replaces the entire object with the data provided
    - PUT/resource/new-id: If there is no resource for a given ID, it will be created
- PATCH: This is used to do partial updates, instead of replacing the entire resource with the given data, it won't update or remove properties that do not match with the input
- DELETE: This is used to delete resources and an ID must be provided
- OPTIONS: This returns the allowed HTTP verbs and informs if CORS is enabled

Routing the HTTP verbs

As already exemplified, for our routing strategy, we can use a switch...case statement using httpMethod and resource to identify the path. I suggest adding a try...catch statement to warn the client about unexpected errors instead of letting Lambda swallow the messages.

The following example shows how to implement the routes for the products function:

```
module.exports.handler = (event, context, callback) => {

  const userId = '1'; // TODO: retrieve from authentication headers
  try {
    switch(`${event.httpMethod} ${event.resource}`) {
      case 'GET /products':
        products.retrieveAll(userId, callback);
        break;
      case 'POST /cart':
        const selectedProducts = JSON.parse(event.body).products;
        cart.saveCart(userId, selectedProducts, callback);
        break;
      case 'OPTIONS /cart':
        utils.optionsHandler(callback);
        break;
      case 'PUT /checkout':
        const id = JSON.parse(event.body).id;
        checkout.processCheckout(id, callback);
        break;
      case 'OPTIONS /checkout':
        utils.optionsHandler(callback);
        break;
      default:
        utils.notFoundHandler(callback);
    }
  } catch (err) {
    utils.errorHandler(err, callback);
  }
};
```

 Remember that you need to run serverless deploy to create the Lambda function and endpoints, but after that, the command serverless deploy function --function products can be used for a faster deployment.

The next section will explain how the utils module was created to handle the responses.

Handling HTTP responses

Usually, we need to handle at least four response types:

1. **Success**: Return HTTP 200 OK when the request is processed successfully.
2. **Error**: Return HTTP 500 Internal Server Error when an error happens in the backend.
3. **Not found**: Return HTTP 404 Not Found when the client requests a resource that doesn't exist.
4. **Options**: Return HTTP 200 OK along with the allowed methods for this resource.

There are many other HTTP status codes, like 400 Bad Request when the client sends a request without the necessary parameters, but covering an extensive list of status codes is out of the scope of this book and most of them are not used in the majority of applications.

The following code snippet shows how to implement those handlers:

```
const corsHeaders = {
  'Access-Control-Allow-Origin': '*'
};

module.exports.successHandler = (obj, callback) => {
  callback(null, {
    statusCode: 200,
    headers: corsHeaders,
    body: JSON.stringify(obj)
  });
};

module.exports.errorHandler = (err, callback) => {
  callback(null, {
    statusCode: 500,
    headers: corsHeaders,
    body: JSON.stringify({
      message: 'Internal Server Error',
      error: err.toString()
    })
  });
};

module.exports.notFoundHandler = (callback) => {
  callback(null, {
    statusCode: 404,
    headers: corsHeaders,
    body: JSON.stringify({ message: 'Not Found' })
  });
```

```
    };
```

Regarding the OPTIONS verb, we need to answer the requests with the status code 200 OK and set the allowed methods and headers:

```
module.exports.optionsHandler = (callback) => {
  callback(null, {
    statusCode: 200,
    headers: {
      "Access-Control-Allow-Origin": "*",
      "Access-Control-Allow-Methods":
        "GET, POST, PUT, PATCH, DELETE, OPTIONS",
      "Access-Control-Allow-Headers":
        "Accept, Content-Type, Origin"
    }
  });
};
```

Implementing the Lambda functions

In this section, we are going to see how to implement the backend features. After implementing and deploying the Lambda functions, we can modify the frontend code to make Ajax requests to the backend.

Retrieving all products

This feature has the following three responsibilities:

- Retrieve all products from the products table
- Retrieve all user comments/ratings and join them with the product list
- Retrieve the user Shopping Cart and merge with the product list to identify what products were already selected

Those queries will be created and executed by repository and its implementation will be defined in the next Chapter 7, *Managing a Serverless Database*.

By now, let's use the FakeDB to return hardcoded values:

```
const db = require('../repositories/fakedb');
const utils = require('./utils');

module.exports.retrieveAll = (userId, callback) => {
  db.retrieveAllProducts(userId, (err, res) => {
```

```
      if (err) utils.errorHandler(err, callback);
      else utils.successHandler(res, callback);
   });
};
```

In this case, the FakeDB will just return a list of products:

```
module.exports.retrieveAllProducts = (userId, callback) => {
   const comments = [{
      id: 1,
      username: "John Doe",
      age: "3 days ago",
      text: "I'm using this to decorate my desk. I liked it."
   }];

   const products = [{
      id: "lonely-bird",
      name: "Lonely Bird",
      image: 'https://s3.amazonaws.com/...',
      price: 29.99,
      isSelected: yes,
      comments: comments
   }];

   callback(null, products);
};
```

Saving the Shopping Cart

This request receives as the input a list of selected products and the UserID. In our sample application, the UserID will uniquely identify the shopping cart, which means that each user has just one cart.

If the user is logged in, the frontend knows the UserID. However, we can't receive an ID directly from the client and take actions trusting that this information is valid. We know that a malicious user can modify the JavaScript code to send an ID of another user.

For a reliable operation, we must analyze the authentication tokens that are passed through the headers of all requests from logged users and check if the ID is correct. This step will be implemented in Chapter 8, *Securing the Serverless Application*.

Checking out

Handling payments is a complex feature that won't be covered in this book. So, when the user tries to checkout the Shopping Cart, a message will be displayed to show that this is just a demo application.

However, we can use this feature to learn how serverless notifications work. When the user starts a payment process, the backend receives the credit card information and makes a request to process the payment. As this step can take a long time, instead of using the client to make repetitive requests (polling), we can use WebSockets to notify the user when the response is available. Serverless notifications will be covered using IoT in Chapter 9, *Handling Serverless Notifications*.

Summary

In this chapter, you have learned the serverless architectures such as nanoservices, microservices, monolith, and Graph. For our serverless store, the monolith architecture was selected and used to build the backend. We also covered how to structure the project's code and build RESTful APIs.

In the next chapter, you will learn about the SimpleDB serverless database. Due to the fact that SimpleDB may not be good enough for most applications, we are also going to learn about DynamoDB, which is not a serverless database, but requires minimal management.

7
Managing a Serverless Database

A serverless database is defined like any other serverless service: it needs to have *high availability*, *high scalability*, and the pricing model must consider its *real usage*. Satisfying those conditions is particularly hard for databases since *performance* is a key feature. For a predictable and high performance, databases are usually configured in their own dedicated servers, but serverless requires a shared model to avoid charging the customer for 100% of the time the database is available. In serverless, we want to pay only when a request is done and not when the database is in an idle state.

Currently, only a few services have managed to bring the serverless model to databases. AWS offers just one service: SimpleDB, but it lacks many important features and is extremely limited. For other and better options, you can try FaunaDB, Google Firebase, or Google Cloud Datastore. To continue to use AWS services in this book, we are going to cover DynamoDB, which is an almost serverless database.

Furthermore, we'll see how to use Amazon S3 to store media files since, in most cases, it's better to save files in a cheap storage system than a database server.

In this chapter, we will cover the following topics:

- Using and managing SimpleDB and DynamoDB databases
- Using Amazon S3 to store media files

When you finish this chapter, you'll have implemented the data access layer of the online store and acquired the necessary knowledge to use serverless databases.

Amazon SimpleDB

SimpleDB is an old service (late 2007), and it is the only one offered by AWS that can really be called a serverless database. AWS offers many other managed databases, such as DynamoDB or RDS, but all of them require that you set provisions and pay for 24 hours a day, even when no one is using your system. You *do* need to worry about the servers when you need to constantly check whether the capacity is well designed for your traffic.

SimpleDB is serverless for the following reasons:

- **Totally managed by AWS**: You don't need to spin-up a machine and install/configure a DBMS.
- **Highly available**: AWS manages multiple geographically distributed replicas of your database to enable high availability and data durability.
- **Scalable**: You can grow in size very fast without worrying about provisioning.
- **Cost-efficient**: You pay for the amount of data stored, data transferred, and the CPU time used to run queries. If no one is using the database, you pay only for what is currently stored.

SimpleDB is a NoSQL database, but unfortunately, it is very limited due to the absence of important functionalities. For example, the only data type that you can use is a string. This makes it harder for you to implement a lot of use cases, but we will cover some hacks here to make it feasible. If your application is somewhat complex, I would avoid using SimpleDB. Use it only for small applications.

Modeling the database

First, a little bit of nomenclature: a *domain*, in SimpleDB, is the equivalent of a *table* in the relational world and an *item* is the equivalent of a *row*. They are pretty equivalent, but you need to know what they mean to understand SDK functions. Also, in SimpleDB, each *item* has a list of attribute-value pairs, where the *attribute* is like a *column* and the values are always of the string data type.

For a practical example, we will model the database for the serverless store. We are going to use just two domains such as `Products` and `ShoppingCart`. We will not create a domain to save user account data (e-mail, password, and others) because we are going to use Amazon Cognito in the next chapter and Cognito is responsible for saving and managing user data.

The following table lists the attributes for the `Products` domain. All of them will be created to hold strings due to a SimpleDB restriction, but I've added what would be the ideal data type. And, in the next sections, we will see how to handle this limitation:

Attribute	Desired data type
ID	String
Name	String
Price	Decimal
Image	String
Comments	Array of documents

Some observations about this model are as follows:

- `ID`: The `ID` attribute could be defined as an integer, but I've defined it as a string since we are using the ID in the URL. Instead of showing the URL as `store.com/product/123`, we are using `store.com/product/lonely-bird`.
- `Price`: The `Price` attribute will be saved as a string, although we wanted to save it as a number.
- `Image`: The `Image` attribute will be saved as a string because we will save the URL of a S3 object instead of saving the entire object in the database.
- `Comments`: The `Comments` attribute needs a relation of **one-to-many**, where *one* product has *many* comments. Some NoSQL databases, such as MongoDB, have an "array of documents" data type, which would be helpful here.

The `Comments` field will be a list of:

Attribute	Desired data type
ID	Integer
Username	String
Date	DateTime
Text	String

This model requires other observations:

- The `ID` attribute could be defined as an integer where the `ID` of every new comment would be the value of the last saved comment `ID` plus one unit. However, SimpleDB doesn't offer any feature for auto-incrementing a field. To avoid needing to query the last comment `ID` before saving a new comment, and the conflicts it would cause due to the lack of transactions, we can use this attribute to save an **Universally Unique Identifier (UUID)** as a string value.
- The `Date` attribute will be discussed later.

The following table lists the attributes for the `ShoppingCart` domain:

Attribute	Desired data type
UserID	String
LastUpdate	DateTime
SelectedProducts	Array of documents

As we are going to use Amazon Cognito, the `UserID` was defined as a string. The only problem with this model is that we want a field to store a datetime and another to store an array of data, where `SelectedProducts` are defined by a list of `ProductID` and `Quantity` pairs.

Handling one-to-many relations

In the previous models, we saw that *one* product has *many* comments and *one* cart has *many* selected products. In a relational database, we would model another table to list all comments or selected products and we would use the `join` operator to retrieve all related data when querying for a specific product or cart. However, in NoSQL, we usually don't have a `join` operator so we need to make two separated queries to retrieve what we need *or* we can save all related data in just one field as an array of documents.

In SimpleDB, we don't have an "array of documents" data type, but we have two other options:

- Save a stringified array of JSON objects
- Multi-valued attributes

The first option is a hacky solution where you can stringify an array of JavaScript objects and save it in a single attribute. The problem is that you won't be able to query attributes in this field, so forget queries such as "How many distinct users have ordered ProductID lonely-bird?".

The second option is the best solution since SimpleDB allows you to have multiple attributes with the same name. Take a look at the following dataset for the `ShoppingCart` that uses multi-valued attributes:

UserID	LastUpdate	ProductID	QuantityX	ProductID	QuantityY	ProductID	QuantityZ
A	`<Date>`	X	2	Y	2	Z	4
B	`<Date>`	X	3				
C	`<Date>`	X	1	Y	5		

The `ProductID` attribute repeats with the same name multiple times and this is not an issue because SimpleDB allows two attributes with the same name. What SimpleDB does not allow is two attributes with the same name *and* value. In the first item (`UserID` with value A), we have a `ProductID` with value X and a `ProductID` with value Y, which is valid. The problem would be with the `Quantity` attributes, since two of them have value 2 in the same item. To fix this problem, the `ProductID` value was appended to the attribute name, creating the attributes `QuantityX` and `QuantityY`.

> The SimpleDB domain is schemaless, which means that, when you insert a new item, you say what attributes it has and it won't return an error if you add an attribute name that doesn't exist yet.

Handling numbers

The biggest issue with SimpleDB is not about how to store data as a string but how to retrieve it using queries. You can save the number 27 as `"27"`, but filtering a query with `Quantity > "5"` would not return the desired value.

A solution to handle numerical data as a string is to modify it before saving. Instead of saving `"27"`, use a zero-padding function and store it as `"000027"`. Now query it with `Quantity > "000005"` and you will get the value that you want.

How many zeros do you need to add? It depends. Think about the largest number that your dataset can reach and zero-pad all the other numbers to have the same number of characters.

This trick works for integers. If you have a decimal, as in the `Price` attribute, you need to multiply it by the number of decimal places. In this case, multiply it per 100 before saving the value and divide it by 100 when you retrieve it.

Another issue is handling negative numbers. In this case, you need to add an offset. This offset must be greater than the largest negative number of your entire dataset. For example, if your offset is `100,000`, the value `-27` must be added to `100,000` (resulting in `99973`) and zero-padded with six places, resulting in `"099973"`. If you need to compare whether the number is greater than `5`, you will need to add the offset and zero-pad the comparison value, resulting in `Quantity > "100005"`.

Handling Booleans

You can store Boolean values as either `true`/`false` or 1/0. You can select what you prefer, just define a convention and use the same strategy in all Boolean attributes.

Here's an example of this:

```
const boolean = true;

// save 'true' in the database
const booleanStr = boolean.toString();

// convert 'true' (string) to true (boolean)
const booleanAgain = Boolean(booleanStr);
```

Handling dates

When saving a datetime variable, you can use the ISO 8601 standard format, for example, `5:15:10 PM December 24th 2016 UTC` becomes `2016-12-24T17:15:10.000Z`. This format is queryable using strings. So `Date > "2016-12-24T00:00:00.000Z"` will return the value of the previous example.

Now consider that you have a `LastAccess` attribute and you want to query all the users that accessed your system in the last 5 minutes. In this case, you just need to find the current time, subtract it by 5 minutes, and convert it into the ISO string before querying.

Creating a domain

Creating a domain is pretty straightforward. You just need to set the domain name as the parameter and it will be created with the `createDomain` function.

Here's an example of this:

```
const AWS = require('aws-sdk');
const simpledb = new AWS.SimpleDB();

const params = {
  DomainName: 'Products'
};

simpledb.createDomain(params, (err, data) => {
  if (err) console.log(err, err.stack);
  else console.log(data);
});
```

Regarding the attributes, you don't need to specify them while creating the domain. There is no schema attached. Each item has its own list of attributes that are not necessarily the same as the other attributes.

Limits

SimpleDB was designed for small workloads, so AWS has enforced some limits that may restrict your application. In the following table, I've listed the most important limits that you should be aware of before using SimpleDB in your system. You can find more about this in the official documentation at `http://docs.aws.amazon.com/AmazonSimpleDB/late st/DeveloperGuide/SDBLimits.html`:

Parameter	Restriction
Domain size	10 GB per domain
Domain size	1 billion attributes per domain
Attribute value length	1,024 bytes
Maximum items in the `Select` response	2,500
Maximum query execution time	5 seconds
Maximum response size of `Select`	1 MB

Inserting and querying data

The following example shows how to insert data into a SimpleDB domain. I'm using `batchPutAttributes` because it allows multiple inserts simultaneously, but you could call `putAttributes` to insert a single item:

```
const AWS = require('aws-sdk');
const simpledb = new AWS.SimpleDB();

const insertParams = {
  DomainName: 'Products',
  Items: [
    {
      Attributes: [
        {
          Name: 'Name',
          Value: 'Lonely Bird'
        },
        {
          Name: 'Price',
          Value: '2999'
        },
        // more attributes
      ],
      // needs to be unique
      Name: 'lonely-bird'
    },
    // more items
  ]
};

simpledb.batchPutAttributes(insertParams, (err, data) => {
  if (err) console.log(err, err.stack);
  else console.log(data);
});
```

The following example shows how to query the data that was previously inserted. Despite being a NoSQL database, SimpleDB uses a SQL-like syntax for queries:

```
const AWS = require('aws-sdk');
const simpledb = new AWS.SimpleDB();

const selectParams = {
  SelectExpression:
    'select * from Products where Name = "Lonely Bird"'
};
```

```
simpledb.select(selectParams, (err, data) => {
  if (err) console.log(err, err.stack);
  else if (data.Items) {
    data.Items.map(item => {
      item.Attributes.map(attr => {
        console.log(attr);
      });
    });
  }
  else console.log('No results');
});
```

The preceding code will generate the following output:

```
{ Name: 'Name', Value: 'Lonely Bird' }
{ Name: 'Price', Value: '2999' }
```

Performance and concurrency

AWS will automatically create an index for every attribute that you create, but querying data filtering by dates or integers converted into strings can easily lead to performance issues. You should always be careful of your performance requirements and the size of your domain.

Also, like most NoSQL databases, SimpleDB doesn't support transactions, so concurrency can be a real problem for data consistency. Instead of transactions, SimpleDB offers *conditional operations*. For example, if you need to insert some data, you can place a condition that will execute the operation only if the attribute does not exist yet. Another use case is to implement a counter. You will update the value of the counter to X+1 only if the current value is X. If this condition is not met, it's because another user have already incremented the value and your update will be canceled.

Here's an example of a conditional operation:

```
const AWS = require('aws-sdk');
const simpledb = new AWS.SimpleDB();

const params = {
  Attributes: [
    {
      Name: 'Counter',
      Value: '10', // new value
      Replace: true
    }
  ],
```

```
      DomainName: 'MyCounter',
      ItemName: '123', // identifier
      Expected: {
        Exists: true,
        Name: 'Counter',
        Value: '9' // previous value
      }
    };

    simpledb.putAttributes(params, (err, data) => {
      if (err) console.log(err, err.stack);
      else console.log(data);
    });
```

Managing the database

You can manage your database using the AWS CLI or SDK, but many people prefer to use a tool that provides a user interface. Since AWS doesn't offer a console for SimpleDB, we need to rely on third-party tools. In this case, I can recommend the Chrome extension SdbNavigator. It's a very simple tool but offers a nice user interface with the essential features such as creating domains, inserting items, and making queries.

Take a look at the following steps for managing the database:

1. Using Chrome, you can add the extension from `https://chrome.google.com/webstore/detail/sdbnavigator/ddhigekdfabonefhiildaiccafacphgg`.

2. After installing it, add your AWS keys and select a region to connect. You can add a new domain with the **Add domain** button:

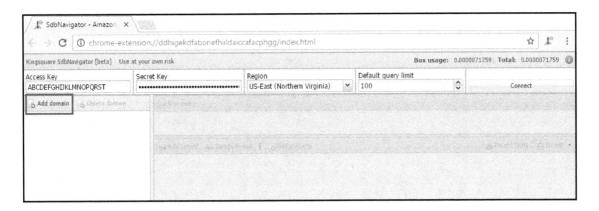

3. This tool has a button to add properties. When you add a new item, these properties will become the items' attributes:

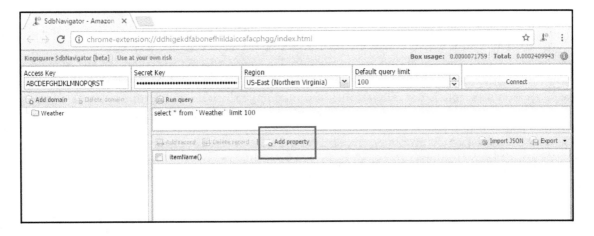

4. The **Add record** button is used to add your domain items:

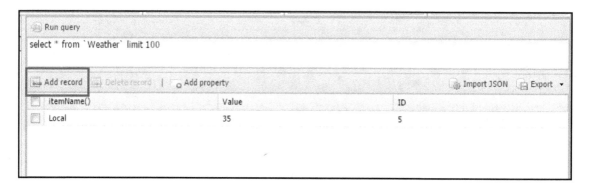

Backing up and restoring data

Unfortunately, there is no native AWS feature to consistently back up and restore SimpleDB domains. The solution is to make queries that will read all of the data (backup) and scripts to insert (restore) this saved data when needed. However, the main issue is consistency. If your application is running while you are copying the data, there is no guarantee that your backup would be consistent. The application may have started a delete operation and your backup may still have some part of the items that should have been deleted.

Besides this consistency problem, you still have issues with copying/inserting data since AWS places many limits on this operation. For example, the maximum number of items in `select` is 2,500 items. To solve this second problem, you can try one of the many third-party tools available to mitigate this burden.

Controlling user access

SimpleDB relies on the AWS security model. So if you want to manage access, you will need to create IAM users and roles. The granularity of this control lies in the domains your users can access and the actions they can execute.

In our Lambda functions, we *must* give permissions *explicitly*. You can't execute a SimpleDB request without setting the restrictions. This configuration is done in the `serverless.yml` file under the `iamRoleStatements` function. In the following example, I'm giving read (`sdb:Select`) and write (`sdb:PutAttributes`) access to the `Products` and `ShoppingCart` domains. If you want to allow full access, use the `"sdb:*"` action and set the domain with `domain/*`:

```
service: simpledb-example

provider:
  name: aws
  runtime: nodejs6.10
  iamRoleStatements:
    - Effect: "Allow"
      Action:
        - "sdb:BatchPutAttributes"
        - "sdb:PutAttributes"
        - "sdb:Select"
      Resource: [
        "arn:aws:sdb:us-east-1:*:domain/Products",
        "arn:aws:sdb:us-east-1:*:domain/ShoppingCart"
      ]

functions:
  query:
    handler: handler.query
```

DynamoDB

DynamoDB is a fully managed, NoSQL database with high availability and that can be configured to scale automatically. The only reason that it can't be considered as a serverless database is due to its pricing model. You must pay for provisioned resources even if no one is using your application.

However, DynamoDB is a great database, with many useful features, and AWS offers a generous permanent free tier. It is being extensively used in many serverless projects because it is cheap, easy to use and offers predictable performance. In this book, we are going to use DynamoDB as our main database. If you browse this chapters' code files, you will see the data layer of the serverless store implemented with SimpleDB and DynamoDB, but DynamoDB will be the default and the database where we will discuss here what features needs to be implemented for the serverless store.

Modeling the database

In DynamoDB, a *table* is a collection of *items* and each item is a collection of key-value pairs called *attributes*. Like most NoSQL databases, DynamoDB is *schemaless*. You just need to define the primary key and you can add items with different attributes.

DynamoDB supports the following data types:

- **Scalar**: Category of data types that store a single value:
    - String: UTF-8 strings with a maximum size of 400 KB.
    - Number: It stores a maximum of 38 digits and accepts negative numbers as well.
    - Boolean: It stores true or false.
    - Binary: It allows binary data to be saved. Due to maximum size of 400 KB, it may not be a good choice for many applications. We are going to use S3 to store product images and a String field in DynamoDB to save the S3 URL.
    - Null: It represents an attribute with an unknown or undefined state.
- **Document**: It is a category of data types that store multiple values:
    - List: It stores an *ordered* collection of values. It's similar to an array where you can store elements of any type. Example: [5, "foo", 2, -4, "bar"].
    - Map: It stores an *unordered* collection of values. It's similar to JSON object. Example: { "Name": "foo", "Address": 123 }.
- **Set**: It's a data type where you store data as an array, but all elements must be unique and of the same data type. Also, the order is not preserved. Example: a set of numbers could be [1, 7, 2, -4].

For the serverless store, we need to create two tables such as Products and ShoppingCart. They will be defined as the following:

- Products: Take a look at the following table depicting its attributes:

Attribute	Data Type
ID	String
Name	String
Price	Number

Image	String
Comments	List of Maps

- `Comments`: Take a look at the following table depicting its attributes:

Attribute	Data Type
ID	String
Username	String
Date	String
Text	String

- `ShoppingCart`: Take a look at the following table depicting its attributes:

Attribute	Data Type
UserID	String
LastUpdate	String
SelectedProducts	List of Maps

- `SelectedProducts`: Take a look at the following table depicting its attributes:

Attribute	Data Type
ProductID	String
Quantity	Number

Some observations about this model are as follows:

- The `Comments` and `SelectedProducts` attributes were defined as a list of map objects, which means that we will save an ordered list of JSON objects
- Just like SimpleDB, there is no auto-increment field for DynamoDB, so we will use UUIDs for the Comment IDs
- DynamoDB doesn't support a datetime data type, so we will need to define the `Date` and `LastUpdate` attributes as a string that uses the ISO format

Creating a table

We are going to create the tables for the serverless store using the AWS SDK. As
DynamoDB is a schemaless database, we just need to set the primary key and the attributes
will be defined when the items are inserted.

Use the following example to create them:

```
const AWS = require('aws-sdk');
const dynamodb = new AWS.DynamoDB();

let params = {
  TableName: 'Products',
  AttributeDefinitions: [
    {
      AttributeName: 'ID',
      AttributeType: 'S' // string
    }
  ],
  KeySchema: [
    {
      AttributeName: 'ID',
      KeyType: 'HASH'
    }
  ],
  ProvisionedThroughput: {
    ReadCapacityUnits: 5, // default value
    WriteCapacityUnits: 5 // default value
  }
};

dynamodb.createTable(params, (err, data) => {
  if (err) console.log(err, err.stack);
  else console.log(data);
});
```

You can use the same code to create the ShoppingCart table. Just change the table name to
ShoppingCart and the primary key name to UserID.

Limits

DynamoDB imposes some limits that you need to consider before building your application. They are listed as follows:

Parameter	Restriction
Number of tables	256 per account
Table size	There is no limit in the number of items
Provisioned throughput	Up to 40,000 read and 40,000 write capacity units
Item size	The sum of the size of all attributes of one item must not exceed 400 KB
Secondary indexes	5 local and 5 global secondary indexes per table
API BatchGetItem()	Maximum of 100 items or 16 MB retrieved
API BatchWriteItem()	Maximum of 25 put or delete requests or 16 MB sent
API Query or Scan	The result set is limited to 1 MB

Inserting and querying data

We are going to this discuss in this section how to insert and query data with DynamoDB.

Inserting data

DynamoDB offers two ways to insert data such as `putItem()` and `batchWriteItem()`. The difference between them is that `putItem` allows you to create one new item or update an existing item, while `batchWriteItem` allows you to create or delete multiples items, but doesn't support the update operation.

The following is an example of the `putItem` method:

```
const AWS = require('aws-sdk');
const dynamodb = new AWS.DynamoDB();

const params = {
  TableName: "Products",
  Item: {
    ID: { S: "lonely-bird" },
    Name: { S: "Lonely Bird" },
    Price: { N: "29.99" },
```

```
      Image: { S: "https://s3.amazonaws.com/..." },
      Comments: {
        L: [
          {
            M: {
              ID: { S: "ABC"},
              Username: { S: "John Doe"},
              Date: { S: "2016-12-24T17:15:10.000Z" },
              Text: { S: "I liked it." }
            }
          },
          {
            M: {
              ID: { S: "XYZ"},
              Username: { S: "Jane Smith"},
              Date: { S: "2016-12-24T18:15:10.000Z" },
              Text: { S: "I liked it too." }
            }
          }
        ]
      }
    }
  };

  dynamodb.putItem(params, (err, data) => {
    if (err) console.log(err, err.stack);
    else console.log(data);
  });
```

The Document Client API

As you can see, the previous example shows how to insert a single item, but the syntax is very complicated. To define a string attribute, we need to create a JSON object where the key is "S" (string) and the value is the desired data.

To make this task easier, we can use the Dynamo's Document Client API to abstract the attribute values by using native JavaScript types for read and write operations.

The following example shows how to insert the same item using this API. Note that we need to retrieve the client using new AWS.DynamoDB.DocumentClient() and the command is put instead of putItem:

```
  const AWS = require('aws-sdk');
  const documentClient = new AWS.DynamoDB.DocumentClient();

  const params = {
    TableName: "Products",
```

```
Item: {
  ID: "lonely-bird",
  Name: "Lonely Bird",
  Price: 29.99,
  Image: "https://s3.amazonaws.com/...",
  Comments: [
    {
      ID: "ABC",
      Username: "John Doe",
      Date: "2016-12-24T17:15:10.000Z",
      Text: "I liked it."
    },
    {
      ID: "XYZ",
      Username: "Jane Smith",
      Date: "2016-12-24T18:15:10.000Z",
      Text: "I liked it too."
    }
  ]
}
};

documentClient.put(params, (err, data) => {
  if (err) console.log(err, err.stack);
  else console.log(data);
});
```

Querying data

To query the item that we have just inserted, DynamoDB offers two methods such as
scan() and query(). We will see how they work in the next sections. For both of them, we
are going to use the Document Client.

The scan method

The scan method is used to retrieve all items of a table without needing to filter by a key.
Filtering is possible, but is optional. The problem with this method is that, for a large table,
you need to make multiple requests because it will interrupt the operation when it scans
more than 1 MB of data. When the scan operation is interrupted, the result set will contain a
LastEvaluatedKey parameter that can be used for further requests:

```
const AWS = require('aws-sdk');
const documentClient = new AWS.DynamoDB.DocumentClient();

const params = {
```

```
    TableName: 'Products'
};

documentClient.scan(params, (err, data) => {
  if (err) console.log(err, err.stack);
  else console.log(data);
});
```

The query method

The `query` method finds items based on the hash key. It is similar to the `scan` method since a query will be interrupted if it reads more than 1 MB of data, returning a `LastEvaluatedKey` parameter, but the main difference between `query` and `scan` is that `query` will consider the filter conditions before reading the data and `scan` will apply the filters after the table is read.

The following is an example to query only the `Lonely Bird` product:

```
const AWS = require('aws-sdk');
const documentClient = new AWS.DynamoDB.DocumentClient();

const params = {
  TableName: "Products",
  KeyConditionExpression: "ID = :id",
  ExpressionAttributeValues: { ":id": "lonely-bird" }
};

documentClient.query(params, (err, data) => {
  if (err) console.log(err);
  else console.log(data);
});
```

Performance and concurrency

Like most NoSQL databases, there is no support for transactions in DynamoDB. Atomic operations can only be done on the item level, which means that you can atomically change two attributes of a single item, but you can't update two distinct items in a single operation. Like SimpleDB, DynamoDB supports conditional updates to implement counters.

Regarding performance, DynamoDB creates indexes for the hash key and one optional range key, but if you need to query data filtering by other fields, you need to create additional indexes. For example, if you want to find all products that cost more than US$ 10, you need to create an index for the Price attribute. That's something that we don't need in our serverless store model, since we will query only by the hash keys for both tables, but we will describe here how to add extra indexes.

First, you need to understand that DynamoDB has the following two types of index:

- **Local secondary index**: An index that has the same partition key as the base table
- **Global secondary index**: An index that is not restricted to the same partition of the base table

One difference between them is that local indexes uses the same provisioned throughput of the hash key and global indexes requires that you pay for an extra provisioned throughput for them. The benefit of global indexes is that you don't need to include a filter by the hash key, and you can filter directly by the key that you have specified. In the previous example, if you want to query all products with a price above US$ 10, you need to create a global index for the Price attribute.

Now suppose that you have a table for Orders that saves the OrderID, ProductID, Price, and other information. The OrderID would be the hash key and, for a single order, we would have many items. For example, take a look at the following table:

OrderID	ProductID	Price
1	77	15.99
1	88	18.99
1	23	12.99
2	18	15.00

In this model, if you want to query by the OrderID with number 1 and filter by Price greater than 15, you would create a *local* secondary index for the Price attribute and not a *global* index.

The following example shows the syntax to create local and global indexes:

```
const params = {
  TableName: 'TableWithIndexes',
  AttributeDefinitions: [
    { AttributeName: 'ID', AttributeType: 'S' },
    { AttributeName: 'MyOtherAttribute', AttributeType: 'S' },
    { AttributeName: 'MyLocalAttribute', AttributeType: 'S' },
```

```
      { AttributeName: 'MyGlobalAttribute', AttributeType: 'S' }
    ],
    KeySchema: [
      { AttributeName: 'ID', KeyType: 'HASH' },
      { AttributeName: 'MyOtherAttribute', KeyType: 'RANGE' }
    ],
    ProvisionedThroughput:
      { ReadCapacityUnits: 5, WriteCapacityUnits: 5 },
    LocalSecondaryIndexes: [
      {
        IndexName: 'MyLocalIndex',
        KeySchema: [
          { AttributeName: 'ID', KeyType: 'HASH' },
          { AttributeName: 'MyLocalAttribute', KeyType: 'RANGE' }
        ],
        Projection: { ProjectionType: 'ALL' }
      }
    ],
    GlobalSecondaryIndexes: [
      {
        IndexName: 'MyGlobalIndex',
        KeySchema: [
          { AttributeName: 'MyGlobalAttribute', KeyType: 'HASH' }
        ],
        Projection: { ProjectionType: 'ALL' },
        ProvisionedThroughput:
          { ReadCapacityUnits: 5, WriteCapacityUnits: 5 }
      }
    ]
  }
};
```

 You can use `DynamoDB.updateTable()` to add *global secondary indexes* after a table is created, but you can only add *local secondary indexes* during the creation of a table. It is not possible to update a table to add local indexes.

Managing the database

AWS has a management console for DynamoDB where you can configure the capacity of your tables, create indexes, and view CloudWatch metrics. In the following steps, I will show how you can see and manipulate your table's data:

1. Browse the Management Console at this link `https://console.aws.amazon.com/dynamodb`.

2. In the left menu, click on **Tables**:

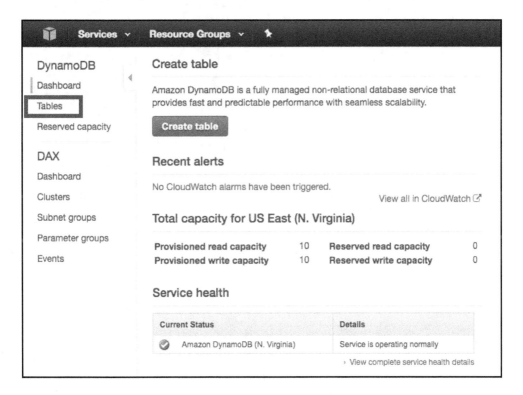

3. Now click on your table **Name** and in the **Items** tab. In this tab, you can create, delete, or update items. A scan query will be executed automatically, but you can change the query parameters if you want to see other items. Click on the item **ID** to open the edit modal:

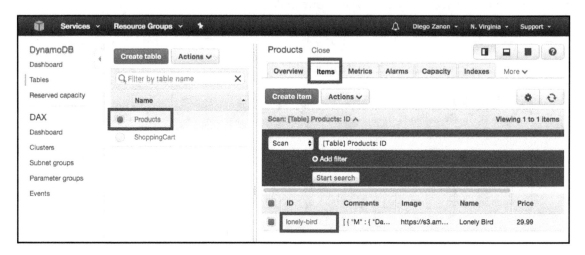

4. The **Edit item** modal allows you to see all properties of an item and update the attributes if required:

Provisioned throughput

DynamoDB performance is based on provisioned throughput for read and write operations. One *read capacity unit* represents one strongly consistent read per second or two eventually consistent reads per second for objects with up to 4 KB in size, while one *write capacity unit* means that you can write one 1 KB object per second. You need to define those values when you create your table, but you can update them if you want later. In this chapter's example, the table was created with five read units and five write units for each key.

If your system requests more read/write operations than expected by your provisioned capacity, AWS will allow the operations to be executed without errors for a short period of time. If you continue to exceed the provisioned capacity, some requests will fail with the `ProvisionedThroughputExceededException` error. The good news is that the AWS SDK has built-in support for retrying throttled requests, so we don't need to write the logic for this.

Auto scaling

You can configure CloudWatch to send e-mail alerts when your DynamoDB usage is higher than your provisioned throughput and manually update the capacity when necessary *or* you can configure auto scaling. As we want to avoid worrying about servers and scalability, we will configure auto scaling to handle this burden for us.

Auto scaling will actively manage the throughput capacity to scale up and down to match your application utilization when your workload increases or decreases. What we need to configure is a range (upper and lower limits) for read and write capacity units and a target utilization percentage within this range. You can access the auto scaling configuration through the Management Console. Click in the table where you want to enable this setting and select the **Capacity** tab.

The following screenshot shows an example of auto scaling configuration:

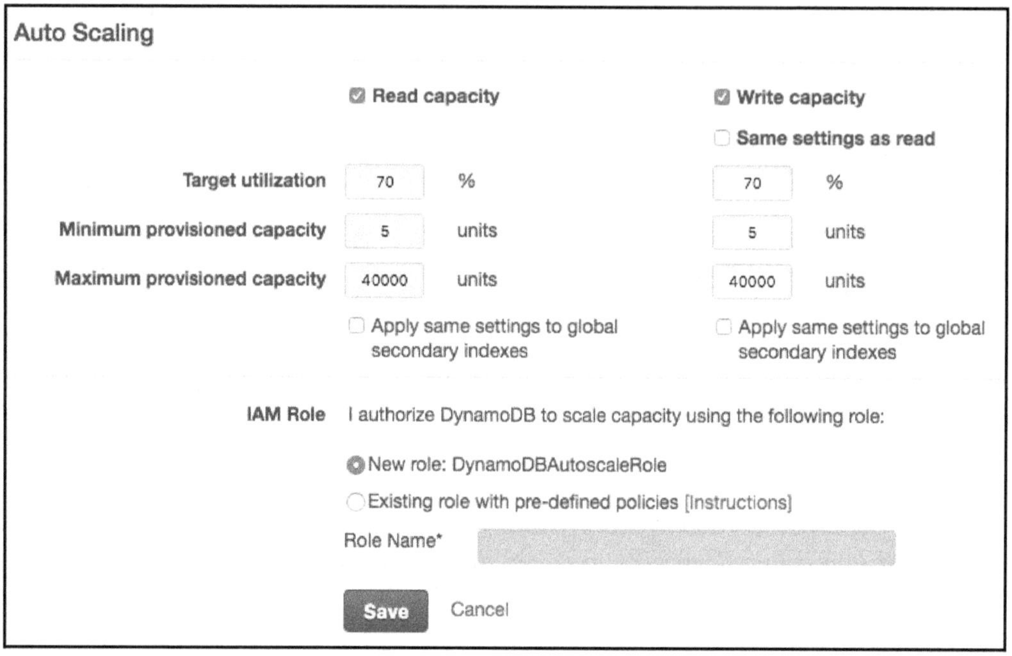

Backing up and restoring data

Unfortunately, DynamoDB doesn't provide a simple feature for backup and restore. What AWS proposes is to use other two services for this task such as **AWS Data Pipeline** and **Amazon Elastic MapReduce** (**EMR**). Due to the complexity and length of this configuration, it won't be covered in this book. You can follow the AWS tutorial to implement a task for this:

```
http://docs.aws.amazon.com/datapipeline/latest/DeveloperGuide/dp-importexpor
t-ddb.html
```

In short, what you need is to use a AWS Data Pipeline template for DynamoDB and schedule a task that will start an EMR with Hive to save/restore a DynamoDB table.

Controlling user access

Just like SimpleDB, we manage DynamoDB user access through IAM roles. We must give permissions *explicitly* to the Lambda functions to be able to execute the requests. This configuration is done in the `serverless.yml` file under the `iamRoleStatements` function:

```
service: dynamodb-example

provider:
  name: aws
  runtime: nodejs6.10
    iamRoleStatements:
    - Effect: "Allow"
      Action:
        - "dynamodb:Scan"
        - "dynamodb:Query"
        - "dynamodb:PutItem"
        - "dynamodb:DeleteItem"
        - "dynamodb:BatchWriteItem"
      Resource: [
        "arn:aws:dynamodb:us-east-1:*:table/Products",
        "arn:aws:dynamodb:us-east-1:*:table/ShoppingCart"
      ]

functions:
    query:
      handler: handler.query
```

Improving the serverless store

In this book's GitHub repository, you will find a `scripts` folder that you can use to create the tables for DynamoDB and SimpleDB, along with sample data to be used in our tests. Also, in the root directory, you will find a `backend` folder that contains a `repositories` folder with the `dynamodb.js`, `simpledb.js`, and `fakedb.js` files. The sample application uses `fakedb` as the default database, because it doesn't require any configuration since it provides only hardcoded data.

We are going to implement the DynamoDB code now. In the `lib` folder, we are going to change the dependencies from `const db = require('../repositories/fakedb')` to `const db = require('../repositories/dynamodb')` and in the `dynamodb.js` file, we need to develop four methods such as `retrieveAllProducts`, `retrieveCart`, `saveCart`, and `processCheckout`.

Retrieving all products

Retrieving all products is a simple function that will execute a `scan` operation. As we have just a few items, we don't need to worry about the 1 MB limit in this case:

```
module.exports.retrieveAllProducts = (callback) => {

  const params = {
    TableName: 'Products'
  };

  documentClient.scan(params, callback);
};
```

Retrieving the user's shopping cart

Retrieving the user's cart uses a simple query where we will filter by `UserID`:

```
module.exports.retrieveCart = (userId, callback) => {

  const params = {
    TableName: "ShoppingCart",
    KeyConditionExpression: "UserID = :userId",
    ExpressionAttributeValues: { ":userId": userId }
  };

  documentClient.query(params, callback);
});
```

Saving the user's shopping cart

The `saveCart` function receives the `userId` and `selectedProducts` as arguments, where the `selectedProducts` is a pair of `ProductId-Quantity` elements:

```
module.exports.saveCart = (userId, selectedProducts, callback) => {

  const params = {
    TableName: "ShoppingCart",
    Item: {
      UserID: userId,
      LastUpdate: new Date().toISOString(),
      SelectedProducts: selectedProducts
    }
  };
```

```
    documentClient.put(params, callback);
};
```

Processing the checkout

Handling payment data is a complex process and is out of scope for this book. In this case, we are going to implement a function that will just execute the callback passing `null` as the error parameter:

```
module.exports.processCheckout = (callback) => {
  // do nothing
  callback(null);
};
```

Amazon S3 (for media files)

S3 is not a database, it is only a storage system. It lacks a database engine and many storage features, but it can be pretty useful for saving media files such as photos, videos, and music.

This approach is already very popular. For example, if you develop an application that uses a MongoDB database, you could use MongoDB GridFS to store large binary data. However, the most efficient solution is to offload this kind of data to cloud services because the machines responsible for your database are usually the most expensive ones. It means that the cost per gigabyte in a database is usually higher than a cloud storage service, such as S3.

In our serverless store, we are storing the product images in SimpleDB/DynamoDB as string fields. Instead of saving the full binary data, we save just the URL of the image file. Example:

```
https://s3.amazonaws.com/serverless-store-media/product-images/lonely-bird.j
pg
```

When we receive this information in the frontend, the `<img>` element has the `src` attribute referencing this S3 URL:

```
<img src={this.props.product.imageURL} alt="product" />
```

Instead of downloading the image from the database, the user will download the image from S3, thus relieving the database.

This is one use case for S3. There are two other common usages:

- **The user needs to upload his avatar image**: Instead of saving in the database, we can generate a temporary permission for the user to upload the file directly to S3
- **The user wants to see his private album**: Instead of requesting a Lambda function to download the files from S3, we can generate private temporary links from where he will be able to download the files

We will discuss in this section how to handle these examples and how to use S3 as a database for media files.

Uploading and downloading files

If your bucket stores public files, you can configure it to allow anonymous requests to upload and download files. However, if the files are private, you need to give pre-signed URLs to the client to ensure privacy and security. Both the actions, namely upload and download, must be signed.

These keys are generated at the backend because you need to use the SDK with credential access to the bucket. Let's take a look at the following steps to upload and download files:

1. Create a Lambda function and expose an endpoint to allow it to be called by the frontend code. Use the `getSignedUrl` function of the S3 object to obtain the signed URL:

```
const AWS = require('aws-sdk');
const s3 = new AWS.S3();

const params = {
  Bucket: 'bucket',
  Key: 'key'
};

const operation = 'putObject'; // upload operation
// const operation = 'getObject'; // download operation

s3.getSignedUrl(operation, params, (err, url) => {
  // return the url
});
```

2. If the operation is to download a private file, render the HTML with an anchor tag that uses this pre-signed URL in the `href` attribute and set the attribute `target` to `_blank` in order to carry out the download:

```
<a href="PRE-SIGNED-URL" target="_blank">Download</a>
```

3. If the operation is to upload a file, add an `input` element to receive the file:

```
<input type="file" />
```

4. And upload the file with an Ajax request using the pre-signed URL:

```
$.ajax({
    url: preSignedUrl, // use the signed URL in the request
    type: 'POST',
    data: file,
    // ...
    success: () => { console.log('Uploaded') },
    error: err => { console.log(err) }
});
```

5. As you have generated the pre-signed URL using a Lambda function, you will know the filename and where the file will be stored, however, you won't know exactly when the file upload will finish if it is really started by the user. One option that you have is to add another Lambda function to receive the object created event, which will be triggered by the S3 bucket.

Enabling CORS

The previous code will only work if we enable CORS for the S3 bucket. CORS headers are necessary because we are going to make upload and download requests from a domain that is different from the S3 domain. This setting can be configured using the S3 Console: `https://console.aws.amazon.com/s3`. Open your bucket properties and select **Permissions**, followed by **CORS Configuration,** as shown in the following screenshot:

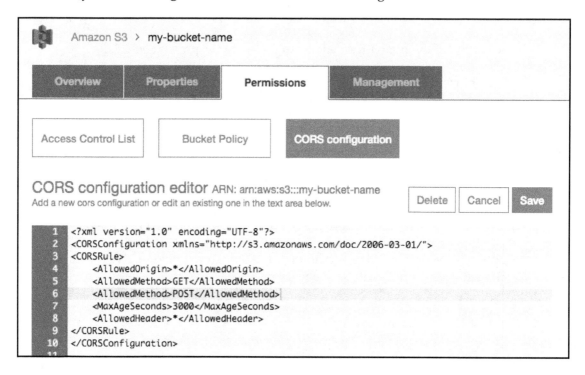

This command will add a CORS configuration for GET requests. Before saving, we need to add one line to include authorization for POST requests and change the Allowed Header to * (all):

```
<CORSConfiguration>
  <CORSRule>
    <AllowedOrigin>*</AllowedOrigin>
    <AllowedMethod>GET</AllowedMethod>
    <AllowedMethod>POST</AllowedMethod>
    <MaxAgeSeconds>3000</MaxAgeSeconds>
    <AllowedHeader>*</AllowedHeader>
  </CORSRule>
</CORSConfiguration>
```

Backing up and restoring data

Amazon S3 was designed to provide up to 99.999999999% of durability, which means that AWS makes a huge effort to replicate your data and keep it safe from disk failures. Although you can rest assured that your data is safe on S3, you must consider that it is not so safe against your own mistakes. For example, if you have a feature that deletes specific files from S3, you can make a mistake and delete a wrong file or, even worse, delete all of them. So, making backups is important to ensure a safer operation for your business.

You can back up files locally (downloading) or make copies in other external services (such as Azure or Google Cloud), but it is usually not necessary. You can save all files of a bucket in another bucket using a command of the AWS CLI:

```
aws s3 sync s3://original-bucket s3://backup-bucket
```

If you want to restore all files that were saved at specific time to the backup bucket, you would need to add a `--delete` option to remove files in the target bucket that do not exist in the backup bucket:

```
aws s3 sync s3://backup-bucket s3://bucket-to-be-restored --delete
```

Using S3 versioning

S3 versioning is another way to protect your data. Once enabled, every time you modify an object, a new one will be saved, and when you delete an object, S3 will just place a delete mark on it. Versioning allows you to recover files that were accidentally deleted, but you will pay more to keep those files available.

To configure S3 versioning, go to the Management Console and select the bucket **Properties**. You will see an option to enable versioning:

You can reduce costs by configuring life cycle rules to delete old versioned files. This setting can be found under the **Management** tab:

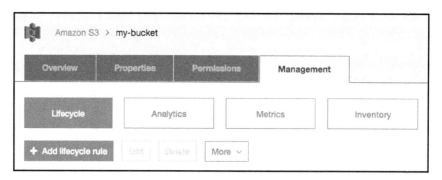

To finish this section, an observation about security: if your AWS access keys get compromised, a malicious user could delete the files in the S3 bucket and also remove versioned files. To prevent this, you can add an extra layer of protection by enabling **MFA Delete**. With this setting, you can only permanently delete a file if you have access to the AWS account *and* if you are able to provide an access code from an authentication device.

Summary

In this chapter, you learned how to model, query, and insert data using serverless databases. We saw how SimpleDB works, but due to its lack of features, we also covered how to use DynamoDB. Plus, you learned more about Amazon S3 and how to use it to store media files.

In the next chapter, we are going to learn how to use authentication and authorization on AWS and also check out standard security practices to build a serverless project.

8
Securing the Serverless Application

Handling security is an extensive and complex topic. If you don't do it right, you may be hacked. Even if you do everything right, you may be hacked. So it's important you understand the common security mechanisms to avoid exposing your website to vulnerabilities, and also, always follow the recommended practices and methodologies that have been largely tested and proven to be robust.

In this chapter, we will cover the following topics:

- Basic security practices and concepts
- Learning how to use Amazon Cognito
- Developing the signup and login pages of the serverless store
- Handling authorization and authentication of users in the backend

By the end of this chapter, you will have acquired basic knowledge on how to handle security on AWS to build a serverless website.

Security basics

One of the mantras of security experts is this: *don't roll your own*. It means you should never use in a production system any kind of crypto algorithm or security model that you developed by yourself. Always use solutions that have been highly used, tested, and recommended by trusted sources. Even experienced people may commit errors and expose a solution to attacks, especially in the cryptography field, which requires advanced math. However, when a proposed solution is analyzed and tested by a great number of specialists, errors are much less frequent.

In the security world, there is a term called **security through obscurity**. It is defined as a security model where the implementation mechanism is not publicly known, so there is a belief that it is secure because no one has prior information about the flaws it has. It can be indeed secure, but if used as the only form of protection, it is considered as a poor security practice. If a hacker is persistent enough, he or she can discover flaws even without knowing the internal code. In this case again, it's better to use a highly tested algorithm than your own.

Security through obscurity can be compared to someone trying to protect their own money by burying it in the backyard when the common security mechanism would be to put the money in a bank. The money can be safe while buried, but it will be protected only until someone finds about its existence and starts to look for it.

Due to this reason, when dealing with security, we usually prefer to use open source algorithms and tools. Everyone can access and discover flaws in them, but there are also a great number of specialists that are involved in finding the vulnerabilities and fixing them.

In this section, we will discuss other security concepts that everyone must know when building a system.

Information security

When dealing with security, there are some attributes that need to be considered. The most important ones are the following:

- **Authentication**: Confirm the user's identity by validating that the user is who they claim to be
- **Authorization**: Decide whether the user is allowed to execute the requested action
- **Confidentiality**: Ensure that data can't be understood by third-parties
- **Integrity**: Protect the message against undetectable modifications
- **Non-repudiation**: Ensure that someone can't deny the authenticity of their own message
- **Availability**: Keep the system available when needed

These terms will be better explained in the next sections.

Authentication

Authentication is the ability to confirm the user's identity. It can be implemented by a login form where you request the user to type their username and password. If the hashed password matches what was previously saved in the database, you have enough proof that the user is who they claim to be. This model is good enough, at least for typical applications. You confirm the identity by requesting the user to provide what *they know*. Another kind of authentication is to request the user to provide what *they have*. It can be a physical device (like a dongle) or access to an e-mail account or phone number.

However, you can't ask the user to type their credentials for *every* request. As long as you *authenticate* it in the first request, you must create a security token that will be used in the subsequent requests. This token will be saved on the client side as a cookie and will be automatically sent to the server in all requests.

On AWS, this token can be created using the Cognito service. How this is done will be described later in this chapter.

Authorization

When a request is received in the backend, we need to check if the user is allowed to execute the requested action. For example, if the user wants to checkout the order with ID `123`, we need to make a query to the database to identify who is the owner of the order and compare if it is the same user.

Another scenario is when we have multiple roles in an application and we need to restrict data access. For example, a system developed to manage school grades may be implemented with two roles, such as `student` and `teacher`. The teacher will access the system to insert or update grades, while the students will access the system to read those grades. In this case, the authentication system must restrict the actions *insert* and *update* for users that are part of the *teachers* group and users in the *students* group must be restricted to *read* their own grades.

Most of the time, we handle authorization in our own backend, but some serverless services don't require a backend and they are responsible by themselves to properly check the authorization. For example, in the next chapter, we are going to see how serverless notifications are implemented on AWS. When we use AWS IoT, if we want a private channel of communication between two users, we must give them access to one specific resource known by both and restrict access to other users to avoid the disclosure of private messages. This kind of authorization will be detailed in the next chapter.

Confidentiality

In Chapter 4, *Hosting the Website*, we learned how to use AWS Certificate Manager to request TLS certificates for free and how to add them to CloudFront distributions. Developing a website that uses HTTPS for *all* requests is the main drive to achieve confidentiality in the communication between the users and your site. As the data is encrypted, it's very hard for malicious users to decrypt and understand its contents.

Although there are some attacks that can intercept the communication and forge certificates (man-in-the-middle), those require the malicious user to have access to the machine or network of the victim user. From our side, adding HTTPS support is the best thing that we can do to minimize the chance of attacks.

Integrity

Integrity is related to confidentiality. While confidentiality relies on encrypting a message to prevent other users from accessing its contents, integrity deals with protecting the messages against modifications by encrypting messages with digital signatures (TLS certificates).

Integrity is an important concept when designing low level network systems, but all that matters for us is adding HTTPS support.

Non-repudiation

Non-repudiation is a term that is often confused with authentication since both of them have the objective to prove who has sent the message. However, the main difference is that authentication is more interested in a technical view and the non-repudiation concept is interested in legal terms, liability, and auditing.

When you have a login form with user and password input, you can authenticate the user who correctly knows the combination, but you can't have 100% certain since the credentials can be correctly guessed or stolen by a third-party. On the other hand, if you have a stricter access mechanism, such as a biometric entry, you have more credibility. However, this is not perfect either. It's just a better non-repudiation mechanism.

Availability

Availability is also a concept of interest in the information security field because availability is not restricted to how you provision your hardware to meet your user needs. Availability can suffer attacks and can suffer interruptions due to malicious users. There are attacks, such as **Distributed Denial of Service (DDoS)**, that aim to create bottlenecks to disrupt site availability. In a DDoS attack, the targeted website is flooded with superfluous requests with the objective to overload the systems. This is usually accomplished by a controlled network of infected machines called a **botnet**.

On AWS, all services run under the AWS Shield service, which was designed to protect against DDoS attacks with no additional charge. However, if you run a very large and important service, you may be a direct target of advanced and large DDoS attacks. In this case, there is a premium tier offered in the AWS Shield service to ensure your website's availability even in worst case scenarios. This requires an investment of US$ 3,000 per month, and with this, you will have 24x7 support of a dedicated team and access to other tools for mitigation and analysis of DDoS attacks.

Security on AWS

In this book, we use AWS credentials, roles, and policies, but security on AWS is much more than handling authentication and authorization of users. This is what we will discuss in this section.

Shared responsibility model

Security on AWS is based on a shared responsibility model. While Amazon is responsible for keeping the infrastructure safe, the customers are responsible for patching security updates to software and protecting their own user accounts.

AWS's responsibilities include the following:

- Physical security of the hardware and facilities
- Infrastructure of networks, virtualization, and storage
- Availability of services respecting **Service Level Agreements (SLAs)**
- Security of managed services such as Lambda, RDS, DynamoDB, and others

A customer's responsibilities are as follows:

- Applying security patches to the operating system on EC2 machines
- Security of installed applications
- Avoiding disclosure of user credentials
- Correct configuration of access policies and roles
- Firewall configurations
- Network traffic protection (encrypting data to avoid disclosure of sensitive information)
- Encryption of server-side data and databases

In the serverless model, we rely only on managed services. In this case, we don't need to worry about applying security patches to the operating system or runtime, but we do need to worry about third-party libraries that our application depends on to execute. Also, of course, we need to worry about all the things that we need to configure (firewalls, user policies, and so on), the network traffic (supporting HTTPS) and how data is manipulated by the application.

The Trusted Advisor tool

AWS offers a tool named Trusted Advisor, which can be accessed through `https://consol e.aws.amazon.com/trustedadvisor`.

It was created to offer help on how you can optimize costs or improve performance, but it also helps identify security breaches and common misconfigurations. It searches for unrestricted access to specific ports on your EC2 machines, if Multi-Factor Authentication is enabled on the root account and if IAM users were created in your account.

 You need to pay for AWS premium support to unlock other features, such as cost optimization advice. However, security checks are free.

Pen testing

A penetration test (or pen test) is a good practice that all big websites must perform periodically. Even if you have a good team of security experts, the usual recommendation is to hire a specialized third-party company to perform pen tests and to find vulnerabilities. This is because they will most likely have tools and procedures that your team may not have tried yet.

However, the caveat here is that you can't execute these tests without contacting AWS first. To respect their user terms, you can only try to find breaches on your own account and assets, in scheduled time frames (so they can disable their intrusion detection systems for your assets), and only on restricted services, such as EC2 instances and RDS.

AWS CloudTrail

AWS CloudTrail is a service that was designed to record all AWS API calls that are executed on your account. The output of this service is a set of log files that register the API caller, the date/time, the source IP address of the caller, the request parameters, and the response elements that were returned.

This kind of service is pretty important for security analysis, in case there are data breaches, and for systems that need the auditing mechanism for compliance standards.

MFA

Multi-Factor Authentication (MFA) is an extra security layer that everyone must add to their AWS root account to protect against unauthorized access. Besides knowing the user and password, a malicious user would also need physical access to your smartphone or security token, which greatly restricts the risks.

On AWS, you can use MFA through the following means:

- **Virtual devices**: Application installed on Android, iPhone, or Windows phones
- **Physical devices**: Six-digit tokens or OTP cards
- **SMS**: Messages received on your phone

Handling authentication and authorization

In this section, we are going to use Amazon Cognito to create the users for our application and to be able to handle their login. After authenticating the user, we will be able to give proper authorization for the tasks that they are allowed to execute.

Amazon Cognito

Cognito provides two services such as **User Pools** and **Identity Pools**. The first is where you create and store user credentials, the latter is where you set the permissions for the user to access AWS resources.

We will start by creating a user pool, so we can add signup and signin features to our website. We will add the user pool ID to our frontend code and requests will be done directly to the User Pool service, without needing to be executed from a Lambda function.

Later, we will configure an identity pool, which will be needed to give to the users temporary access to AWS resources. In our example, the user will be able to subscribe to IoT notifications directly, without requesting the backend to give this authorization.

Creating a user pool

Let's take a look at the following steps to create a user pool:

1. To create a user pool, we will use the console, which can be accessed through `htt ps://console.aws.amazon.com/cognito`. Select the **Manage your User Pools** option:

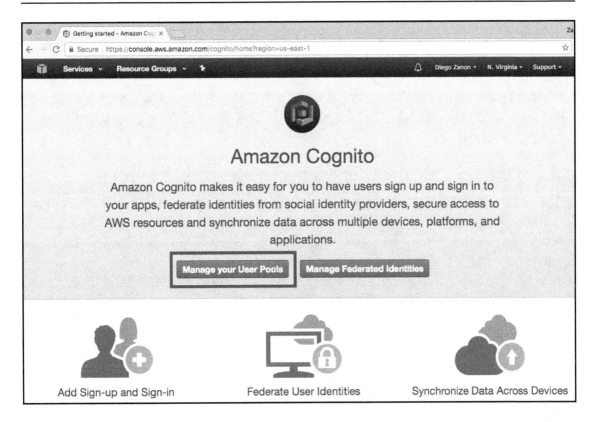

2. Click on **Create a User Pool** on the next screen, as shown in the following screenshot:

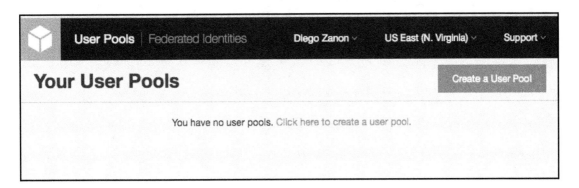

3. Now define a pool name for your user pool resource and check whether you want fast creation (using defaults) or whether you want to step through each setting. I've selected the former (**Review defaults**):

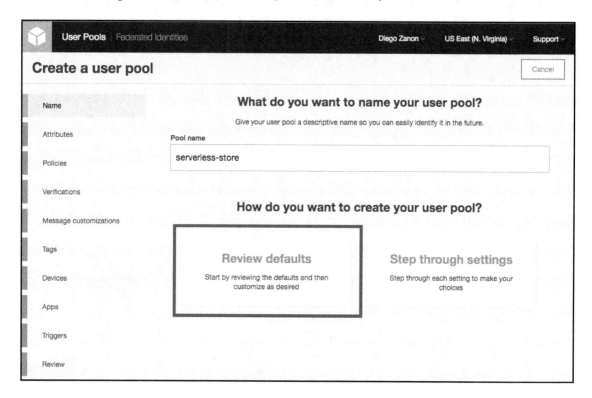

4. The next screen will be a list of defaults that you need to revise before hitting
   Create pool:

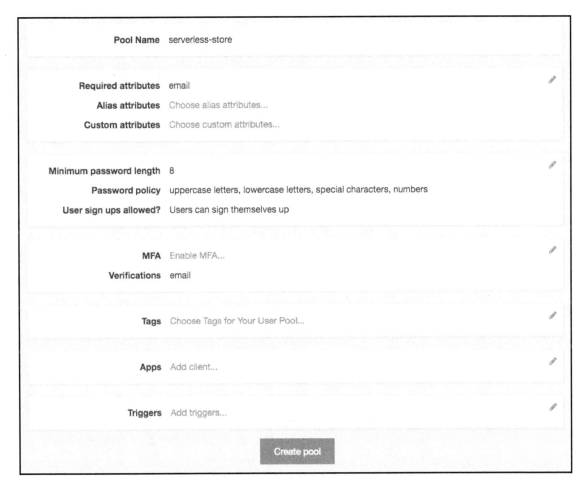

- The following is a list of options and what you need to consider in each of them:
  - **Attributes**: This displays a list of user attributes that you can select
    as required options for login. Usually, only an e-mail is enough for
    most applications, but you can include attributes like username,
    phone number, or user picture. Also, you may set custom user
    attributes to be saved in your user profile.

- **Policies**: This defines how strict the user's password must be. For example, if you require a minimum length, special characters, and upper or lower cases. Also, you can restrict user creation by admins only.
- **Verifications**: You can request the user to verify the ownership of the e-mail address or phone number (SMS) upon registering. Cognito will send a message with a code for validation. Also, you can enable MFA for your users as a second layer of security. This feature is very important nowadays to prevent accounts being hacked and is already implemented by Cognito, making it very easy to integrate with your application. You can enable MFA by e-mail or phone.
- **Message customizations**: This is related to the previous configuration where you can request users to validate their e-mails or phone numbers. The text of these messages is configurable here. Besides, you can set the e-mail messages to use your domain address, if it was already verified and configured in Amazon SES.
- **Tags**: This option is useful if you want to associate the user pool with a tag that will show up in your billing data. With this option, you can create a tag with a cost center or application name for better management of cost allocation.
- **Devices**: You can allow the device to be remembered for future accesses. This feature is useful as a convenience and you can also suppress MFA requests if the device has already been authenticated with MFA in the past.
- **Apps**: You need to create an application specification to restrict the applications that will be able to handle the login process and handle forgotten passwords for your application. This feature creates an application key and secret.
- **Triggers**: You can trigger Lambda functions in pre-signup, pre-authentication, post authentication, create authorization challenge, and other options. Basically, you can have control of server-side procedures to handle the user authentication.

5. After creating the user pool, you can see the assigned **Pool Id** and **Pool ARN**. Write down those values because they will be needed later:

6. There is still one more thing before we complete this configuration. As we want our website to handle signup/signin, we need to create an application ID. Browse the **App clients** field to add an application for our website and uncheck the **Generate client secret** option, since this feature is not supported by the JavaScript SDK:

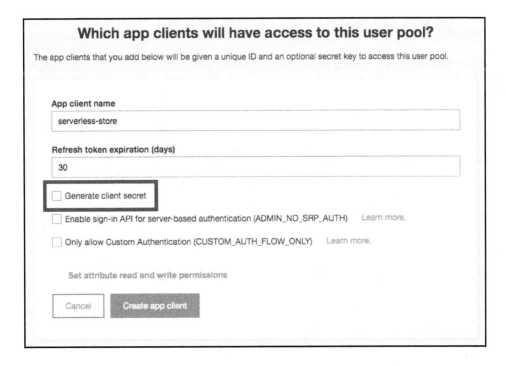

7. After creating the **app client**, write down the **App client id**:

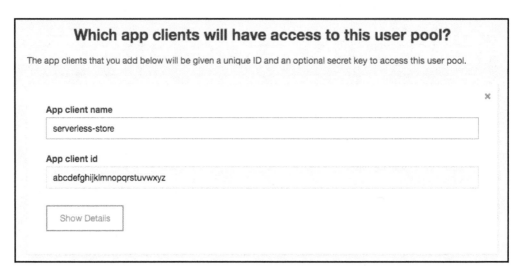

Creating an identity pool

Now we are going to create an identity pool. Let's take a look in the following steps:

1. The first step is to browse to the **Federated Identities** page that can be found in Cognito home or from the user pool that we have just created:

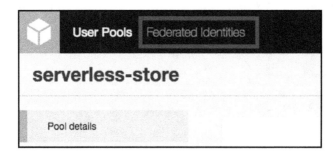

2. When creating a new identity pool, check the box **Enable access to unauthenticated identities**. We will configure later what resources an unsigned user can access, which will be different to the level of access that a signed user can have. Take a look at the following screenshot:

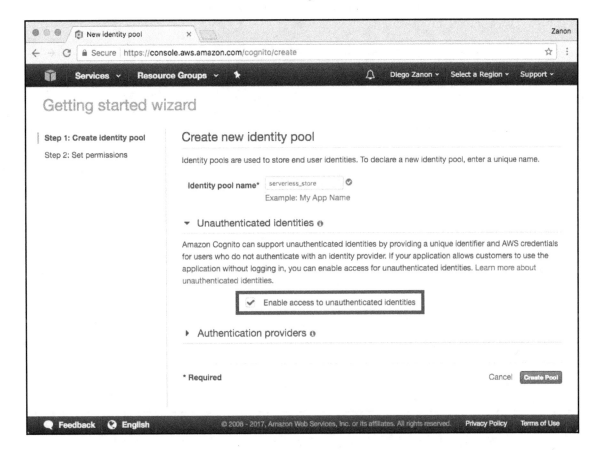

3. The next field is to set the **Authentication providers** parameter. Cognito Identity Pool is an *authorization* service that needs to receive as input the users from an *authentication* service. In our example, we will use the Cognito User Pool that we have just created by filling out the **User Pool ID** and the **App Client ID** fields, but if you want, you can add support for other providers as well, such as Facebook, Google+, or Twitter:

4. Now we need to configure the access of our authenticated and unauthenticated users. As an example, we could allow access to a folder of a S3 bucket to allow the user to directly upload photos from the website, without needing the backend to execute this action. In our serverless store, we need to handle notifications with IoT. So that's what we are going to configure next:

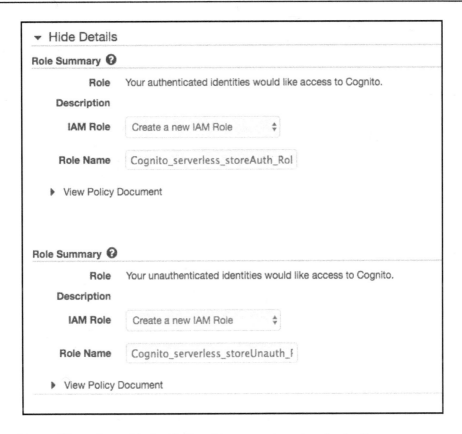

5. You will need to edit the **Policy Document** option for both types
   (unauthenticated and authenticated). Start modifying the document for
   authenticated users:

```
{
  "Version": "2012-10-17",
  "Statement": [
    {
      "Effect": "Allow",
      "Action": [
        "mobileanalytics:PutEvents",
        "cognito-sync:*",
        "cognito-identity:*"
      ],
      "Resource": ["*"]
    },
    {
      "Effect": "Allow",
      "Action": [
```

```
      "iot:Connect",
      "iot:AttachPrincipalPolicy"
    ],
    "Resource": ["*"]
  },
  {
    "Effect": "Allow",
    "Action": ["iot:Subscribe"],
    "Resource": [
     "arn:aws:iot:<region>:<account>:topicfilter/<public-topic>",
     "arn:aws:iot:<region>:<account>:topicfilter/<private-topic>"
    ]
  },
  {
    "Effect": "Allow",
    "Action": [
      "iot:Publish",
      "iot:Receive"
    ],
    "Resource": [
      "arn:aws:iot:<region>:<account>:topic/<public-topic>",
      "arn:aws:iot:<region>:<account>:topic/<private-topic>"
    ]
  }
 ]
}
```

iot:Connect and iot:AttachPrincipalPolicy requires access to every resource (*), while we need to restrict the iot:Subscribe to a topicfilter/<topic> resource and the iot:Publish and iot:Receive to a topic/<topic>.

6. When building the ARNs, replace the <region> with the region of the AWS IoT that you are going to use, <account> with your Account ID, <public-topic> with serverless-store-comments and <private-topic> with serverless-store-${cognito-identity.amazonaws.com:sub}. The private topic will allow the authenticated user to access a topic defined by their federated identity.
7. For unauthenticated access, use the same policy document, but remove the extra ARN that was added for the private topic. You can also remove the iot:AttachPrincipalPolicy since it will not be necessary for unauthenticated users.

8. After creating the identity pool, go to the **Dashboard** option and click on **Edit identity pool**. You will see the **Identity pool ID** option in this screen. Write it down because it will be needed later:

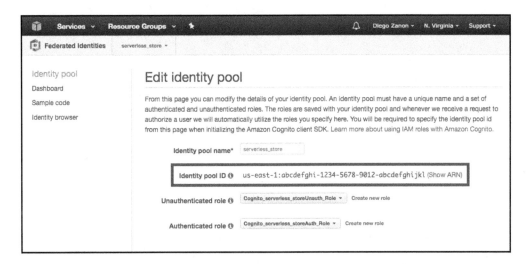

Using Cognito in our serverless store

Now we are going to integrate our React frontend with Cognito to implement the signup and login pages. The authentication methods will be done directly with Cognito, without using a Lambda function for this. To make this work, we need to configure our React application:

1. First, install the module `amazon-cognito-identity-js` in our frontend folder by running the following command:

   ```
   npm install amazon-cognito-identity-js --save
   ```

2. Inside the `lib` folder, create a `config.js` file to store our Cognito IDs:

   ```
   export default {
     "cognito": {
       "USER_POOL_ID": "YOUR_USER_POOL_ID",
       "APP_CLIENT_ID": "YOUR_APP_CLIENT_ID",
       "IDENTITY_POOL_ID": "YOUR_IDENTITY_POOL_ID",
       "REGION": "YOUR_COGNITO_REGION"
     }
   };
   ```

3. As we did in previous chapters, we have created a `services.js` file inside the
    `lib` folder to make all Ajax requests. We need to import the following from the
    Cognito module:

```
import {
  AuthenticationDetails,
  CognitoUser,
  CognitoUserAttribute,
  CognitoUserPool
} from 'amazon-cognito-identity-js';
```

Now we have prepared our frontend to use Cognito.

The Signup page

The signup form was created in Chapter 5, *Building the Frontend,* and it has the appearance
as shown in the this screenshot:

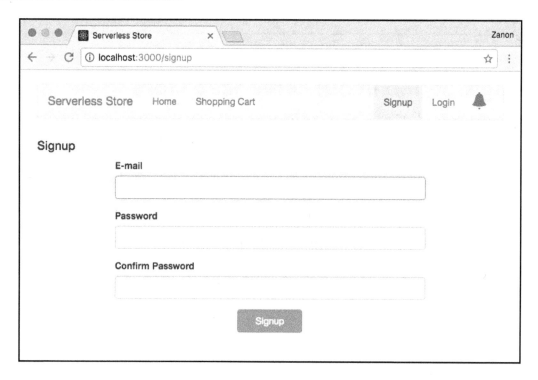

We are going to implement the handler for the **Signup** button by performing the following steps:

1. We start by creating a method in our `services.js` file that will execute a request to Cognito, invoking the `signUp` function that will use the e-mail and password provided by the form:

```
signup(email, password, callback) {
  const userPool = new CognitoUserPool({
    UserPoolId: config.cognito.USER_POOL_ID,
    ClientId: config.cognito.APP_CLIENT_ID
  });

  const attributeEmail = [
    new CognitoUserAttribute({
      Name: 'email',
      Value: email
    })
  ];

  userPool.signUp(email,
                  password,
                  attributeEmail,
                  null,
                  callback);
}
```

2. The `App` component will call this function and it will save the resulting user object in its state:

```
handleSignup(email, password) {
  Services.signup(email, password, (err, res) => {
    if (err) alert(err);
    else this.setState({newUser: res.user});
  });
}
```

3. After registering the user successfully, we need to re-render the signup component to display a confirmation request. The user will be asked to fill the text input with the value sent to their e-mail:

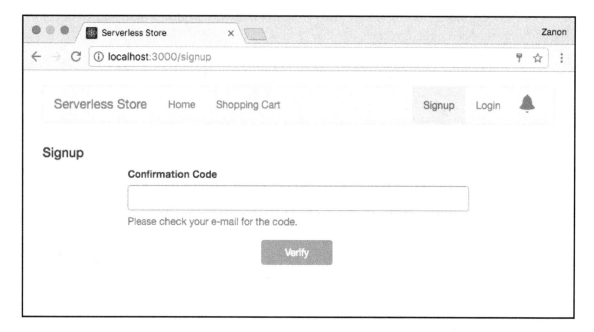

4. The request to Cognito will use the same `user` object that was returned in the signup result:

```
confirmSignup(newUser, code, callback) {
    newUser.confirmRegistration(code, true, callback);
}
```

5. If the confirmation code is correct, we can use the e-mail and password that the user has provided and authenticate his access, without asking the user to type them again.

How to authenticate will be defined in the next section.

The Login page

Implementing the **Login** page to authenticate users requires a few steps. Let's see how this is done by performing the following steps:

1. The **Login** page was also created in `Chapter 5`, *Building the Frontend* and it has this look:

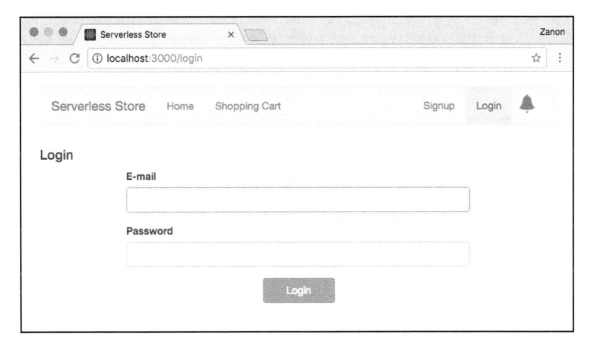

2. The `Login` button will trigger a request to Cognito defined in the `services.js` file:

```
login(email, password) {
  const userPool = new CognitoUserPool({
    UserPoolId: config.cognito.USER_POOL_ID,
    ClientId: config.cognito.APP_CLIENT_ID
  });

  const user = new CognitoUser({
    Username: email,
    Pool: userPool
  });

  const authenticationData = {
```

```
      Username: email,
      Password: password
    };

    const authDetails =
      new AuthenticationDetails(authenticationData);

    return new Promise((resolve, reject) => {
      user.authenticateUser(authDetails, {
        onSuccess: (res) =>
          resolve(res.getIdToken().getJwtToken()),
        onFailure: (err) => reject(err)
      });
    });
  }
```

3. This `login` function will be used by the `App` component. After signing successfully, we need to save `userToken` in the state of `App`:

```
  handleLogin(email, password) {
    Services.login(email, password)
      .then(res => {
        this.setState({userToken: res});
      })
      .catch(err => {
        alert(err);
      });
  }
```

Persisting the user token

Fortunately, the Cognito SDK will persist the user token automatically in the browser local storage. If the user browses your website again before the token expiration, the data will be there, available, without the need to request the user to type the e-mail/password again.

This token can be retrieved with the following code:

```
  getUserToken(callback) {
    const userPool = new CognitoUserPool({
      UserPoolId: config.cognito.USER_POOL_ID,
      ClientId: config.cognito.APP_CLIENT_ID
    });
    const currentUser = userPool.getCurrentUser();

    if (currentUser) {
      currentUser.getSession((err, res) => {
```

```
    if (err)
      callback(err);
    else
      callback(null, res.getIdToken().getJwtToken());
  });
} else {
  callback(null);
}
}
```

Logging out

As the user token is being persisted, we can check its existence in the App initialization (componentDidMount) and display a **Logout** button instead of a **Login** button in the navigation bar:

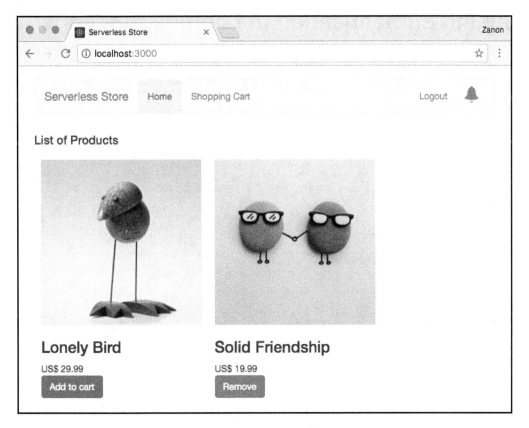

When clicking in this **Logout** button, we can clear the token executing the following code:

```
handleLogout() {
  const userPool = new CognitoUserPool({
    UserPoolId: config.cognito.USER_POOL_ID,
    ClientId: config.cognito.APP_CLIENT_ID
  });

  const currentUser = userPool.getCurrentUser();
  if (currentUser !== null) {
    currentUser.signOut();
  }

  this.setState({userToken: null});
}
```

Handling authentication in Lambda functions

API Gateway has a nice integration with Cognito Pools for user authentication. We can configure it through the Serverless Framework to retrieve the user data from Cognito whenever a request with a token ID is provided. Let's see how this is done by executing the following steps:

1. Modify the `serverless.yml` file to use the Cognito User Pool authorizer:

```
functions:
  products:
    handler: functions/products.handler
    events:
      - http:
          method: POST
          path: cart
          authorizer:
            arn: YOUR_COGNITO_USER_POOL_ARN
      - http: OPTIONS cart
```

2. Include `Authorization` as a valid header when the Lambda function answer an `OPTIONS` request:

```
"Accept-Control-Allow-Headers":
  "Accept, Authorization, Content-Type, Origin"
```

3. Deploy the backend again by running the following command:

```
serverless deploy
```

4. Modify the frontend to always include the `userToken`, if it is available, in an `Authorization` header by executing the following code:

```
headers: {
  "Authorization": userToken
}
```

5. Now we have access to the user information in the backend. If we analyze the `event` object, we can retrieve the `userId` variable by executing the following code:

```
module.exports.handler = (event, context, callback) => {

  let userId = null;

  if (event.requestContext.authorizer)
    userId = event.requestContext.authorizer.claims.sub;

  // ...
}
```

The `userId` term is a **Universally Unique Identifier (UUID)**. An example of `userId` is as follows:

b90d0bba-0b65-4455-ab5a-f30477430f46

The `claims` object offers more user data, like the e-mail, using the `email` property.

Summary

In this chapter, we have discussed the basic security concepts and how to apply them in a serverless project. For our demo application, we have used Amazon Cognito to handle the authentication and authorization of users, so you have learned how to implement signup, signin, and logout features.

In the next chapter, we will use the Cognito credentials to access AWS IoT resources to handle serverless notifications. We will see how the backend can send messages to an authenticated user and how to provide real-time notifications to anonymous users.

9
Handling Serverless Notifications

Push notifications are a common use case for modern applications. They are important not just for mobile devices, but also for websites. When you are browsing your Facebook timeline and receive a notification that a friend has commented on one of your photos, this is a push notification. In this chapter, you will learn how to implement this feature in a serverless solution.

We will cover the following topics in this chapter:

- Implementing serverless notifications using AWS IoT
- Public and private notifications

By the end of this chapter, you'll have learned how to handle real-time notifications in a serverless application.

AWS IoT

It may sound strange to use the Internet of Things as a service for websites, but AWS IoT is the only service offered by Amazon that supports WebSockets in a serverless model. Without WebSockets, we need to rely on *polling*. Polling is the process where the client needs to make repeated and frequent requests to the server, checking whether a new message is available, while WebSockets are used to create a link between the client and the server where the server can send the message directly to the client without the need of being constantly requested. WebSockets are used to implement the *publish-subscribe* pattern, which is more efficient than *polling*.

Besides AWS IoT, another candidate to implement real-time serverless notifications is Amazon **Simple Queue Service** (**SQS**). You can create a queue of messages that are destined for a single user and wait for this user to request SQS looking for new messages. While polling is necessary for this solution, Amazon offers a feature named *long-polling*. With this feature, when you request a message to SQS, AWS will hold your request up to 20 seconds, waiting for a new message to arrive. If one arrives while waiting, you will receive the response immediately. If no message appears, after 20 seconds, you will receive an empty response and will need to make a new SQS request. This approach reduces the total number of requests and the costs associated with a frequent polling approach.

One advantage that SQS has over IoT is the guarantee that a message will be read. If you place a message in SQS, it will be removed only when someone receive it, while with IoT, the user must be connected to receive the message.

Another service that is used for notifications is Amazon **Simple Notification Service** (**SNS**). Although the name sounds like an obvious choice for serverless notifications, it does not support WebSockets and you can't hook a browser client to receive notifications on demand. However, for mobile applications, you can use it with push notifications services, such as **Google Cloud Messaging** (**GCM**), for real-time messages without polling.

You may not like the name "IoT", but it is a great service and solves our use case of getting notifications respecting the serverless model. AWS IoT is a simple messaging service. You can have *devices* subscribed to *topics* to receive messages that will be published by other devices. In our examples, you will consider a *device* as a user connected through a web browser that will receive messages from other users or from a Lambda function.

Protocols

AWS IoT supports *HTTP*, *MQTT*, and *MQTT over WebSockets* protocols. HTTP uses a RESTful endpoint and **Message Queue Telemetry Transport** (**MQTT**) is a lightweight messaging protocol that was created for small sensors and constrained devices.

You may think that using HTTP would be the easiest option for us who already know how to use RESTful endpoints, but HTTP support is restricted to publishing messages. In a REST architecture, you can't subscribe to messages, since the server can't initiate transmissions. The server is only able to answer requests.

MQTT over WebSockets is an enhancement to the MQTT protocol with the objective of supporting browser-based applications. It supports the *subscribe* feature, so your user can be hooked waiting for messages instead of being constantly polling for updates every few seconds. Avoiding a polling mechanism is strictly necessary for efficiency and to allow scalability when you want to serve thousands of users simultaneously.

Finding the IoT endpoint

To use the AWS IoT service, you must provide the IoT endpoint of your account from the region that you want to use this service. Let's execute the following steps to find the IoT endpoint:

1. You can find this information using the IoT Management Console, which is available at `https://console.aws.amazon.com/iot`.
2. In the top-right corner, you can change the service region. Click on **Get started** to move to the next screen:

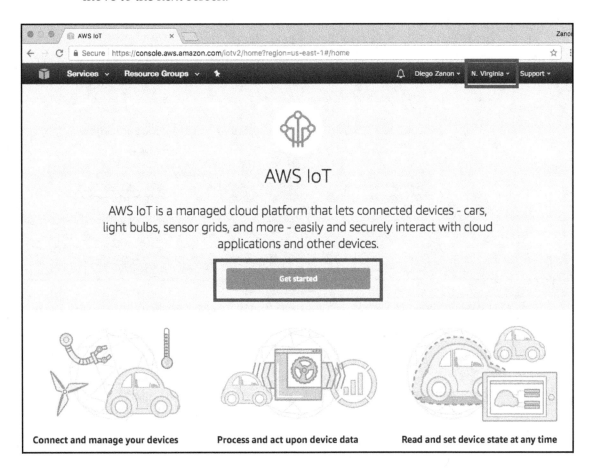

3. On the console screen, choose the **Settings** option located in the bottom-left corner:

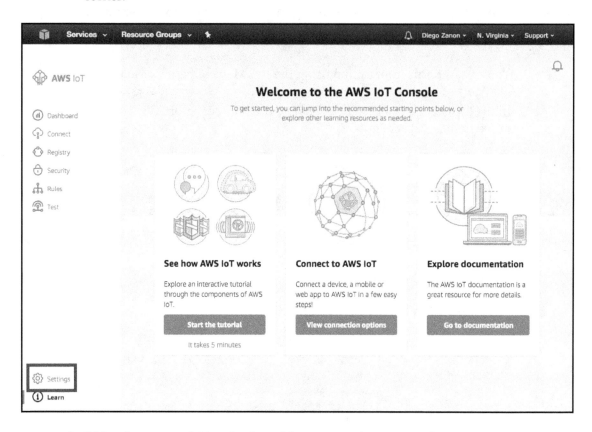

4. Write down your IoT endpoint address to use in your application:

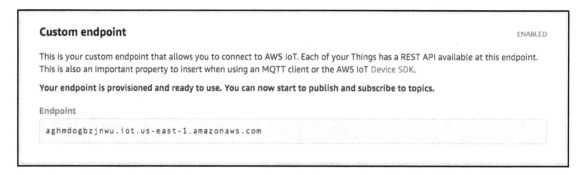

Security observation: the endpoint address doesn't need to be private. You can hardcode it in your application and distribute it to your clients, since the frontend code needs to know this address to access IoT messages.

5. For our demo application, the frontend code we will have this information in the `config.js` file:

```
"iot": {
  "REGION": "us-east-1",
  "ENDPOINT": "abcdef.iot.us-east-1.amazonaws.com"
}
```

AWS IoT SDK

Handling the MQTT protocol and signing each request can be a troublesome task. Fortunately, we don't need to *reinvent the wheel*. AWS offers an SDK that implements the MQTT protocol for us and offers all the features that we need to use. You can find the source code on GitHub at `https://github.com/aws/aws-iot-device-sdk-js`.

You can install the module using npm by executing this command:

```
npm install aws-iot-device-sdk --save
```

To use this SDK, we need to pass the following information:

- **Credentials**: The SDK will need to know the AWS access key, AWS secret access key, and session token to be able to sign the requests and get the authorization to access the AWS resources. We are going to use Cognito later to dynamically retrieve temporary credentials.
- **Region**: The region of the AWS IoT service that we are going to use.
- **IoT endpoint**: The IoT endpoint that we have just retrieved.
- **IoT topic**: You don't need to explicitly create an IoT topic beforehand. Just choose a word and use it as a channel to exchange messages. However, your credentials must have authorization to this topic or to * (all topics).

For our example, we are going to create a class in a `iot.js` file inside the frontend's `lib` folder:

```
import awsIot from 'aws-iot-device-sdk';
import config from './config';

export default class IoT {
  constructor(keys, messageCallback) {
    this.client = null;
    this.accessKey = keys.accessKey;
    this.secretKey = keys.secretKey;
    this.sessionToken = keys.sessionToken;
    this.messageCallback = messageCallback;
  }

  connect() {
    // TODO
  }

  publish(topic, message) {
    // TODO
  }

  subscribe(topic) {
    // TODO
  }
}
```

This class has a constructor which receives the necessary credentials and a `messageCallback` function that will be used as a dependency injection. Whenever we receive a new message, we are going to call this `messageCallback` function to execute the desired logic by the one that has created the new object instance of the IoT class.

Let's now see how to implement the `connect`, `publish`, and `subscribe` methods:

```
connect() {
  this.client = awsIot.device({
    region: config.iot.REGION,
    host: config.iot.ENDPOINT,
    accessKeyId: this.accessKey,
    secretKey: this.secretKey,
    sessionToken: this.sessionToken,
    port: 443,
    protocol: 'wss' // WebSocket with TLS
  });

  this.client.on('connect', this.handleConnect);
```

```
    this.client.on('message', this.handleMessage);
    this.client.on('close', this.handleClose);
  }

publish(topic, message) {
  this.client.publish(topic, message);
}

subscribe(topic) {
  this.client.subscribe(topic);
}
```

In the previous code, the `connect` method subscribes the `client` object to three events:

- The `connect` event
- The `message` event
- The `close` event

There are also three more events that you can subscribe to make your application more robust:

- The `error` event
- The `reconnect` event
- The `offline` event

The last step is to define the methods that will handle these events. They are defined as the following:

```
handleConnect() {
  console.log('Connected');
}

handleMessage(topic, message) {
  this.messageCallback(topic, message);
}

handleClose() {
  console.log('Connection closed');
}
```

Implementing serverless notifications

In the previous section, you learned about the AWS IoT SDK, we just haven't tested it yet. In this section, we will use it in the following two features of our serverless store:

- Live comments in a product review page
- Notifications after a payment has been accepted

The first feature is a type of a **public notification**, as it uses an IoT topic that all users can read. The second one is a **private notification**, so only one person and the Lambda backend are allowed to access the IoT topic to subscribe or publish messages. We will cover both of them to learn how to give proper access for each case.

Those two examples will illustrate how you can work with IoT to serve notifications, but it does not limit what you can do with it. You can think in other use cases. For example, IoT can also be used for serverless multiplayer games. You could build an HTML5 game that could make requests to a Lambda backend to execute some logic (for example, find a room to play) and an IoT topic to exchange messages between players. It may not be well suited to very dynamic games like FPS games, but could be pretty useful and cheap for card games, puzzles, and games where you don't need extremely low and predictable response times.

Public notifications

In Chapter 5, *Building the Frontend*, we defined the product details view and it has a list of all customer reviews. What we are going to implement here is *live comments*. When a user adds a new review, another user that is browsing the same page will see the message at the same moment that it is posted. It may not seem to be so important for a customer review page, but this is the kind of feature that is extremely important for chat systems, forums, and social networks.

Adding a comment box

The following screenshot shows the current state of our product details page:

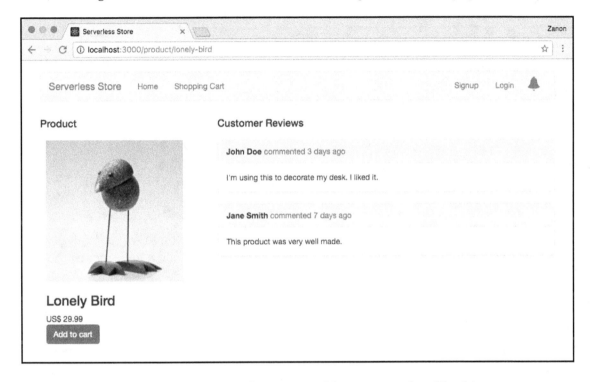

We are going to modify the React application to add a comment box like this one:

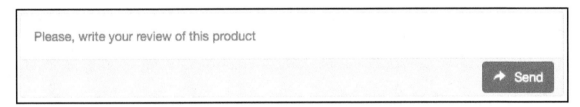

For this task, we need to create a `CommentBox` component that will be rendered as input text and a button:

```
return (
  <div className="comment-box">
    <input type="text" onChange={this.handleChange}
           value={this.state.input} />
    <button onClick={this.handleClick}>
```

```
        <i className="glyphicon glyphicon-share-alt">
        </i> Send
      </button>
    </div>
  );
```

When defining the elements, we have placed an `onChange` event to the input text to save the input value and an `onClick` event to send the information to the `App` component. They are implemented as the following:

```
handleChange(e) {
   this.setState({ input: e.target.value });
}

handleClick() {
   this.props.onComment(this.state.input, this.props.productId);
   this.setState({ input: '' });
}
```

This completes the `CommentBox` implementation. What we are going to see next is how the `App` component will handle these events to update the page and send a message to other users that are on the same page.

Updating the list of comments

In the `App` component, we need to handle comment creation. In the following code excerpt, we are creating a new comment object and adding it to the beginning of the comment list array:

```
handleComments(comment, productId) {
  const newComment = {
    id: uuid(),
    username: 'user1337',
    age: 'a few seconds ago',
    text: comment
  };

  const product = this.state
                      .products
                      .find(p => p.id === productId);

  // add to the comment to the beginning of the array
  product.comments.unshift(newComment);

  this.setState({
    products: this.state.products
```

```
    });

    // TODO: send the new comment to IoT
}
```

 To set the ID of the comment, I've used the `UUID` module (`npm install uuid --save`) to create a random value. Example of an UUID: `110ec58a-a0f2-4ac4-8393-c866d813b8d1`

What we need to do now is to send the new comment to the IoT service, so it can be shared with other users on the same page and saved in the database. For now, our comment feature should be working and updating the list of customer reviews:

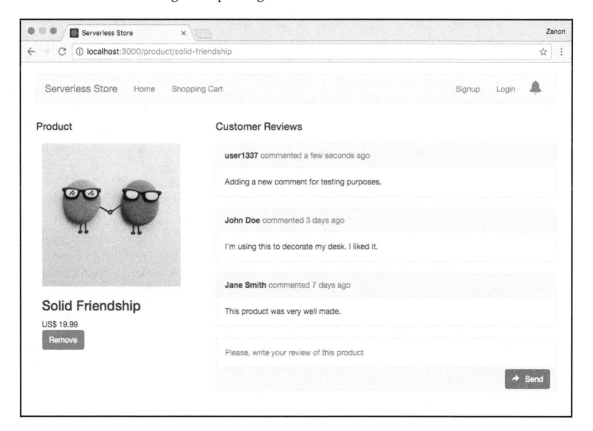

Creating a new instance of the IoT SDK

In this section, we are going to create a new instance of the IoT class that uses the IoT SDK. This class needs AWS access keys to connect with the IoT services. As we are handling public notifications that don't need an authenticated user, we need to create credentials for anonymous users.

Let's create a new instance of the IoT SDK by performing the following steps:

1. We will start adding the AWS SDK to our frontend project using npm:

```
npm install aws-sdk --save
```

2. With the AWS SDK, we can request anonymous access to Cognito using the following code:

```
AWS.config.region = config.cognito.REGION;
AWS.config.credentials =
  new AWS.CognitoIdentityCredentials({
    IdentityPoolId: config.cognito.IDENTITY_POOL_ID
  });

AWS.config.credentials.get(() => {
  const keys = {
    accessKey: AWS.config.credentials.accessKeyId,
    secretKey: AWS.config.credentials.secretAccessKey,
    sessionToken: AWS.config.credentials.sessionToken
  }
});
```

3. As we configured in the previous chapter, this identity pool gives access to anonymous users to the IoT topic `serverless-store-comments`. With those keys in hand, we are ready to create an instance of the IoT class, connect, and subscribe with this topic:

```
const getIotClient = (messageCallback, callback) {
  retrieveAwsKeys(keys => {
    const client = new IoT(keys, messageCallback);
    client.connect();
    client.subscribe('serverless-store-comments');
    callback(null, client);
  });
}
```

Sending and receiving new comments

The App component is our entity responsible for managing the application state. Therefore, it will be responsible for sending and receiving comments. To implement this, we need to make the following three changes:

1. Modify the componentDidMount to create an instance of the IoT class:

```
componentDidMount() {
  getIotClient(
    this.handleIotMessages,
    (err, client) => {
      if (err) alert(err);
      else this.setState({iotClient: client})
    });
}
```

2. Modify the handleComments function to send new comments using IoT:

```
handleComments(comment, productId) {
  const newComment = {
    id: uuid(),
    username: 'user1337',
    age: 'a few seconds ago',
    text: comment
  };

  const topic = 'serverless-store-comments';
  const message = JSON.stringify({
    comment: newComment,
    productId: productId
  });

  this.state.iotClient.publish(topic, message);
}
```

3. Create the handleIotMessages function to receive the messages and update the list of comments:

```
handleIotMessages(topic, message) {
  const msg = JSON.parse(message.toString());

  if (topic === 'serverless-store-comments') {
    const id = msg.productId;
    const product = this.state
                        .products
                        .find(p => p.id === id);
```

```
        product.comments.unshift(msg.comment);
        this.setState({
          products: this.state.products
        });
      }
    }
```

Test the application, running it using two browser tabs. When you add a comment in one tab, the same comment must appear immediately in the other tab.

Triggering a Lambda function with IoT

The IoT service is being used to exchange live messages between connected users. However, the information is not being persisted. What we are going to do here is to trigger a Lambda function when a new message arrives to an IoT topic, so this message can be persisted.

We can trigger a Lambda function by configuring an event in the `serverless.yml` file:

```
functions:
  comments:
    handler: functions/comments.handler
    events:
      - iot:
          sql: "SELECT * FROM 'topic-name'"
```

 For our example, replace `topic-name` with `serverless-store-comments`.

IoT uses an SQL-like syntax to trigger the Lambda function and to select which content will be sent. In the preceding example, we are passing all contents of the message to the Lambda function.

This SQL statement can be very useful for filtering messages to only trigger a Lambda function when necessary. For example, suppose that we send a message with the following JSON object:

```
{
  "comment": "this is a bad product",
  "rating": 2
}
```

We could use the SQL statement to trigger another Lambda function, for example `handle-bad-reviews`, only when the rating is low:

```
"SELECT * FROM 'topic-name' WHERE rating < 3"
```

Going back to our serverless store example, we have defined the trigger to the Lambda function. Now we can implement the function to save the data into the database. As using a serverless database was already covered in Chapter 7, *Managing a Serverless Database*, the next example will just log the contents of the `event` object for testing purposes:

```
const utils = require('../lib/utils');

module.exports.handler = (event, context, callback) => {
  console.log(event);
  utils.successHandler(event, callback);
};
```

You can test if it is working using the `logs` command of the Serverless Framework:

```
serverless logs --function comments
```

Private notifications

In Chapter 8, *Securing the Serverless Application*, we defined a policy document for authenticated users to include an authorization to the following IoT topic:

serverless-store-${cognito-identity.amazonaws.com:sub}

This means that an authenticated user will have access to an exclusive topic, the name of which is defined by its own federated identity. What we are going to implement next is a *private notification*, where a Lambda function will publish a message to an IoT topic and just one user will be able to receive it.

Using credentials of an authenticated user

For an unauthenticated user, we saw that we set credentials using the following code:

```
AWS.config.region = config.cognito.REGION;
AWS.config.credentials =
  new AWS.CognitoIdentityCredentials({
    IdentityPoolId: config.cognito.IDENTITY_POOL_ID
  });
```

However, for an authenticated user, the `credentials` object needs to be set with an extra property: `Logins`. The following code shows how this is done:

```
const region = config.cognito.REGION;
const pool = config.cognito.USER_POOL_ID;
const authenticator =
  `cognito-idp.${region}.amazonaws.com/${pool}`;

AWS.config.credentials =
  new AWS.CognitoIdentityCredentials({
    IdentityPoolId: config.cognito.IDENTITY_POOL_ID,
    Logins: {
      [authenticator]: userToken
    }
  });
```

Updating the logout feature

When we use the AWS credentials feature, the AWS SDK saves user data to local storage. To avoid another user logging on the same browser to use the credentials of the previous user, we need to clear that data on logout. This is done by adding the following piece of code to the `Logout` handler:

```
if (AWS.config.credentials) {
  AWS.config.credentials.clearCachedId();
}
```

Creating an IoT policy

Using an authenticated user to connect to IoT requires an extra step: we need to attach an IoT security policy. Without this attachment, the IoT service will reject all requests.

Let's see how to create this policy by performing the following steps:

1. Open the IoT Console at `https://console.aws.amazon.com/iot`.
2. In the left-hand menu, navigate to **Security | Policies** and then click on **Create a policy**:

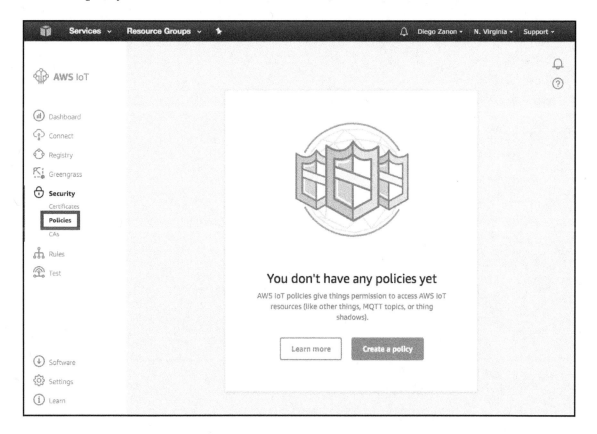

3. Choose a policy name, use the **Action** iot:Connect, iot:Subscribe, iot:Publish, and iot:Receive, type * for the **Resource**, and check **Allow** for the **Effect**:

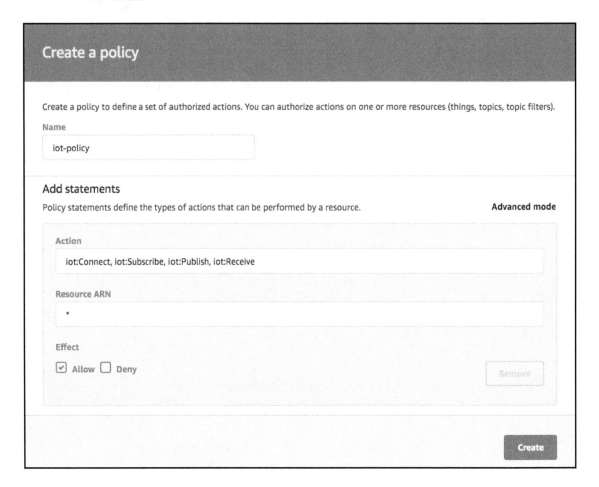

4. Click on **Create** to finish.

 Security observation: although we have selected the * resource, we won't be able to subscribe or publish to all topics because AWS will use the Cognito roles to check permissions and this policy document was set with restricted access.

Attaching an IoT policy and connecting

In the previous chapter, we set the Cognito policy document to allow access to the action
`iot:attachPrincipalPolicy`. Now we are going to use it. After getting the AWS
credentials, we are going to use the `AWS.Iot` module and the `attachPrincipalPolicy`
function to attach the IoT policy that we have just created to the authenticated user. After
setting the policy, we are going to connect to IoT and subscribe to the public and private
topics:

```
AWS.config.credentials.get(() => {
  const keys = {
    accessKey: AWS.config.credentials.accessKeyId,
    secretKey: AWS.config.credentials.secretAccessKey,
    sessionToken: AWS.config.credentials.sessionToken
  }

  const awsIoT = new AWS.Iot();
  const params = {
    policyName: 'iot-policy',
    principal: AWS.config.credentials.identityId
  }

  awsIoT.attachPrincipalPolicy(params, (err, res) => {
    if (err) alert(err);
    else {
      const client = new IoT(keys, messageCallback);
      client.connect();

      // subscribe to the public topic
      client.subscribe('serverless-store-comments');

      // subscribe to the private topic
      const id = AWS.config.credentials.identityId;
      client.subscribe('serverless-store-' + id);

      callback(null, client);
    }
  });
});
```

Passing the Cognito Identity to the Lambda function

In the previous chapter, when we have defined the restricted access to IoT resources, we have used the `${cognito-identity.amazonaws.com:sub}` IAM policy variable to define the IoT topic name. This parameter uses the Cognito Identity, but the backend code doesn't know this value. The Lambda function will retrieve a User ID through the authorizer (`event.requestContext.authorizer.claims.sub`), but the Authorizer ID is different from the Cognito Identity.

To pass this value from the frontend code to the backend, AWS recommends we send a signed request using its **Signature Version 4 (Sigv4)** signing process. Furthermore, instead of setting the Cognito authorizer in the API Gateway, you need to use the **AWS_IAM** authorizer. It's the safest way to pass this information to the backend because this method guarantees that only the real user will be able to send its Cognito ID.

However, we won't cover this topic here. Signing the request with **Sigv4** and using **AWS_IAM** authorizer is much more complicated than using the the Cognito authorizer and our demo application doesn't need this because we use the Authorizer ID to identify a user and not the Cognito ID. Besides, as we have configured the IoT role policy, it's impossible for one user to receive a message created to another user, even if a malicious user knows the other user's Identity. The worst case scenario would be for a malicious user to trigger unwanted messages to other users, which will happen only if the other user credentials were compromised.

So, in our case, we are going to send Cognito ID from the frontend to the backend using the `AWS.config.credentials.identityId` parameter in the `Checkout` request.

Sending IoT messages with Lambda

We have modified the application to subscribe the authenticated user to a public and a private topic. What we are going to look at now is how to send a message to this private topic using a Lambda function by performing the following steps:

1. The first step is to modify the `serverless.yml` file to give explicit permissions to allow access to `iot:Publish`:

```
provider:
  name: aws
  runtime: nodejs6.10
  iamRoleStatements:
    - Effect: "Allow"
      Action:
        - "iot:Publish"
      Resource:
        "arn:aws:iot:<region>:<account>:topic/*"
```

2. For our example, we are going to use the `processCheckout` function. The user will click on **Checkout** and this action will trigger a Lambda function that will publish a message to the user topic. The result will be the notification icon changing color to notify the user that a new message is available:

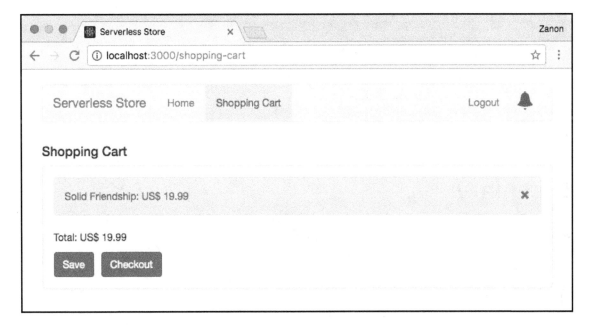

3. Changing the frontend application is a simple task, so it will be an exercise for the reader. Regarding the backend code, we are going to use the following code for the `processCheckout` function:

```
const AWS = require('aws-sdk');
const utils = require('./utils');

module.exports.processCheckout = (cognitoId, callback) => {
  const iotdata = new AWS.IotData({
    endpoint: 'YOUR_IOT_ENDPOINT'
  });

  const params = {
    topic: 'serverless-store-' + cognitoId,
    payload: 'Your payment was confirmed.'
  };

  iotdata.publish(params, (err, res) => {
    if (err) utils.errorHandler(err, callback);
    else utils.successHandler(res, callback);
  });
};
```

 Remember that the `userId` variable was retrieved in the previous chapter by analyzing the `event` object:
`event.requestContext.authorizer.claims.sub`

Summary

In this chapter, you learned how to create serverless notifications using the AWS IoT service. We covered how to implement a live comment system and push notifications for individual users. You already know how to use the AWS IoT Device SDK and how to use the IoT to trigger Lambda functions or to use a Lambda to send messages to an IoT endpoint.

In the next chapter, we will finish the online store, showing how to test our serverless application, followed by the definition of a deployment workflow for development and production environments, and we will finish off by showing what you can (and should) monitor in a serverless solution.

10
Testing, Deploying, and Monitoring

We are approaching the end of this book, but we can't finish without discussing some aspects that are beyond coding a solution. We need to understand how you can test functions that run in an environment that you don't own, what is a good development workflow to deploy and deliver new versions of your solution, and, although we don't need to worry about servers when building a serverless project, we need to understand what is the minimal monitoring that we need to configure to provide a cost-efficient and reliable solution.

In this chapter, we will cover the following topics:

- Testing a serverless solution
- Defining how to handle the deployment and delivery of new versions
- Monitoring errors, performance, and costs

After this chapter, you'll have completed the book and will be prepared to build your next solution with serverless components or enhance an existing one benefiting from the serverless concept.

Testing your solution

Testing a serverless project can be a challenging experience, since we rely on many different cloud services that are hard to emulate locally and, besides testing individual services, we need to test how they work together.

However, the practices that you have already used in traditional projects can all be used for serverless applications. To improve the quality of your software, you may use **Test-Driven Development (TDD)**, **Behavior-Driven Development (BDD)**, or any other development process that fundamentally relies on automating tests. Although we don't have access to the machines that will execute the code, we can simulate many things locally and we can run integrations tests from time to time to assert that everything works as expected.

In the following sections, we are going to see how to create tests for the backend and frontend. To make this topic simpler, we are going to create tests for trivial functions. If you want more extensive examples, you can browse the code files of this chapter to see how the serverless store was tested.

Unit testing Lambda functions

Since a Lambda function is defined in a common JavaScript file, you just need to set your testing tool to load this file and test the function locally. To simulate the input data that is set by the API Gateway or another trigger, you need to set the event variable of your test according to the expected input.

Let's perform the following steps to see how to unit test a Lambda function:

1. First, let's create a new serverless project by running the following command:

   ```
   serverless create --template aws-nodejs --name testing
   ```

2. Now, let's modify the serverless.yml file to the following:

   ```
   service: testing-service

   provider:
     name: aws
     runtime: nodejs6.10

   functions:
     hello:
       handler: functions/greetings.hello
   ```

3. In this project, we have only one Lambda function, and this `hello` function is defined by a `greetings.js` file inside a folder named `functions`. Consider the following simple implementation:

```
module.exports.hello = (event, context, callback) => {
  const message = `Hello, ${event.name}!`
  callback(null, message);
};
```

4. This `hello` function is the function that we want to test. Now, let's create our testing code. In the following screenshot, we show the project tree, where a folder named `test` was created and it contains a `mocha.opts` file, along with two other folders, `unit` and `integration`. Since this sample code doesn't interact with any other service, we can call it a `unit` test and the file `test-greetings.js` is where it will be implemented:

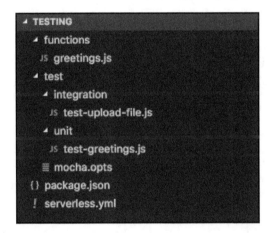

5. We can exclude this `test` folder and all of its contents from the deployment package by adding an exclude rule at the end of the `serverless.yml` file:

```
package:
  exclude:
    - test/**
```

6. Regarding the `mocha.opts` file, it was included to configure the options for the Mocha test framework (`https://mochajs.org/`), but you can use any other testing tool.

7. In this `mocha.opts` file, I've added only one line of code to specify which folder must be used to run tests:

```
test/unit
```

The `unit` folder will hold unit tests, which are tests that must execute in milliseconds so that the developer can immediately assert the state of the code with each modification. The `integration` folder holds tests that access external services and are allowed to complete in seconds/minutes. These are designed to execute occasionally, usually once a day, and not as frequently as unit tests. So, they were not included in the options.

8. Mocha is installed through npm, so we need to add a `package.json` file and execute the following command:

```
npm install mocha --save-dev
```

9. In the `package.json` file, add a `test` command with the `mocha` value in the `scripts` field. It will be helpful later, since you can run the `npm test` command to execute the unit tests:

```
{
    "name": "testing",
    "version": "1.0.0",
    "scripts": {
        "test": "mocha"
    },
    "devDependencies": {
        "mocha": "^3.2.0"
    }
}
```

10. Now that we have properly set up the test environment, we can implement the test file named `test-greetings.js`. To use Mocha, we need to use the `describe` function to list the test cases and the `it` function to implement a test case:

```
const assert = require('assert');

// list the unit tests of the greetings function
describe('Greetings', () => {

    // this is the only test that we have for this file
    describe('#hello()', () => {
```

```
    // the `done` argument must be used only for
    // async tests, like this one
    it('should return hello + name', (done) => {

        // the test code will be defined here

    });
  });
});
```

11. For this Lambda function, we can implement the following test:

```
// load the Lambda function
const greetings = require('../../lib/greetings');

// set the event variable as expected by the function
const event = {
  name: 'John'
};

// context can be null in this test
const context = null;

// invoke the function locally
greetings.hello(event, context, (err, response) => {
  const expected = 'Hello, John!';
  const actual = response;
  // testing if the result is the expected
  assert.equal(expected, actual);

  // exiting successfully if `err` variable is null
  done(err);
});
```

12. To execute the tests, run `npm test`. You should receive the following output:

```
●  ●  ●                    backend — -bash — 80×24
MacBook:backend zanon$ npm test

> testing@1.0.0 test /Users/zanon/Desktop/testing/backend
> mocha


  Greetings
    #hello()
      ✓ should return hello + name


  1 passing (11ms)

MacBook:backend zanon$
```

13. As a good practice, you should always *test* the test. You can do this by changing the expected result from `Hello, John!` to `Bye, John!`, which will obviously make the assert fail, resulting in the following output:

```
●  ●  ●                    backend — -bash — 80×24
  Greetings
    #hello()
      1) should return hello + name


  0 passing (13ms)
  1 failing

  1) Greetings #hello() should return hello + name:

      AssertionError: 'Bye, John!' == 'Hello, John!'
      + expected - actual

      -Bye, John!
      +Hello, John!

      at greetings.hello (test/unit/test-greetings.js:29:24)
      at Object.module.exports.hello (functions/greetings.js:5:5)
      at Context.it (test/unit/test-greetings.js:23:23)


MacBook:backend zanon$
```

Mocking external services

Sometimes, you can't unit test a Lambda function directly simply because, sometimes, you can't consider the function as a *unit*. If the function interacts with external services, like sending a notification or persisting some data in a database, you can't consider it as a unit of logic. In this case, you can only unit test the function if you remove such dependencies from the test, and you do so by *mocking* them.

Mocking is the act of building an object to simulate the behavior of another object. When we need to test a complex service, there are many underlying behaviors that we may not be interested in testing. For example, if I use an external service to process credit card payments and I want to test whether it processes correctly for a given input, I don't want to handle unexpected events such as connectivity issues. In this case, I could create a fake object that would imitate the expected behavior and my test case would return success or failure if a specific condition is met.

To be able to mock services, we need to separate the business logic from external services. With this approach, we can write unit tests and keep the solution less dependent of cloud services, which helps if one day you need to migrate from one cloud provider to another.

The following code shows an example where there **isn't** a clear separation of the business logic and services. Therefore, it is harder to test:

```
const db = require('db');
const notifier = require('notifier');

module.exports.saveOrder = (event, context, callback) => {

  db.saveOrder(event.order, (err) => {
    if (err) {
      callback(err);
    } else {
      notifier.sendEmail(event.email, callback);
    }
  });
};
```

This example receives an order information, saves it in a database, and sends an e-mail notification. There are two main problems here such as the code is bound to the input (how it handles the `event` object) and you can't unit test the inner contents of the Lambda function without triggering requests to the database and the notification service.

A better implementation is to create a separated module that will control the business logic, and to build this module allowing you to inject the dependencies:

```
class Order {

  // Dependency Injection
  constructor(db, notifier) {
    this.db = db;
    this.notifier = notifier;
  }

  save(order, email, callback) {
    this.db.saveOrder(order, (err) => {
      if (err) {
        callback(err);
      } else {
        this.notifier.sendEmail(email, callback);
      }
    });
  }
}

module.exports = Order;
```

Now, this code can be unit tested since the database and notifier services are passed as input values, so they can be mocked.

Regarding the Lambda code, it becomes much simpler:

```
const db = require('db');
const notifier = require('notifier');
const Order = require('order');

const order = new Order(db, notifier);

module.exports.saveOrder = (event, context, callback) => {
  order.save(event.order, event.email, callback);
};
```

Using Sinon.JS for mocking

In the previous example, we improved the Lambda function by creating an external module, named `Order`, to handle all actions related to orders. This was necessary because we can only mock the objects that we have access to. We won't be able to test the Lambda function directly because we don't have access to the services that it uses (database and notifications), but at least we will be able to test the `Order` class, since it allows the services to be injected.

For our mocking example, we are going to use Sinon.JS. It can be installed with the following command:

```
npm install sinon --save-dev
```

Sinon will be used along with Mocha. So, we will need to create a test case like the following one:

```
const assert = require('assert');
const sinon = require('sinon');
const Order = require('./order');

describe('Order', () => {
  describe('#saveOrder()', () => {
    it('should call db and notifier', (done) => {
      // the test code will be defined here

    });
  });
});
```

We can implement this test as the following:

```
// define the behavior of the fake functions
const dbMock = {
  saveOrder: (order, callback) => {
    callback(null);
  }
}

const notifierMock = {
  sendEmail: (email, callback) => {
    callback(null);
  }
}

// spy the objects to identify when and how they are executed
sinon.spy(dbMock, 'saveOrder');
```

```
    sinon.spy(notifierMock, 'sendEmail');

    // define the input event
    const event = {
      order: { id: 1 },
      email: 'example@example.com'
    };

    // inject the mocked objects
    const order = new Order(dbMock, notifierMock);

    // execute the function
    order.save(event.order, event.email, (err, res) => {

      // assert if the mocked functions were used as expected
      assert(dbMock.saveOrder.calledOnce, true);
      assert(notifierMock.sendEmail.calledOnce, true);
      assert(dbMock.saveOrder.calledWith(event.order), true);
      assert(notifierMock.sendEmail.calledWith(event.email), true);

      done(err);
    });
```

This example shows that you can use Sinon.JS to check whether your dependencies are being called as expected and with the correct parameters. You can improve this example, adding fake responses and testing different behaviors, but we won't go deeper into this subject because those features are not strictly related to serverless. The objective here is to show that common testing frameworks can be used with serverless without needing anything special to configure them.

Testing the frontend

We have developed the frontend using React, so we will build a simple example to show how you can test it. The objective is to see if a simple component renders correctly and if it displays a text as expected.

Let's take a look at the following steps to create this example:

1. We will start by creating a new React project executing the following command:

   ```
   create-react-app frontend-test
   ```

2. Create React App uses Jest as its test runner. As a convention, it will always looks for files that end with `.test.js` to execute the tests. In the default template, we have the `App.js` and `App.test.js` files. If you run `npm test`, Jest will execute the sample test that was created in `App.test.js` and it will output the following result:

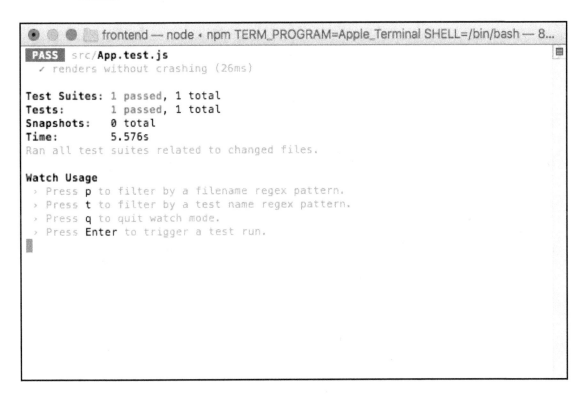

```
● ● ●    frontend — node ‹ npm TERM_PROGRAM=Apple_Terminal SHELL=/bin/bash — 8...
PASS  src/App.test.js
  ✓ renders without crashing (26ms)

Test Suites: 1 passed, 1 total
Tests:       1 passed, 1 total
Snapshots:   0 total
Time:        5.576s
Ran all test suites related to changed files.

Watch Usage
 › Press p to filter by a filename regex pattern.
 › Press t to filter by a test name regex pattern.
 › Press q to quit watch mode.
 › Press Enter to trigger a test run.
```

 After running `npm test`, Jest will be watching for changes, so you can continue developing your frontend and Jest will execute all test cases whenever you save a file.

3. Inside `App.js`, we have an `App` component defined by the following code:

```
render() {
  return (
    <div className="App">
      <div className="App-header">
        <img src={logo} alt="logo"/>
        <h2>Welcome to React</h2>
      </div>
    </div>
  );
}
```

4. And `App.test.js` is defined by the following code, which is just a smoke test to see if the component can be rendered without crashing:

```
import React from 'react';
import ReactDOM from 'react-dom';
import App from './App';

it('renders without crashing', () => {
  const div = document.createElement('div');
  ReactDOM.render(<App/>, div);
});
```

5. Now we are going to improve this test case and we will need to install two helper tools such as Enzyme and react-test-renderer:

```
npm install enzyme react-test-renderer --save-dev
```

6. With Enzyme, we can simplify the previous example by using the `mount` function instead of `ReactDOM.render`:

```
import React from 'react';
import ReactDOM from 'react-dom';
import App from './App';
import { mount } from 'enzyme';

it('renders without crashing', () => {
  mount(<App/>);
});
```

7. To finish this example, we are going to add another test case to see if a given element, `<h2>Welcome to React</h2>`, was rendered within this component as we are expecting:

```
it('renders with "Welcome to React"', () => {
  const wrapper = mount(<App/>);
  const welcome = <h2>Welcome to React</h2>;
  expect(wrapper.contains(welcome)).toEqual(true);
});
```

Simulating AWS services locally

One of the drawbacks of using cloud services is that they offer products that you can't install on your own machine. If you could install them, your development speed would increase because testing locally is faster them connecting to them through the Internet.

To solve this limitation, there are many tools that have been created by the community to help you to simulate AWS services by running them locally. You can find some of them in the following links:

- **Lambda functions**: `https://github.com/lambci/docker-lambda`
- **API Gateway and Lambda**: `https://github.com/dherault/serverless-offline`
- **Scheduled Lambda functions**: `https://github.com/ajmath/serverless-offline-scheduler`
- **DynamoDB**: `https://github.com/mhart/dynalite`

There are some benefits and drawbacks with this strategy. Particularly, I don't buy this idea and I don't use them. You can find my view of the pros and cons as follows and decide for yourself if those tools may improve your development workflow:

Pros:

- **Speed**: It is faster to run locally than using the Internet.
- **Tests**: Some tools are just mocks that simulate the behavior of a real service without making any I/O operations, which means that you can test your services without changing your code. Others are similar implementations that allows you to debug your code.
- **Costs**: You can run them for free using your own machine.

Cons:

- **Speed**: Most services need extra configuration steps. For a small project, you may take more time configuring and troubleshooting issues with the fake services than you will benefit from faster tests.
- **Tests**: It is hard to feel confident in your tests if you are using only simulated services. You need to run integration tests with real services from time to time. Also, you may not be able to do some tests. For example, simulating IAM permissions is really hard.
- **Costs**: You may spend more developer-hours configuring those tools than you will save on cloud costs. Most cloud providers have adopted a pricing schema where they offer a free tier that allows developers to build and test their products for free and the providers just start to charge money when the service is used intensively.

Deploying your application

In this section, we will discuss the deployment of a serverless application. I'm not referring to just running the `serverless deploy` command, what I mean is that you need to know and define how to handle and manage new versions of your application in the production environment.

Can you hit the deploy button at any time of the day? What are the implications? How can you create a replica of the production environment just for testing? Those are the kind of things that will be discussed in this section.

Development workflow

Deploying a new version of a Lambda function is a simple task. We run a command and the framework is responsible for packaging the contents and uploading them to AWS. However, running the `serverless deploy` command usually takes a couple of minutes. The problem is not the time to upload the ZIP file, but what the framework needs to update using CloudFormation. A new CloudFormation template needs to be issued asking AWS to update all related resources of a specific zone, which takes time. As our codebase grows, we may need to create dozens of API Gateway endpoints, many different IAM roles, or other kinds of AWS resources. Managing them can be troublesome, as they increase the deployment time to an unpleasant duration.

Reducing this time can be achieved using selective deployment. If you have modified just a specific function, you can make a fast deploy by referencing it using the following command:

```
serverless deploy function -f myFunction
```

Blue-green deployment

Blue-green deployment is a common technique to deploy a new version of software without generating unavailability. Consider that you're running an application of the 3.0 version and you want to deploy the new 3.1 version. Before you start updating your machines, all of them are using the 3.0 version and we say that they are in a *blue* state. We start by creating new machines with the updated code, version 3.1, and these machines are in a *green* state. The next step is to modify the load balancer to redirect all new connections to the new machines (green) while it keeps on running requests to the old machines (blue). After the previous calls finish running, the *blue* machines won't receive any new requests, and they can be shutdown.

Blue-green is important because, in the past, as we usually had just one web server machine to handle an application, the common practice was to stop the web server, update the code, and start it again. Those few seconds of unavailability were acceptable in the past, but today, with automation and the possibility of distributing the load among multiple servers, it is not necessary anymore to disrupt the service for an update or maintenance routine.

This concept is equivalent in the serverless world. When you update the code of a Lambda function, AWS will use it to handle new incoming requests while the previous one will keep running with the previous code. The API Gateway will also handle modifications in the endpoints behaviors without causing unavailability:

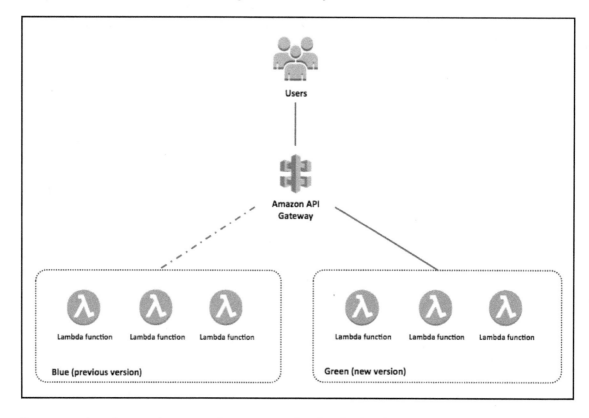

So, answering the previous question: can you hit the deploy button at any time of the day? Yes, you can deploy new versions of your application without worrying about availability. However, during the deployment of a new version, we can have different versions running simultaneously. You should pay attention to this case, especially regarding versions that require changes to the database model.

Deploying new versions with a different database model

In serverless, we usually run code that executes in fractions of a second. So, running two different versions simultaneously may take less than a second, but how do we apply databases changes in a model? Renaming a column may break the execution of a previous version.

Ideally, we would all be using NoSQL databases with flexible schemas, but that's not true. Some business cases are better handled by relational databases or NoSQL databases with a restrict schema.

When modifying a schema, there are three operations that require our attention such as create, rename, and drop.

Creating a new table or column

Adding a table or a column in a pre-existing table shouldn't break any kind of application. However, there are some ORM tools, such as the Entity Framework (for .NET), that associates each schema version with a migration ID. In this case, when you run a migrate command to upgrade a database schema, it adds a new migration ID that will be checked by the application code. If you run the previous version of the code, the ID will not match and it will return an error.

This kind of restriction was created as a safety measure to avoid a deprecated code from running in production and causing inconsistencies when the expected model is different. Though, if you have proper control over your deployments, you can disable this restriction to avoid unavailabilities while upgrading versions.

Also, we need to pay attention when we add constraints or foreign keys. If you modify a table with thousands of rows to add a new foreign key, the alter table command may need some significant time to process. While processing, the table will be locked for selects and this can lead to some query timeouts.

Renaming a table or column

Suppose you need to rename a column from name A to B. If you make this change, the previous code may not work properly, since it won't find the column with name A and the newest code may not work if deployed before the rename happens.

The proposed solution here is to make this change by performing the following steps:

1. Run a script to create a new column named B.
2. Add a temporary trigger that will execute every time that you modify some data in the A column to apply the same modifications to the B column.
3. Duplicate all contents from A to B.
4. Deploy a new code version that is exactly like the previous one, but read/write using the column B and not A.

5. Wait a bit to ensure that all requests are using the new Lambda code and not the previous one. You may need to wait for the maximum timeout of your Lambda functions.
6. Run another script that will remove column A and the temporary trigger.
7. Deploy your up-to-date code that uses column B and adds new features to your application.

Dropping a table or column

Dropping a table or column is a little bit easier. You just need to deploy a new application code that doesn't use the table or field that you want to remove. After waiting a little bit to ensure that the previous code has finished being executed, you can safely execute a script that will delete the table or remove the field.

Rollback a deployment

Sometimes, we deploy a new version of an application that may introduce a buggy feature. Depending on the error severity, you may need to rollback the application before starting to fix the error for a new deployment. You have two options for this rollback:

1. Version control all deployments in tags. When you need to rollback, select the code from the previous tag and run `serverless deploy` again.
2. Use the `serverless rollback` command to change your functions to a previous version.

AWS has a versioning system for our deployments, so using the `serverless rollback` command is safe and fast. This command should be used passing a `timestamp` parameter, like the following:

```
serverless rollback --timestamp <timestamp>
```

To find the timestamp information of our last deploy, we need to run the following command:

```
serverless deploy list
```

It will give you the following output:

```
● ● ●                  backend — -bash — 80×24
MacBook:backend zanon$ serverless deploy list
Serverless: Listing deployments:
Serverless: --------------
Serverless: Timestamp: 1499216161420
Serverless: Datetime: 2017-07-05T00:56:01.420Z
Serverless: Files:
Serverless: - compiled-cloudformation-template.json
Serverless: - testing.zip
Serverless:
Serverless: Timestamp: 1499216616127
Serverless: Datetime: 2017-07-05T01:03:36.127Z
Serverless: Files:
Serverless: - compiled-cloudformation-template.json
Serverless: - testing.zip
Serverless: --------------
Serverless: Timestamp: 1499217093742
Serverless: Datetime: 2017-07-05T01:11:33.742Z
Serverless: Files:
Serverless: - compiled-cloudformation-template.json
Serverless: - testing.zip
MacBook:backend zanon$
```

In the previous screenshot, we would use the value `1499216616127` for the `timestamp` parameter. Note that we need to select the penultimate version and not the last one.

> The command `serverless rollback` will rollback all functions for a previous deployment that was done with the command `serverless deploy`. If you used `serverless deploy function`, this change won't be versioned.

Creating staging environments

Best practice says that we must have different environments for development and production. You can also add a third environment, usually named *staging*, for testing:

- **Development**: This is where you deploy code as a work in progress, testing that it works together with other services
- **Staging**: This is usually necessary to validate the build by customers or a quality assurance team
- **Production**: This is where your application is visible by end users

All software that we develop is highly dependent on the environment, such as the operating system, runtime version, installed modules and dlls, external services, configuration files, and others. Therefore, it was a pretty common excuse, at least some years ago, for a developer to explain production errors saying that "it works on my machine". Mirroring the development environment with the production setting was a very difficult task. Sometimes, changes applied to one were not reflected to the other, causing strange errors.

With virtual machines, and more recently with Docker containers, this issue has greatly diminished, since we can now trust that we can perfectly reproduce production errors in our development machines and that what we build will work exactly as expected, regardless of the machine that executes it.

With cloud providers, all of our infrastructure can be scripted. So, we can automate how an environment can be created through code. In this case, you just need to change a variable value and deploy it again to mirror your development code with the production code. In your `serverless.yml` file, there is an option under `provider` that allows you to name your current environment and easily mirror it to others simply by choosing a new name for the `stage` property:

```
service: serverless-app

provider:
  name: aws
  runtime: nodejs6.10
  stage: dev
  region: us-east-1
```

Being careful with the production environment

Being able to easily mirror the development environment to production is a very powerful feature that needs to be used wisely. In my earlier days as a developer, I had the unfortunate habit of having the staging and production virtual machines open simultaneously. Which, of course, I stopped doing the day I messed with a production service thinking that I was changing the staging version.

What I recommend is to use the staging option to mirror the *development* environment with the *testing* environment. You can easily deploy a new version for your customer or for your quality assurance team, but you should *never* use your development machine to apply updates in production to avoid the associated risks.

Creating a new environment is as simple as choosing a new name for the stage. So, you can name it with things like test-2017-08-02 or test-feature-x to create new endpoints with a specific test environment.

You can designate someone in the team who will be the only person responsible for deploying a new production version. Restricting the responsibility to just one person will reduce the chance of accidents. Another option is to have one machine with the sole purpose of production deployments. Needing an extra step, which is to connect with the machine, helps because it forces you to be focused on the task and you won't accidentally select the wrong environment.

Furthermore, I also recommend that you have two different AWS accounts, one for development and testing, and another one exclusively for production. Although it is possible to configure the IAM roles to protect your environment and prevent the same user from modifying both environments, it is still risky. The IAM restrictions may be incorrectly configured, or you could add a new resource and forget to set the proper access, allowing undesired changes.

Test data

When you have your entire infrastructure scripted, the only difference between the development and production environments is the associated data. The test environment usually has its own fabricated data, but sometimes we can't reproduce errors, for example, performance issues or inconsistencies, because the underlying data is different.

However, making a backup of the production data and directly restoring a copy into the testing environment can be a bad practice for the following reasons:

- Production data contains real e-mails. Running test code may send accidental e-mails to real people.
- Production data contains sensitive data such as real names, e-mails, phone numbers, and addresses. Sharing this data with all developers is unnecessary and risky. The developer machine is much more unsafe and susceptible to being hacked than the production environment.

In this case, I recommend using fabricated data for most of the tests, and when you need to make performance tests or analyze a specific issue, you use a production backup but you need to have a procedure in place to modify the content, removing sensitive data before sharing the data with all developers.

Keeping your functions warm

As we have discussed in past chapters, one of the problems with serverless functions is the cold starts. When your Lambda function is triggered, AWS will find its package, unzip, and install it in a container to be executed. These steps takes some time (usually 5 seconds) and they delay the execution of your function.

After executing a function, AWS will keep it in a suspended state for a while. If a new request is done a few minutes later, it won't suffer from the cold start delay because the package will be readily available. After 15 minutes of inactivity, it will *freeze* again.

If your application needs to ensure low response times, you can deploy them with a configuration to keep them *warm*. There is a plugin for the Serverless Framework called **WarmUP** (`https://github.com/FidelLimited/serverless-plugin-warmup`) that will create a scheduled Lambda function that will be responsible by invoking the other functions from time to time (default it to 5 minutes).

Let's follow the following steps to see how to use it:

1. Create a new serverless project by executing the following command:

   ```
   serverless create --template aws-nodejs --name warmup
   ```

2. Create a `package.json` file.
3. Install the WarmUP plugin by executing the following command:

   ```
   npm install serverless-plugin-warmup --save-dev
   ```

4. Add the following reference to the end of the `serverless.yml` file:

   ```
   plugins:
     - serverless-plugin-warmup
   ```

5. For each function that you want to keep warm, add the `warm: true` pair:

   ```
   functions:
     hello:
       handler: handler.hello
       warmup: true
   ```

6. This plugin will invoke other functions, so we need to give it the necessary permission:

```
iamRoleStatements:
  - Effect: 'Allow'
    Action:
      - 'lambda:InvokeFunction'
    Resource: "*"
```

7. The last step is to modify the Lambda function to ignore requests created by this plugin:

```
module.exports.hello = (event, context, callback) => {

  if (event.source === 'serverless-plugin-warmup') {
    console.log('WarmUP - Lambda is warm!')
    return callback(null, 'Lambda is warm!')
  }

  callback(null, { message: 'Hello!' });
};
```

Monitoring the operation

The serverless concept is defined as running your code without worrying about the infrastructure that will be responsible for supporting it. This still holds true, but there are some DevOps tasks that may improve your application's efficiency and stability. Therefore, you should not confuse serverless with NoOps. You just don't need to worry *that* much about the infrastructure.

Since we are using AWS, we are going to use its monitoring tool: Amazon CloudWatch. There are some other paid and free tools that can also be used for this task, so feel free to compare them before selecting your own tool.

To use CloudWatch, open the Management Console at `https://console.aws.amazon.com /cloudwatch`, and let's see in the following subsections how we can monitor our Lambda functions:

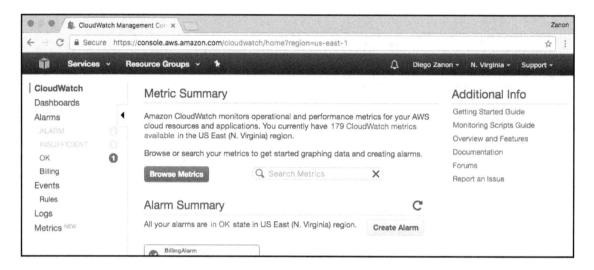

Monitoring costs

Estimating costs in serverless is a difficult task, since it depends highly on usage. Also, deploying a new function may result in unexpected costs due to programming errors. For example, consider that you set a function with a timeout of 5 minutes and 1 GB of RAM. Maybe it is supposed to execute in a few milliseconds 95% of the time, but due to an error, it may freeze every time and run indefinitely, just stopping after the timeout is reached.

Another scenario is when you use a Lambda function to call another Lambda function, but a programming error may create an endless loop causing your Lambda functions to execute constantly. In fact, AWS has some limits and measures to prevent these kind of errors, but that's something that we should pay attention to avoiding.

You can always open your AWS Billing dashboard to track your monthly expenses, but when these kind of issues occur, you want to be at least warned as soon as possible. In this case, you can set a billing alert to send an e-mail if the monthly cost reaches an unexpected level.

Let's monitor the costs by performing the following steps:

1. Open your **CloudWatch** console and browse the **Billing** link in the left-hand side menu, followed by **Create Alarm:**

2. On the next screen, select **Billing Metrics:**

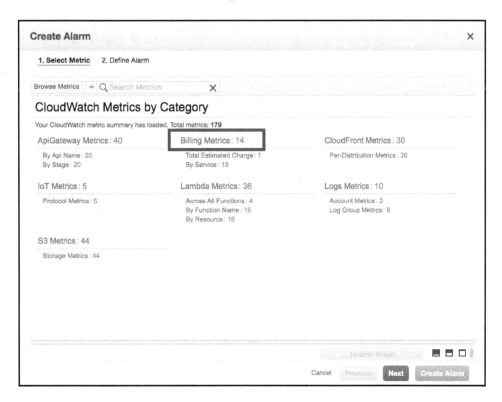

3. CloudWatch allows you to create a billing alert for the entire account or to filter the alert by service. In this case, you can select the **AWSLambda** service and click on **Next:**

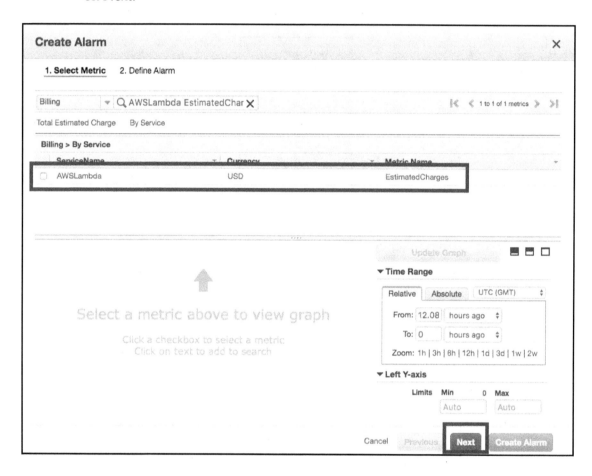

4. On the last screen, you can set a threshold for the alarm and define which persons it should notify if it goes beyond an acceptable value:

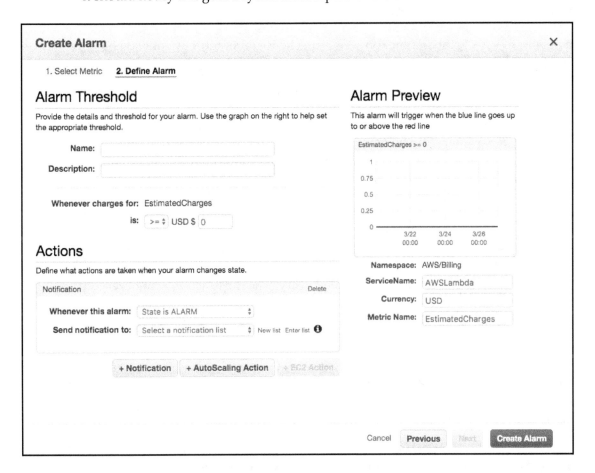

Monitoring errors

Going back to the **CloudWatch** console home screen, click on the **Browse Metrics** button located at the center. It will redirect you to another page where you can select all the metrics available to your Lambda functions. You can choose to monitor by function name, resource, or across all functions. The available metrics are as follows:

- **Errors**: This is the metric of the number of times that the Lambda function stopped prematurely due to an error, or it has stopped after reaching the timeout limit. This is an important metric because, ideally, you expect to see zero errors in production and will want to be warned when an error is detected.
- **Invocations**: This is the metric of the number of times that your Lambda function was invoked. If this function is executed by a schedule, you may want to be notified if it executes more times than expected. Also, using this metric, you may track when executions go out of control if the function is executed more times than a reasonable value.
- **Duration**: With this metric, you can track if your function is taking longer than expected to execute.
- **Throttles**: This metric is counted every time the function is not executed because the limit of concurrent Lambda functions is reached. This value can be increased if you open a support ticket to AWS, but the default value is 1,000 and it can be very low for some use cases.

As you can see, these metrics are automatically monitored and you can build some graphs with historical data. If you want to set alarms, go back to the **Console Home** page and click on **Alarms** in the left-hand side menu, followed by **Create Alarms**, and configure the recipients as you wish.

Retrieving metrics with the Serverless Framework

You can use the Serverless Framework to retrieve CloudWatch metrics. It can be a useful feature to take a quick look at the application's operation without browsing the **CloudWatch** console.

The following screenshot shows the output of the `serverless metrics` command:

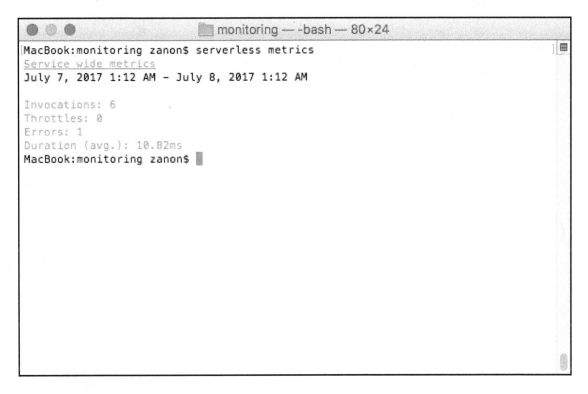

This command can be used to see the combined operation of all functions (`serverless metrics`) or the stats of just one function (`serverless metrics --function <your-function>`).

Also, you can filter by a date range using the arguments `--startTime` and `--endTime`. The following command will include only stats related to events that happened in the last 30 minutes:

```
serverless metrics --startTime 30m
```

Streaming Lambda logs

When an error occurs in a Lambda execution, the error message is usually insufficient. For example, consider the following error message:

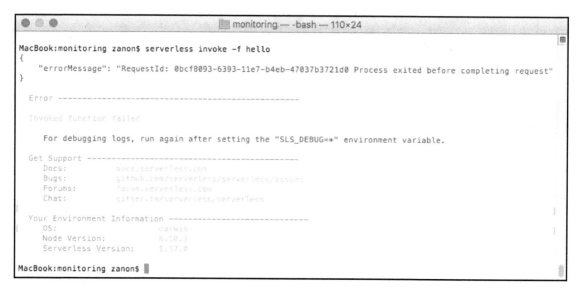

You can retrieve more details about the error message by streaming logs to the terminal. You can hook to a specific function and receive the history of error messages and live errors. For this, run the following command:

```
serverless logs -f myFunction --tail
```

The `--tail` argument indicates that you want to listen to new error messages. You can also use `--filter word` to show only messages that match the filter or `--startTime` to specify the range of logs that you want to see. For example, `--startTime 2h` shows logs from the last two hours.

The log messages show the stack trace of the errors, which is much more useful to understand the root cause of an issue:

```
monitoring — node /usr/local/bin/serverless logs -f hello --tail — 76×24
MacBook:monitoring zanon$ serverless logs -f hello --tail
START RequestId: 8346f110-6399-11e7-9bca-a1b7de191984 Version: $LATEST
2017-07-08 01:54:24.379 (-03:00)        8346f110-6399-11 7-9bca-a1b7de191984
TypeError: Cannot set property 'name' of undefined
    at module.exports.hello (/var/task/handler.js:7:25)
REPORT RequestId: 8346f110-6399-11e7-9bca-a1b7de191984  Duration: 28.89 ms
Billed Duration: 100 ms  Memory Size: 1024 MB   Max Memory Used: 19 MB

RequestId: 8346f110-6399-11e7-9bca-a1b7de191984 Process exited before comple
ting request
```

Handling errors

When a function executes with errors, Lambda offers two handlers such as SNS and SQS. You can use them to handle events that have failed, so you may try them again later or retrieve additional information to understand what caused the issue.

SNS is used to notify on errors and SQS is used to create a queue of failed Lambda tasks that can be processed by another service:

```
functions:
  hello:
    handler: handler.hello
    onError: <ARN>
```

You should set the ARN of the SNS topic as SQS queue.

 SQS is currently not supported due to a bug in the Serverless Framework v.1.18, but this error is already a known issue and should be fixed soon.

Monitoring performance

As we already discussed, you can find how long it takes for a function to execute through the duration metric in the CloudWatch option or by running the `serverless logs` command of the framework. Ideally, there is no difference if the code is executed during work hours, at midnight, or on weekends. AWS strives to always provide a constant experience at any time of the day.

In practice, this is not always true. There is no known pattern for this behavior, but you can expect large differences in the execution time. Without considering cold start delays, your function can take 50 milliseconds to execute, and 1 minute later, it can take 400 milliseconds to execute the same code with the same input. It is much more difficult to provide a constant experience in serverless sites than when using a traditional infrastructure. This is because your infrastructure is always shared between other customers.

Though you can see discrepancies, it is a good practice to monitor the duration. Instead of setting an alarm considering the *maximum* duration, you can set the *average* or *percentile*, where a percentile is a statistic unit, which means the percentage of observations that fall in a category. For example, a p90 of 100 milliseconds means that you expect that 90% of the requests will take less than 100 milliseconds to execute and you should receive an alarm message if this is not true for a given period of time.

Setting alarms is especially important when our Lambda function relies on external services. If the function reads data from a database table, it may take 200 milliseconds if the table has 10 records and 1 minute if it has 1,000,000 records. In this case, an alarm may be useful to alert you that it's time to clean some old data or improve the query.

Monitoring efficiency

Monitoring the efficiency means that you want to certify that you are using your resources in the best way possible. When you create a new Lambda function, there are two important options to configure such as the timeout value and the RAM memory to allocate.

Having a long timeout value will not impact the efficiency, but setting the wrong RAM memory will really affect the function performance and costs.

For example, consider the logs of the function executed in the following screenshot:

It has an allocated memory size of 1,024 MB (default) while `Max Memory Used` was only 19 MB. In this case, it clearly shows that you can reduce the allocated memory to minimize costs.

I recommend that you always test your code with different memory sizes and track the duration time. Running with less memory than needed results in much higher times to process. If your Lambda function is used to answer user requests, you may think of paying for a little more memory to process the requests faster while, if it is a background task, you may use the minimum necessary to save money.

Also, when benchmarking your own code to see how fast it is for different memory sizes, pay attention to which scenario it is running. If your project architecture is a Monolith, it may be very fast to retrieve some user data using just a few megabytes of memory, but it may have trouble processing the sales report of a given period.

Summary

In this chapter, you learned how you can test serverless code in the frontend and backend. Also, we have discussed some key concepts that you must consider in your deployment workflow, and showed how you can monitor serverless applications using Amazon CloudWatch.

Now the book has finished. I hope that you have enjoyed reading through the chapters and have learned enough to build your next awesome application using serverless. You can use the serverless store demo as a reference for your future projects, but don't feel limited to it. Use your own preferred tools to test, to develop the frontend, and to access the database. My objective with this book is not to define a strict pattern of how you should build a serverless application, but to give you an example to prove that the concept is valid and may be a good one for many applications.

Finally, I encourage you to try other cloud providers. This book focuses on AWS due to my own positive experiences, but there are other excellent services out there. When evaluating a provider, don't just pay attention to the price tag. Look at the tools that are offered that will make it easier for you to build your application. Mixing services from different providers is also viable. Good luck!

Index

S

www.ingramcontent.com/pod-product-compliance
Lightning Source LLC
LaVergne TN
LVHW081332050326
832903LV00024B/1124